THE LIFE OF
Elreta Melton Alexander

THE LIFE OF
Elreta Melton Alexander
ACTIVISM WITHIN THE COURTS

Virginia L. Summey

THE UNIVERSITY OF
GEORGIA PRESS
ATHENS

© 2022 by the University of Georgia Press
Athens, Georgia 30602
www.ugapress.org
All rights reserved
Designed by Kaelin Chappell Broaddus
Set in 9.5/13.5 Miller Text Roman by Kaelin Chappell Broaddus

Most University of Georgia Press titles are
available from popular e-book vendors.

Printed digitally

Library of Congress Cataloging-in-Publication Data

Names: Summey, Virginia L., author.
Title: The life of Elreta Melton Alexander : activism within the courts /
    Virginia L. Summey.
Description: Athens : The University of Georgia Press, [2022] |
    Based on author's thesis (doctoral—University of North Carolina at
    Greensboro, 2017) issued under title: Fighting within the bar :
    Judge Elreta Alexander and civil rights advocacy in Greensboro, North Carolina. |
    Includes bibliographical references and index.
Identifiers: LCCN 2021050564 | ISBN 9780820361925 (hardback) |
    ISBN 9780820361932 (paperback) | ISBN 9780820361949 (ebook)
Subjects: LCSH: Alexander-Ralston, Elreta, 1919-1998. | African American
    women judges—North Carolina. | Criminal defense lawyers—North Carolina. |
    LCGFT: Biographies.
Classification: LCC KF373.A394 S86 2022 | DDC 347.756/0234 [B]—dc23/eng/20220131
LC record available at https://lccn.loc.gov/2021050564

IN MEMORY OF
MY FRIEND
Nichole Mikko-Causby

CONTENTS

INTRODUCTION   An Individualistic Activist   1
CHAPTER 1   A Respectable Childhood   12
CHAPTER 2   Between Two Worlds   35
CHAPTER 3   Changing the System   57
CHAPTER 4   Turbulence at Home   78
CHAPTER 5   A Reluctant Pioneer?   94
CHAPTER 6   Attempting the Impossible   119
CONCLUSION   Remembering "Judge A"   143

Acknowledgments   151

Notes   155

Bibliography   179

Index   189

THE LIFE OF
Elreta Melton Alexander

INTRODUCTION
An Individualistic Activist

U PON THE RETIREMENT OF A local district court judge, the *Greensboro Record* reflected on her career: "If Webster's Dictionary provided living definitions, then Elreta Melton Alexander-Ralston would be a choice representative for the word, 'individual.' Since her childhood, people began taking notice of the youngest daughter of Rev. and Mrs. J. C. Melton. They haven't stopped since." Indeed, it was apparent that young Elreta was destined for big things as a child. And as an adult, as evident from such things as her expensive wardrobe, her clever repartee, and the fact that she allegedly made grown men cry when they discovered she was the judge presiding over their divorce case, Elreta Melton Alexander was undoubtedly an individual. Almost everyone who encountered her walked away with a story to tell.[1]

This book explores the life of this groundbreaking attorney.[2] In 1945 Alexander became the first African American woman to graduate from Columbia Law School. In 1947 she was the first African American woman to practice law in North Carolina, and in 1968 she was the first African American woman to become an elected district court judge. Despite her accomplishments, Alexander is little known to scholars outside her hometown of Greensboro, North Carolina. Yet this is not a story about her impressive list of firsts. This is a story about an African American woman who achieved these firsts during a time when social and institutional barriers rendered them almost impossible.

Born in 1919, Elreta Melton came of age during the era of Jim Crow. Her middle-class childhood was steeped in the politics of respectability, with a heavy emphasis on education. This arguably more conservative approach to race relations remained Alexander's approach to civil rights. After graduating from what is now known as North Carolina Agricultural and Technical State University, a historically Black university that would later become an integral setting in the civil rights movement, she embarked on a teaching career before marrying her college sweetheart, Girardeau "Tony" Alexander. During World War II she became the first African American woman to be accepted to Columbia Law School, which set her on a pioneering path. After graduating, she returned to Greensboro, where despite a turbulent marriage, she established a successful law career, became a judge, and achieved recognition as an important and prominent figure in North Carolina, all in the midst of the overt and institutionalized racism designed to prevent her success.

I first became familiar with Judge Alexander while a master's student at the University of Montana researching for a class called Writing Women's Lives. I wanted to write about someone from my native North Carolina. When I came across Alexander, I was surprised that I had never heard of her, having grown up not far from Greensboro. As I researched more, I became captivated by her life story. Alexander was bold yet elegant, brilliant yet funny, open-minded yet firm in her convictions, but it was her unique approach civil rights activism that really caught my attention. She brazenly announced in front of white men that, as a Black woman, she would drink from white water fountains to see the difference between "this white water and this colored water." She attempted to do her job as an attorney from the segregated section of the courtroom, highlighting that the law required Black citizens to sit in that section while saying, "I want to be with my people."[3] Even when her approach to barrier breaking seemed at odds with other civil rights advocates, she was exceedingly authentic. Her language, her wardrobe, her use of performance as a form of activism, all demonstrated that Elreta Alexander was a unique woman living—and succeeding—during turbulent times.

Alexander's use of performance was part of her civil rights advocacy and a necessary part of her career, which forced her to assimilate into a legal community dominated by white men. According to E. Patrick Johnson, the "black [person] who has been accepted into the elite circle of whiteness is expected to bracket the blackness that proffered his or her (temporary) invitation to the welcome table of whiteness."[4] In other words, for African Americans to make it into elite establishments (Columbia University is a good example), there is some requirement for them to check their Blackness at the door. As a result, a certain amount of performance is required. Individuals adjust their behaviors to fit in as the circumstances dictate. Poor African American children sometimes fail to assimilate or fit in with the dominant culture of the United States because of their failure to adopt middle-class white values. Conversely, Black leaders who have been accepted in the American mainstream have been accused of losing the ability to understand what it would take to connect the African American community to the dominant society. Alexander grew up in an educated, middle-class household, so her assimilation into mainstream America was probably easier than that of someone who came from poverty. However, for Alexander to establish a career in the segregated South, a certain amount of performance was necessary.

There is little question among those who knew her that Elreta Alexander had performance down to a fine art. Alexander used it to highlight the contradictions inherent in a segregated society. When a white woman once complained that her daughter was "runnin' around with colored boys," Alexander peered down from the bench and said, "Darlin', have you looked at your judge?"[5]

The complexities and contradictions of Alexander's life and politics also intrigued me. While Alexander achieved tremendous professional success, the rise of her career coincided with the downfall of her turbulent and violent marriage. While she spoke at length about her personal life, she rarely elaborated on professional hardships she encountered. As an attorney she defended members of the Ku Klux Klan while also claiming that nobody in Greensboro had done more for civil rights than she had. She ran for judgeships as a Republican at a time when African Americans were fleeing the GOP. And while Alexander undoubtedly broke professional barriers for Black women, her approach was decidedly more conservative than other civil rights activists, as she embraced the politics of respectability of her childhood throughout her adulthood.

In the introduction to her book about Ella Baker, Barbara Ransby states that "biography is a profoundly personal genre of historical scholarship. As biographers, we ask questions about lives that the subjects themselves may never have asked outright and certainly did not consciously answer." Ransby also notes one of the dangers of writing a biography: "imposing our contemporary dilemmas and expectations on a generation of women who spoke a different language, moved at a different rhythm, and juggled a different set of issues and concerns."[6] Individuals are complicated, contradictory, and ever evolving. The life of Judge Elreta Alexander was no different. While many times I was able to find an explanation or rationale for her actions in her oral histories or in the available historiography, some questions remain unanswered. Alexander revealed much of herself in interviews, but the aspects of her life about which she remained quiet would likely reveal much more about her inner thoughts and feelings.

Like any work that attempts to encapsulate an individual's life, this book explores many subjects that intersected and shaped Alexander's life. Elreta Alexander's story encompasses major themes of the twentieth-century South, from Jim Crow to civil rights, including legal and political history. Several historians have laid the foundation for my work, focusing their efforts on subjects that help contextualize Alexander's story. Jennifer Ritterhouse writes of "growing up Jim Crow," describing the challenges parents, such as the Meltons, faced raising a Black child in the South. The Meltons worked to instill in their children what Stephanie Shaw calls "socially responsible individualism," the idea that those blessed with educations should use their abilities to help others in the Black community. Elreta Alexander carried this concept with her throughout her career. Additionally, Stephen A. Berrey discusses performance in *The Jim Crow Routine*, describing the daily interactions between white and Black people in the Jim Crow South. While Alexander had minimal contact with whites in Greensboro during her childhood, what interactions she did have there and in law school gave her a keen sense of performance, which she later developed into a form of activism.[7]

The work of Black feminists also provides a framework for much of the lived experiences of Black women like Alexander. As she left Greensboro to attend law school and later returned to establish her career, Alexander, like many Black women, had to embody a "multiple consciousness" as she dealt with issues of race and gender in her daily life. According to Patricia Hill Collins, "On certain dimensions, Black women may more closely resemble Black men; on others, white women; and on still others, Black women may stand apart from both groups."[8] As Alexander entered a largely white, male field, both her gender and her race were at times held against her. At other times, they were in conflict with each other. Nowhere was this more evident than in a 1964 trial in which she defended a Black man accused of raping a white woman. Postmodernist theories of intersectionality and assemblage examine how these multiple consciousnesses inform our understanding of women like Alexander. Kimberlé Crenshaw argues that Black women are "sometimes excluded from feminist theory and antiracist policy discourse because both are predicated on a discrete set of experiences that often does not accurately reflect the interaction of race and gender."[9] The experiences of Black women are at times influenced by their race, at times influenced by their gender, and at times both. At multiple points in her life and career, Alexander had to navigate this intersection.

Several groundbreaking Black women attorneys before Alexander navigated race and gender in both their personal and professional lives, helping to pave the way for her. Most did so, however, outside the confines of the oppressiveness of Jim Crow. Sadie Tanner Mossell Alexander, the first Black woman in the United States to earn a Ph.D. (1921), described working with a "double handicap," suffering indignities in the workplace because of her race and gender. In 1927 she became the first African American woman to graduate from the University of Pennsylvania Law School and subsequently be admitted to the Pennsylvania bar. Sadie Alexander ultimately joined her husband in private practice because of the discrimination she experienced.[10]

Similarly, Judge Jane Bolin in 1931 became the first African American woman to graduate from Yale Law School and in 1939 became the first African American woman judge in the country, when New York City mayor Fiorello La Guardia appointed her to the domestic relations court. Bolin was inspired to activism by the treatment of African Americans in the South but did not directly experience Jim Crow segregation. Bolin inspired Judge Constance Baker Motley, a Connecticut native who was the second African American woman, after Elreta Alexander, to graduate from Columbia Law School in 1945. Motley went on to have a prestigious career with the NAACP Legal Defense and Educational Fund, as a New York state senator, and as a federal judge nominated by Lyndon B. Johnson.[11]

While no African American woman could easily blaze a groundbreaking legal career in the early twentieth century, unlike the pioneers preceding her, Elreta Alexander did so in the midst of Jim Crow and the civil rights period in the South. While Motley openly discussed the inspiration provided by Bolin, Alexander had no mentors who also had to overcome pervasive and violent southern racism and segregation to establish a career, although other Black southern women had been admitted to their respective state bars before Alexander.[12] Lutie Lytle, raised in Kansas, was the first African American woman admitted to the Tennessee bar (1898); however, she established her practice in New York. Cassandra E. Maxwell in 1939 became the first Black woman to practice law in South Carolina. After teaching at South Carolina State University School of Law, she practiced in Georgia and later Pennsylvania.[13] While these women are all extraordinary, it is more than Alexander's impressive list of firsts in the legal field that make her worthy of study.

Alexander's form of activism was different than the methods of other Black women during the civil rights movement. For example, Ella Baker and Alexander had many things in common, most notably their middle-class childhoods in North Carolina and the politics of respectability, which was emphasized in their Black Baptist churches. They both attended historically Black colleges in North Carolina, but after their respective graduations the similarities end. While they both remained committed to Black advancement, Baker rejected respectability politics and became integral in the establishment of civil rights organizations, such as the Southern Christian Leadership Conference and the Student Nonviolent Coordinating Committee.[14] Alexander, on the other hand, embraced the concept of respectability and became a pioneering attorney. While they both contributed to the advancement of African Americans, they did so in very different manners.

Ransby and historian Katherine Charron demonstrate in their biographies of civil rights leaders that there were multiple approaches to combating segregation and systematic white repression in the South. In *Freedom's Teacher*, for example, Charron demonstrates how Septima Clark used education to combat racial injustice. These biographies use the lives of individuals as a lens through which to examine different aspects of the civil rights movement and activism. My work on Alexander moves civil rights historiography in a new direction. Historians often focus on individuals who push societal boundaries. Ella Baker, Fannie Lou Hamer, Rosa Parks, and other prominent women of the civil rights movement all changed society by working against the status quo. Alexander, on the other hand, is an example of someone who defied racial stereotypes. She changed society and the legal system by working within it, removing barriers and clearing paths for future African American professionals.

In addition to working within the existing structure of the legal system, Alexander attempted to create change within the political system. In her political campaigns for judgeships, Alexander ran as a Republican at a time when African Americans were increasingly attracted to the Democratic Party. While she was part of a minority in the Republican Party, there were still other African Americans committed to civil rights who saw the GOP as a potential conduit for change. Several political historians have written about this, notably Joshua D. Farrington in *Black Republicans and the Transformation of the GOP* and Leah Wright Rigueur in *The Loneliness of the Black Republican*. Alexander's life supports the analyses of Farrington and Rigueur in that she, like other notable Black Republicans such as James Meredith and James Farmer, believed that no group should be completely beholden to one political party.

While the 1964 Barry Goldwater campaign may have permanently alienated Black voters on the national level, as Farrington explains and as Alexander's life demonstrates, the Black vote was still unsolidified as a Democratic bloc on the state and local levels.[15]

Judge Alexander's career achievements took place in the city of Greensboro, North Carolina, a key site of the civil rights movement. During Alexander's legal career, on February 1, 1960, four young men from her alma mater, NC A&T, launched the first sit-in at the Woolworth's downtown. Yet Greensboro's civil rights history is deeper and more nuanced than is typically acknowledged. Much of that history is covered in William Chafe's 1980 book, *Civilities and Civil Rights: Greensboro, North Carolina, and the Black Struggle for Freedom*. In 2013, addressing the long-overlooked role of women in Greensboro's civil rights history, Linda Beatrice Brown published *Belles of Liberty: Gender, Bennett College, and the Civil Rights Movement*. Further, the movement in Greensboro went beyond the work of college students and included a small network of Black professionals, including Dr. George Simkins Jr., who led the charge to desegregate many of the city's recreational facilities and served as the lead plaintiff in the Supreme Court case *Simkins v. Cone* (1963). In her roles as an attorney and judge, Alexander used her professional achievements and middle-class status to advocate for individuals who lacked a voice in the southern legal system. Alexander and Black professional women like her were integral to the civil rights movement. Even if they did not pick up signs and publicly protest, they used the law, worked behind the scenes, and quietly integrated white professional spaces.[16] Changes in the law were vital to the accomplishments of the civil rights movement and the women's movement. Alexander was able to combat segregation by demonstrating that Black women were worthy and capable of successful careers alongside white men, thereby creating environments in which other African Americans could succeed. Her legal expertise and ability to reach across racial boundaries thus made her an important figure in the civil rights movement in Greensboro.[17]

Beyond the intersecting themes and accompanying analyses helping to contextualize her life, Elreta Alexander herself guides much of the narrative in this book. The local newspapers extensively covered her personal and professional activities, and trial transcripts reveal some of her tactics as an attorney. Even more important, her own words are prominent in the telling of her story. Her extensive unpublished interviews and her published book of poetry, *When Is a Man Free?* reveal Alexander's personal motivations and thoughts on the civil rights movement. Like all people, Alexander was a multifaceted and occasionally contradictory individual. Her own words sometimes clarify and sometimes confuse. But her words also validate my thesis that she was a unique activist. Alexander was afforded intelligence and a middle-class status, which could have made her complacent. But when she found herself in the position to confront racial or gender discrimination, she accepted the challenge head on and in the process broke down barriers and fundamentally changed the treatment of race and gender in the North Carolina legal system.

I present these themes in a mostly chronological account of Alexander's life. Chapter 1 focuses on Elreta Melton's childhood and ancestry and explores issues of class and race in the Jim Crow South, particularly in the 1920s and early 1930s in Greensboro, North Carolina. I examine how Elreta's childhood laid the foundation for her future activism. She was the product of two biracial parents who grew up in the Reconstruction South. Elreta's father, J. C. Melton, was a graduate of historically Black Shaw University in Raleigh, North Carolina, and served as a Baptist minister, providing his wife and three children with a comfortable home life. The importance of education was reinforced by her mother, Alain, who was a teacher and worked on her college education at the same time as her children. At school, Elreta learned about colorism and the class issues that often divided the African American community, but her family's focus on respectability politics influenced her more conservative approach to racial justice. Greensboro, North Carolina, fostered a sense of activism in its young Black students. Chafe argues in *Civilities and Civil Rights* that Greensboro had a "progressive mystique," but the city's reputation did not match the reality for many of its Black citizens. My view is that while Greensboro was certainly not as progressive as its white citizens wanted to believe, there were more opportunities for African American citizens than in other southern cities, largely because of its two historically Black colleges.

Chapter 2 introduces Alexander's legal career. Following the advice of a friend, she decided to pursue a career in law and became the first African American woman admitted to Columbia Law School. Perhaps because of the lightness of Alexander's skin, or perhaps because of her status as a law student, Alexander was accepted by the white establishment at Columbia University. Because of her legal training in a white environment, her notion of aesthetics, her style of speech, and her professional positions, her race was seen as secondary by many whites. During her time in New York, World War II raged on, and African Americans at home found new, albeit short-lived, job opportunities. After practicing law in Harlem, Alexander in 1947 became the first African American woman to practice law in North Carolina, but this presented new challenges. Alexander established her career in Greensboro and took up controversial cases dealing with integration and defending Black clients. One of her primary goals was to prove that "brains are not sex or color coded." I argue that in these early years Alexander formed her judicial philosophy and unique style of performance activism. She always considered herself a "showman" and stated that "it always seemed kind of stupid to me for people to treat people as second-class citizens and expect a first-class performance." Having been musically trained as a child, Alexander was familiar with the stage. In her legal career, she often saw courtrooms and meeting rooms as her stage, using performance to change the attitudes of individuals in North Carolina.[18]

In law school, Alexander completed a rigorous course of study on the U.S. legal system, which discriminated against African Americans and particularly African American men. Alexander took this knowledge into what became one of her most significant cases as an attorney. Chapter 3 focuses on an interracial rape trial that fundamentally changed the justice system in Guilford County, North Carolina. On the afternoon of June 21, 1964, four African American young men went out to drink some beers and do some target shooting. What allegedly started out as a prank on the part of the four Black men to scare a white couple turned into a racially charged rape case. Alexander defended the young men, and the trial changed the trajectory of her career. It brought out her commitment to civil rights as she revealed disparities in sentencing, bias in the jury selection process, and other racial issues in the judicial system.

The fourth chapter focuses on Alexander's turbulent marriage. Like most individuals, Elreta Alexander could be a woman of contradiction. While she exuded confidence and power in the courtroom, her personal life was tumultuous. These were not aspects of her life that she kept hidden. Through letters written at the time and in interviews given retrospectively, she openly discussed her marital troubles. In oral histories I conducted with her colleagues and friends the nature of her personal life was an open secret. Alexander suffered domestic abuse at the hands of her first husband, Dr. Girardeau Alexander. Her reasons for staying in a bad marriage were rooted in racial pride and the couple's professional standing in the community. I explore the pressures Alexander faced in balancing a family and career as an African American woman. While the Alexanders were a professionally successful couple, their marriage was plagued with violence, infidelity, and the stress of raising a son with paranoid schizophrenia. Following the work of Darlene Clark Hine and her term "culture of dissemblance," I argue that Alexander carefully compartmentalized her personal and professional lives so as to not jeopardize her pioneering accomplishments.

Little has been written about African American marriages in the postwar period. Anastasia C. Curwood's *Stormy Weather: Middle-Class African American Marriages between the Two World Wars* is one of the few in-depth studies available. In chapter 4, I build on Curwood's analysis, extending it into the postwar era to address the unique challenges faced by Black women in their personal lives during the mid-twentieth century. This chapter highlights Alexander's complexity as a human being. Nobody can definitively say why she stayed in her abusive marriage for so long, but there was obviously a mutual affection.

Chapter 5 challenges Elreta Alexander's 1968 assertion that she was a "reluctant pioneer." In 1967, she published a book of poetry revealing her frustrations with race relations in the United States, and in 1968 she was the first African American woman in the country to become an elected district court judge. From the bench, she established the Judgment Day program, a forerunner of modern deferred-sentencing programs. The Judgment Day program targeted young first-time offenders at the same time that police tactics were targeting young African American men and their incarceration rates began to rise. As Alexander achieved career milestones, Greensboro and the South were embroiled in the civil rights movement. I situate Alexander and her brand of activism within the movement and examine how she challenged the status quo within the confines of the law.

Finally, in chapter 6 I focus on Alexander's career in the 1970s and 1980s. As much as Alexander accomplished, societal and institutional structures still prevented her from reaching certain career heights. I examine race, gender, politics, and how Alexander challenged the North Carolina Republican Party. In February 1974, Alexander filed as a Republican candidate for the position of chief justice of the North Carolina Supreme Court. But she did not receive the Republican nomination, losing to a white fire extinguisher salesman with no college degree. This result highlights the prejudices that existed concerning gender and race in politics. The loss precipitated a difficult time in Alexander's career, leading to her retirement from the bench in 1981.

Elreta Alexander's life and career had incredible highs and some very difficult lows. While not every case she tried is significant to civil rights history, she consistently gave a voice to the marginalized at a time when those voices were systematically excluded. During her highs, she removed obstacles for the Black women who followed her. During her lows, she persevered while remaining dedicated to her family and career. There are no pictures of Alexander marching with civil rights protesters in downtown Greensboro. But there are many of her in judicial robes. Those are the pictures that gave inspiration to future Black women attorneys and judges.

Ultimately this is the story of one Black woman who lived a life that took some extraordinary turns. Some may argue that Alexander did not serve the civil rights movement as an activist because she did not publicly protest, or that her lucrative career as an attorney placed her in the ranks of the middle class and thus out of touch with the plight of working-class Black people. Elreta Alexander was not the perfect civil rights activist, or the perfect women's activist, if there was ever such a thing. But by choosing a career in law, she became an activist for all marginalized people. She worked to make sure the law, as written, worked for all individuals regardless of race. Her life and career coincided with a time when African Americans protested against their legal and social condition and women fought for opportunity and equality both inside and outside the home. That historical era makes her public accomplishments and unique style all the more noteworthy. And yet this remains a deeply personal story filled with triumph, tragedy, and a bit of drama. Her professional accomplishments make Elreta Alexander an important historical figure and initially brought her to my attention. But what she endured personally, in addition to her accomplishments, make this story worth reading.

CHAPTER I
A Respectable Childhood

WHEN ELRETA MELTON WAS AROUND nine years old, her father asked her older brother, Judson, to put the family car in the garage. Beating her brother to the car, Elreta decided to put it in the garage herself. "I had watched Daddy drive it, and I thought I knew how." As it turns out, young Elreta did not know how to use the brakes. "Daddy saw me in the car, although he could only see the top of my head. I steered the car into the wooden garage." Fortunately, the garage took the brunt of the damage.[1] But the incident serves as an apt metaphor for the rest of Elreta Melton Alexander's life. She always attempted to reach her goals regardless of the barriers that stood in her way. Her childhood prepared her to overcome obstacles surrounding gender and race in her adulthood.

In many ways, Elreta Melton's upbringing resembled that of many children coming of age in the early twentieth-century South. She was born without material wealth and privilege, but her family always had a nice, clean house, food on the table, clothes on their backs, and access to education. This level of comfort put her family within the realm of the Black middle class. With an emphasis on respectability, education, and racial uplift, middle-class Black parents groomed children like Elreta to be the leaders of their race. Most of these middle-class Black children were destined to become teachers or ministers, charged with the responsibility of passing on their values to the next generation of African American children. Elreta Melton, however, took the lessons of her childhood and turned them into a groundbreaking career as an attorney and judge that would test antiquated Jim Crow policies.

Growing up in the segregated South prepared her for the difficult legal situations she would later confront. A native North Carolinian, young Elreta was acutely aware of the treatment of African Americans in the South. Her upbringing taught her how to navigate—and at times defy—the segregationist system of Jim Crow. She was also introduced to issues that would become recurring themes throughout her life, such as respectability politics, performance activism, class, and colorism, which laid the foundation for the role she played bridging communities in Greensboro life during the civil rights movement.

Elreta Narcissus Melton was born on March 21, 1919, in Smithfield, North Carolina. Her father, J. C., was a Baptist minister and her mother, Alain, a teacher. She was the youngest of three children; her brother, Judson, was four years old, and her sister, Etta, was one year old at the time of her birth. When Elreta was two, the Meltons were victims in a land fraud deal when they unknowingly purchased a home legally belonging to somebody else. Apparently Reverend Melton neglected to have the title searched, and ultimately the family was evicted because they were unable to pay off the legal owners. Elreta recalled her mother crying after the family lost their home. The loss of the money and the house was undoubtedly a blow for both her and Reverend Melton, who worked hard to provide a middle-class upbringing for their children.[2]

Joseph Cleveland "J. C." Melton was the individual who exerted the most influence on Elreta, and he was the primary impetus behind the Melton family's emphasis on middle-class values. Melton was born on February 16, 1882, in Hertford County, North Carolina. According to Elreta, he was the son of an African American man, John Melton, and a white woman, Narcissus A. Flood, who married in Gates County, North Carolina, during Reconstruction. At that time interracial marriages often provoked racial violence.[3] The agricultural area of northeastern North Carolina near the Great Dismal Swamp, where J. C. Melton grew up, however, contained populations of free African Americans even before the Civil War. That population and the rural environment largely shielded them from violence. The descendants of Indigenous people and Black people who escaped enslavement lived as bi- or triracial communities in that same region. Elreta Alexander stated that in the northeastern North Carolina counties, such as Hertford, "You couldn't tell the whites from the Blacks, because the white man had family here and across the street he had his Black family. And the children came out nearly the same; every now and then, there'd be a little brown one in there." While interracial relationships were not the norm, anyone who came to Hertford County would have witnessed many such pairings, and the community largely stayed quiet regarding the illegality of their neighbors' relationships.[4]

Although biracialism and light skin could sometimes prove advantageous for African Americans, and was not unusual where he grew up, life was not easy for J. C. Being the product of an interracial marriage weighed heavily on him. According to Elreta Alexander, he denied that his mother was white. He was the third of five children and the only boy. After his mother died in 1886, his father married a biracial woman, but there was little room and few resources for their combined twenty-one children. So, at the age of nine or ten, J. C. Melton went to work at a logging camp near the Great Dismal Swamp. After years of logging, drinking, and gambling and with only three years of prior education, Melton decided to go to college. Taking a job as a carpenter to pay for school, he finished his secondary education and was subsequently accepted to Shaw University in Raleigh, North Carolina.[5]

Founded in 1865, Shaw University was the first Black collegiate institution to be established in the South by the American Baptist Home Mission Society to help provide education and training for formerly enslaved people and their children. As Shaw grew, it quickly became a model of education dedicated to uplifting African Americans. Shaw expected its students to graduate and be professionally competitive, and the school groomed them to achieve respectable status within the burgeoning Black middle class.[6]

J. C. worked his way through Shaw as a janitor and carpenter. At twenty-three years old, Melton first encountered his future wife. According to Elreta, Alain Reynolds was only around nine years old. Immediately after noticing young Alain, Melton said, "I'm going to marry that girl." After graduating with his mathematics degree, he went to Cofield, North Carolina, to accept a teaching position at Waters Institute—the same school where he had previously been a construction worker.[7] Alain Reynolds, now a teenager, was a pupil in his class. The two began courting, and Reynolds was transferred out of Melton's class. J. C. returned to attend seminary at Shaw and became a Baptist minister, while Alain went on to college. After finishing her second year, the couple married on March 11, 1914. Reynolds was twenty, and Melton was thirty-three. They had their first child, Judson, the next year.

Alain Reynolds, born in 1894 in Cofield, North Carolina, was also the product of a complicated racial lineage common to that area of the state. Alain's mother had light brown skin, and her father, according to Alexander, was a white merchant named Robert Reynolds. Reynolds reportedly enforced segregation in his store, and Alexander recalled that he "had a rule that no Black-skinned people could come in the front door. This carried over to my mother, and when my brother married a dark-skinned girl, it almost broke up the family."[8] For the daughter of an interracial marriage, the maintenance of light skin, which affected how one was treated in southern society, was very important.

With his light skin tone, education, and career, J. C. Melton was an acceptable spouse for Alain Reynolds. After their marriage and the birth of Judson, Melton accepted a pastorate in Reidsville, North Carolina, and Alain became a teacher. While the Meltons were far from wealthy, they were comfortable. They arrived in Smithfield, North Carolina, in 1916, where Elreta would be born in 1919, and then moved to Scotland Neck, North Carolina, before moving to Danville, Virginia, in 1925. In Danville, J. C. assumed the pastorate at Loyal Baptist Church, where he stayed for several years. But as the country entered the Great Depression, the church could no longer afford his salary.[9] With the encouragement of Dr. F. D. Bluford, president of North Carolina Agricultural and Technical University (NC A&T), the Meltons moved with their three children to Greensboro, North Carolina, in 1930 to assume the pastorate at United Institutional Baptist Church. For the rest of Elreta Melton Alexander's life, Greensboro would be the center of her personal and professional worlds.

In 1930, Greensboro was a burgeoning, progressive city that exemplified the "New South." In 1949 political scientist V. O. Key called North Carolina a "progressive plutocracy" and said that the state "has a reputation for fair dealing with its Negro citizens." Known for its textile and insurance industries, as well as its five colleges, Greensboro took pride in being known for its racial tolerance. At the same time, it was a city where African Americans remained dependent on whites for menial service jobs in mills and factories. Greensboro, like the rest of North Carolina, was a paradox. Neither the city's nor the state's reputations reflected the social reality of its African American citizens.[10]

With the support of abolitionist Quakers who had settled in Guilford County, African Americans carved out their own community early in Greensboro's history. By 1923, the city boasted two African American colleges, giving the Black community a sense of pride. As a minister, J. C. Melton and his family contributed to that community. Melton frequently delivered prayers at

African American events at NC A&T and throughout the town. J. C. and Alain Melton also established the first African American Girl Scout troop in Guilford County.[11]

The middle-class Black values embraced by the Melton family are instrumental to understanding Elreta's childhood and early adulthood. Families like the Meltons embraced W. E. B. Du Bois's concept of the "talented tenth," which stated that through continuing classical education, as opposed to the more conservative industrial education advocated by Booker T. Washington, a small percentage of African Americans could go on to become leaders of their race. This "talented tenth" would therefore be in a position to advocate uplift ideology, which for many Black elites meant they would be the "bourgeois agents of civilization" for the Black lower classes.[12]

For African American families at this time, "middle class" was more than just an economic status. For middle-class Black people, the Jim Crow era was about gaining respectability and proving the abilities of the African American race. During the first half of the twentieth century many African Americans focused on the economic and educational viability of their communities. Therefore, the term "middle class" for African Americans was about education, proper decorum, and respectability in an attempt to promote a "better class" of Black people.[13] Education, respectability, and racial uplift became repeated themes throughout Elreta Alexander's life.

Like many middle-class Black parents, and partially in an attempt to foster their own sense of self, the Meltons attempted to shield their children from the humiliating inequities that often accompanied growing up in the Jim Crow South. This period of southern history, which lasted roughly from *Plessy v. Ferguson* in 1896 to *Brown v. Board of Education of Topeka* in 1954 and beyond, included Elreta's formative years. Jim Crow society was based on a rigid system of white-imposed racial etiquette and segregation intended to disempower African Americans. Black parents felt they had to teach their children that to rebel against that system could be potentially dangerous. All children in the South learned about their own racial identities, and Black children found themselves relegated to separate spaces in society.

Segregation was a defining feature of southern society, providing a physically structured racial hierarchy. While interactions between Black and white people were still common, the racial hierarchy was foundational. In an era of lynching and other extralegal methods of enforcing white supremacy, the consequences of contesting that hierarchy could be extreme. While it was impossible to completely shield their children from the difficulties of growing up

Black in the South, middle-class parents like the Meltons emphasized notions of respectability as a means of resistance to white supremacy. J. C. Melton's rule was that his children would walk twenty miles before they would ride on a segregated bus; they would not be treated like second-class citizens.[14] Throughout her life Elreta Alexander resisted segregation and white supremacy, while maintaining the notions of respectability that she grew up with, although that was the more conservative approach among civil rights leaders.

Whites depended on African Americans to work the menial jobs to keep the new southern economy going, which was the result of the decline of an agrarian economy and the rise of industry. Rather than relying on complete racial segregation, Jim Crow depended on a system of race-based etiquette and deference, creating specific roles and expectations for both races. African Americans had to walk a thin line between survival, maintaining self-respect, and complying with the rules. To do this, performance was required. Elreta learned about this type of performance as a child and carried it into her career. According to historian Jennifer Ritterhouse, "Black children, particularly those of educated, middle-class parents, learned to subsume the command performance of racial etiquette in a broader performance of personal dignity." For Black children without the middle-class privileges afforded to the Melton children, Jim Crow performance was required, or else they risked falling victim to racialized extralegal violence.[15]

Many middle-class Black families, such as the Meltons, could afford to avoid whites and the humiliating system of etiquette designed to maintain their inferiority. The Meltons forbade their children from using segregated public accommodations, such as riding segregated buses, although they did attend all-Black schools, since there were no desegregated alternatives. For Black adults, self-segregating their children also took away some of the worry about racism. While still adhering to the Jim Crow rules of racial etiquette, teaching middle-class Black children the concept of respectability and personal dignity made the degradations slightly easier to bear. In their own spaces, Black children were able to develop their sense of self and define their abilities on their own terms, rather than the terms imposed by whites. The methods used by her parents worked for young Elreta Melton. When she recalled as an adult seeing the bigger houses belonging to white people in Greensboro during the Depression, she said she "resented it, [but] not because I wanted to integrate with them. I've always felt they were kind of looney, anybody that felt there was something better about you because of your color and your sex, I thought there was something wrong with your mind."[16] Even if she did not fully understand notions of racial superiority, young Elreta still had normal childhood desires to participate in everyday activities and live in a nice house, even if that meant complying with the rules of segregation.

Regardless of her parents' best efforts, young Elreta sometimes longed to access public facilities not available to her because of her race. The Carolina Theatre in downtown Greensboro, originally billed as the "Showplace of the Carolinas," opened on Halloween night in 1927. With its Greek temple design, bright colors, and air conditioning—a rarity at the time in North Carolina and surely a draw on a hot summer day—the Carolina Theatre was an experience and a sight to behold for Greensboro's citizens. The theater, however, only allowed African Americans to view films from the third balcony. Because of its segregation policies, J. C. Melton forbade his children from patronizing the theater, even if they were allowed on the third balcony. Defying her father, Elreta sometimes snuck into the theater to enjoy the cool air and the latest Hollywood films. Even as a child, Elreta worked around policies that stood in her way. Although the ban on segregated facilities applied to her parents as well, Elreta Alexander stated that the rule was relaxed once, when her parents went to the Carolina Theatre to attend a production of *Porgy and Bess*.[17]

An essential component of respectability and middle-class values during the Jim Crow era was education. Coming of age before integration, the Melton children attended all-Black schools, which were frequently subpar compared to the schools for white children. Local and state governments in the South dedicated little funding for all-Black schools, resulting in inadequate facilities, overcrowding, and out-of-date textbooks. To remedy some of this inequity, the Meltons enrolled their children in music lessons, requiring each child to learn how to play a musical instrument. Elreta excelled at the piano and boasted about her singing voice. Reverend Melton also continued the children's schooling after their formal classes, reiterating the basics, such as reading and mathematics, and also teaching them Greek and Latin.[18] While Latin probably served Elreta Alexander well in her legal career, as a teenager, singing was her passion. When she was a senior at Dudley High School, the president of Bennett College, David Dallas Jones, approached her mother. Having sent his own daughter, Frances, to Paris, he and his wife, Susie, offered to take in Elreta for the summer and financially help with her budding singing career, improving the chances of her gaining a potential spot in Bennett's quartet, which frequently represented the college. Alain Melton replied, "We might not have all the money, but I don't give my children to anyone. When your daughter arrives, Elreta will be already on the scene. We have what it takes to give her."[19] Alain Melton was determined that her daughter would succeed without having to give up any of their respectability by accepting charity, but Elreta's music career never took off.

The emphasis on education was particularly important for Black girls growing up in the Jim Crow South. Sexual and economic exploitation of Black women ran rampant at the time, as many Black women worked in the homes of white families who took advantage of what they saw as cheap labor. Negative associations with the sexuality of Black women were rooted in slavery, when slavers or overseers sexually assaulted enslaved women and girls regularly, and then portrayed them as Jezebel-type figures. A formal education was key for Black women to avoid work in the domestic or agricultural sectors, where they were prone to abuse. Education, with an emphasis on moral and honest behavior, was essential not just for personal uplift, but for uplift of the race. Young women such as Elreta and her older sister, Etta, received educations aimed at teaching them how to avoid unsavory attention and how to counteract negative views of African Americans among whites. With young Black women being particularly vulnerable to sexual abuse by white men, parents taught their daughters to avoid presenting themselves as sexual beings, hoping to affect the impressions of and treatment by whites.[20] Like other middle-class Black parents, Reverend and Mrs. Melton encouraged an education that would lead to achievement and respectable careers. They were extremely successful in this undertaking, as both Melton daughters went on to become attorneys.

In addition to serving as her educator, Reverend Melton was the dominant parent in young Elreta's life. The itinerant life with a minister proved difficult for Alain Reynolds Melton. Elreta Alexander recalled as an adult that her mother was at times absent when she was a child. She stated that for a year Reverend Melton would take the three children to Dudley High School, and then on weekends drive fifty miles north to Danville, the location of their previous home, and bring her mother back to Greensboro. "Daddy," Alexander stated, "during the course of that year . . . was determined to get Mother to live with the children." The relationship between J. C. and Alain Melton was sometimes strained. Alexander recalled after the deaths of both her parents that Alain had never wanted to marry a minister but did so to get away from home. Additionally, she did not want her children to be seen as the "preacher's children" and be associated with the rigid expectations that often entailed. At times, J. C. and Alain discussed separation, and one of the children always accompanied J. C. on his pastoral visits in order to avoid the appearance of any impropriety. Alain's absence reinforced the bond between Elreta and her father, making his guidance all the more influential.[21]

Based on Elreta Alexander's description, it is possible that Alain may have suffered from mental illness, which sometimes created trying situations in the Melton house. After a year of living apart from her children, Alain moved to Greensboro and enrolled at Bennett College to finish her degree, eventually becoming a teacher at J. C. Price School. But professional success did not ensure private happiness. Alain stated that she did not know life could be so hard, and Alexander remembered that "every weekend, Daddy made us go upstairs and sort of sit guard with Mother so she wouldn't jump out the window." Elreta was a teenager during this worrisome period, but as an adult she never displayed any hostility toward her mother. In a 1993 interview she praised her mother for being a progressive woman, saying Alain was "intent upon enjoying the good life, the good life of making contributions."[22] Their mother-daughter relationship was complex, but also demonstrates the heavy burden of respectability. Maintaining such a performance could prove arduous, and with a lack of mental health services at the time, getting to the root of Alain Melton's depression was difficult. Today, mental health studies show the connection between racism and clinical depression.[23] The everyday tasks of proving themselves worthy to white society likely took a toll on some members of the Melton family.

Being the middle-class wife of a Baptist minister brought with it more stress than most middle-class Black women experienced, which also affected Alain Melton and the children. Despite her own issues, Alain was determined that her children would be able to sing and dance, despite traditional expectations that frowned on dancing. Black Baptist women wanted their minister's wife to be an intelligent homemaker who was active in social causes affecting her husband's congregants. These prominent Black Baptist women emphasized respectable behavior, but Alain Melton provided her children with some respite from the demands of respectability. Reverend Melton, on the other hand, with his strong focus on the importance of education, often played the role of disciplinarian. Although he enforced strict rules aimed at respectability, young Elreta idolized her father and particularly recalled the fun times they had when Alain was out of town. As a young child, Elreta had her sights set on becoming a Baptist minister, like her father, but she could not because of her gender. Years later, she credited her father with her success in the legal field and with instilling in her a strong sense of self-esteem.[24]

While Elreta ultimately ended up in the courtroom instead of the pulpit, her upbringing in the Black Baptist church was instrumental to her success. Within the walls of the church, African Americans were free from the worst aspects of Jim Crow. Middle-class families, such as the Meltons, were attracted to the Black Baptist church because of its emphasis on education and racial uplift. After emancipation, the church had served as a house of worship for freed people, but also as a community center, library, meeting place, and thrift store. African Americans were motivated spiritually, politically, and intellectually by the church and could temporarily escape the laws of segregation imposed on them by the outside world. During Jim Crow, the Black Baptist church started placing more importance on the education of its ministers, and many of the church's women started promoting middle-class values in order to gain respectability for themselves and their church family.[25] Elreta's parents allowed singing and dancing, but otherwise they agreed on the importance of respectability as taught by the church.

When the Meltons moved to Greensboro, they even chose their home based on notions of respectability. The family settled in a comfortable house at 400 Beech Street, which they selected and the church rented as a parsonage. The original church parsonage was a half mile away on East Market Street, but according to Elreta Alexander, "Mother wouldn't live there—and that was the only condition that Daddy could come here, because E. Market St. was where all the gamblers hung out, and it was right around Daddy's church, and she didn't want my brother to be in that environment, and all of us. So we lived there [on Beech Street]." The house was situated in the Cumberland neighborhood, just east of Greensboro's downtown, which had developed along with NC A&T. In the 1930s, the Cumberland neighborhood was home to prominent African American citizens, such as James B. Dudley, the second president of NC A&T.[26] During Elreta's youth, she was in close proximity to primary and secondary schools and surrounded by neighbors who emphasized education. East Greensboro, which was predominately African American, provided the Melton children with a strong community and educational opportunities not found in other areas of the South. It was not a safe haven from the horrors of Jim Crow, during which white vigilantes used intimidation, whipping, arson, and at times murder to keep the white patriarchy intact, but in East Greensboro the Melton family found a home and high-quality education.[27]

The education Elreta received in Greensboro became the foundation of her activism. Elreta attended and graduated from Dudley High School (established in 1929), the first Black high school in Guilford County, which served as a model of excellence and a source of pride in the African American community. Dudley High School benefited from the leadership of men like Dr. John Tarpley, who came to Greensboro as a teacher at Bennett College. He honed a reputation as someone who could establish relationships with white leadership to gain necessary funding for Black schools, while also defending the rights of Greensboro's African Americans.[28]

Despite Tarpley's efforts, in Guilford County the twentieth century saw improvements in the education of Black children but on a slower pace than for white children. In many cases, education for African American children depended on private philanthropic efforts, such as those of Julius Rosenwald, who provided matching grants to aid in the construction of eight hundred public schools in North Carolina for Black children from the 1910s to the 1930s. In what historian James Anderson calls a system of "double taxation," African Americans had to pay taxes to support white public schools, while using their own money to support schools for their own children.[29] Many Black students, however, lacked the skills necessary to pursue a higher education, due to subpar primary education. J. C. Melton ensured that would not be a problem for his children.

Elreta enrolled at Dudley when she was only twelve years old. Her mother had taught at a two-teacher school when Elreta was four, enrolling the child in the first grade two years early. As a child, Elreta was curious and determined. After she had an operation at age thirteen to remove a ruptured appendix, the doctor told Reverend Melton that his daughter was precocious, and Elreta "couldn't wait to get out of the hospital to look in the dictionary to see what the word 'precocious' meant." She was involved in Dudley's music programs and joined the drama club. When she served as manager for her friend Juanita Hunter's student government campaign, Elreta labored over the speech she gave in support of her friend. Reverend Melton helped her to write it and taught her when and how to use inflections in her voice. She presented the speech in the Dudley High School auditorium, which Elreta thought "was the biggest thing I [had] ever seen," but because of her nerves, she talked too quickly, and the other kids mocked her. Elreta returned home that evening determined to "conquer that stage." Almost forty years later, as an accomplished judge, Elreta Alexander admitted that "it's always been hard for me to speak on the Dudley High School stage."[30] By then, public speaking was generally not something that bothered Alexander.

Attending all-Black schools did not eliminate students' exposure to discrimination, and reactions to skin color were at play in Elreta's world and in her educational experiences. Elreta Alexander recalled a teacher at Dudley High School, Mrs. Minor, who made fun of the darker children and those whose parents worked in the service industry, calling them names such as "hayseed" in front of the class.[31] Alexander stated these children often came to school without having the opportunity to get the lint out of their hair, indicating that they worked in one of Greensboro's textile factories to help their family. Colorism—discrimination based on skin tone—also existed at Dudley. The color of one's skin, even within the African American community, can affect how a person is treated socially and professionally. Lighter-skinned African Americans have tended to reap the benefits of colorism, while darker-skinned individuals have faced more discrimination even within their own race. Issues of colorism can be prominent among children as well. When discussing her time at Dudley High, Alexander stated, "Discrimination against darker-skinned students by the teachers was typical, unless they had special talents (e.g., athletes).... We had a saying at that time: 'If you're white, you're right; if you're yellow, you're mellow; if you're black, get back.'"[32] As a child, Elreta primarily spent her time with lighter-skinned children, perhaps in an attempt to avoid pejorative comments regarding the color of her skin or a need to be with those most like her.

As a descendant of two white grandparents, Elreta Alexander was extremely light. As an adult, she was acutely aware that the color of her skin affected the way people thought of her. Light skin was symbolic of the upper class, particularly for Black women and girls. Light-skinned Black women found themselves with more educational and professional opportunities; thus, they often ended up in a higher socioeconomic group.[33] While the lightness of Alexander's skin did not ensure her place in middle-class society, she was cognizant of the benefits it provided her.

At Dudley, however, her skin tone did not always help Elreta's position. For some light-skinned African Americans, especially those who do not conform to preconceived notions of Black identity, lightness means having their Blackness challenged. Elreta Alexander recalled other students calling her "high yellow" at times. It also influenced the way teachers treated her. Alexander later stated that while Mrs. Minor treated the darker children as inferiors, she mocked Elreta, referring to her as "Madam Queen" when she did not laugh at Minor's jokes intended to belittle the darker-skinned children. Young Elreta was very talkative and assertive and made sure she expressed her dissatisfaction with Minor's treatment of other children; she even alerted her father and the principal, Dr. Tarpley, to the situation. The principal called Minor into his office, where she was apparently reprimanded. While other teachers whispered that Elreta seemed to think she was as good at their jobs as they were, the situation was quelled. Later, Alexander stated that this incident probably changed the trajectory of her life; she would also face issues of colorism outside the Black community in her graduate career.[34]

Young Elreta was undoubtedly affected by southern society's prevalent racial attitudes, although the nature of her response was complicated. In a 1993 interview, Elreta Alexander was asked if she had thought about segregation as a child. She responded that she had thought about it, but that it did not necessarily have an adverse effect on her. At the same time, she did not long to be associated with white people.[35] When Alexander reflected on the Jim Crow period after a groundbreaking career, she was able to see the rewards of growing up—and persevering—during a trying time. As a Black child and teenager, however, it would have been hard to maintain this level of confidence in an environment designed to degrade and disempower African Americans. The Jim Crow South presented young Elreta with hurdles that she jumped over, establishing a pattern for her adult life and career.

The Meltons were at times disconnected from much of Greensboro's African American community because of class in addition to colorism. While Greensboro had a "small but significant" Black middle class, most African Americans worked in menial jobs serving whites.[36] Indeed, Reverend Melton's middle-class ideals sometimes did not go over well with his working-class parishioners. Despite all African Americans being seen as inferior by whites, the emergence of a Black middle class created friction within the Black community. Middle-class Black people often expressed a desire to reform or improve the lives of working-class Black people, even though many of the latter already emphasized the concept of respectability to their children. With their education and without the responsibility of being burdened by agricultural and domestic labor, many middle-class Black people felt their talents should be used for the sake of racial uplift. But what many viewed as racial uplift and respectability, others viewed as accommodation to white society. Additionally, the emphasis on self-help that accompanied uplift ideology sometimes indirectly faulted lower-class African Americans for their socioeconomic condition. Because he was an educated and well-spoken man, there was sometimes a rift between Melton and his congregants, highlighting the increasing tension between Black socioeconomic classes.

The strain between Melton and his congregants was not uncommon as the increased emphasis on higher education and the more subdued worship style of college-trained ministers clashed with older, untrained ministers and the laity. Many educated and well-trained Black ministers were unprepared for the conflicts they encountered as they attempted to reconcile traditional religious beliefs and practices with the ideals of middle-class respectability. The socioeconomic makeup of the United Institutional Baptist Church in Greensboro consisted of "the 'have nots' with a few educated middle income members," including teachers, a dentist, a college president, and a lawyer.[37] Most members served as domestic workers and laborers.

In the twentieth century, Black ministers found themselves increasingly torn between their spiritual duties and their efforts to uplift the race. While Melton was not the only middle-class Black man in the church, he led a group of people who generally did not have his educational attainment—or his twenty-five-dollar weekly salary. According to a church history, in January 1937, J. C. Melton resigned as the minister of United Institutional Baptist Church.[38] He left because of an inability to connect with his congregants and overcome increasingly fractious class divides.

As an adult, Elreta Alexander stated that her father's departure from United Institutional Baptist was a direct result of class conflict, and she claimed that her father had to leave the church "because he dared to work to send his kids to school."[39] The church members, however, believed the Melton family had more money than they needed. According to Alexander, her father did not willingly resign but left when the church withheld his salary after his wife and three children all graduated from college. The incident highlights class divisions in the African American community, which Elreta would confront head on in her legal career.

The Melton family's racial and class status set the foundation that Elreta built on to become a pioneering attorney and judge. Racial etiquette was an important component of growing up in the Jim Crow South. It determined where you fit in the community and how you would interact with those around you. The Meltons, however, worked to ensure that Elreta was able to determine her own role and place in society while still maintaining notions of respectability and, perhaps most important, respect for herself. In fact, there was a rule regarding education in the Melton household: nobody could sleep under Reverend Melton's roof who did not finish college.[40] The Melton family afforded their children a college education, and ultimately all three offspring were always able to sleep under their father's roof.

After Elreta Melton graduated from Dudley High School in 1934 at age fifteen, she enrolled at North Carolina Agricultural and Technical University. Besides being the local historically Black university and located only a few blocks from the Melton family home, NC A&T was a natural choice for Elreta because both her brother and sister went to school there, as did many mentors and leaders in Greensboro's Black community. The city of Greensboro fostered a sense of activism in its young Black students, including Elreta, and NC A&T would later become an integral part of the civil rights movement. Her collegiate career at NC A&T reinforced the importance of education and respectability in her life, in addition to marking the beginning of her turbulent personal life.

In the early twentieth century, however, a formal education was out of reach for most African Americans. Many whites in Jim Crow society subscribed to the notions of scientific racism, believing those of African descent to be inferior, lazy, and not intelligent enough to receive an education beyond vocational training. A formal education elevated the class status of Black families. At the same time, it placed a heavy burden of responsibility on their shoulders. It was expected that those African Americans who received an advanced education would use that knowledge for the benefit of the race. This concept of "socially responsible individualism," as described by historian Stephanie Shaw, made privileged young African Americans acutely aware that they were not getting an education just for themselves, but their education should be used to change the position of African Americans in society.[41]

North Carolina Agricultural and Technical University started in 1891 in Raleigh as an annex to Shaw University called the Agricultural and Mechanical College for the Colored Race. The school was a land-grant college funded by the second Morrill Act, passed by Congress on August 30, 1890, which provided each state with $15,000 a year for institutions focusing on agriculture, mechanical arts, math, and sciences. The act also stipulated that the money should not go to a college where race was a factor in the admission of students. Separate colleges for Black and white students, however, were in compliance as long as the funds were equally distributed between the Black and white schools. On March 3, 1892, the board voted to relocate the college to Greensboro, and the school began to expand to include courses in the humanities, fine arts, business, and education. In 1915, the school was renamed the Negro Agricultural and Technical College of North Carolina (A&T).[42]

A&T became a cornerstone of Greensboro's Black community. Along with the all-Black private women's college, Bennett, the school became an example of Greensboro's perceived racial progressiveness. The condition of Greensboro's African American community can be traced back to its access to education. From the 1930s through the 1950s, African Americans in Greensboro had a higher median education level than Black people in other North Carolina cities, as well as a higher median income, with 15 percent of African Americans in town working in professional careers. In the Jim Crow era, Greensboro's Black schools were an important source of activism and change. The college, however, maintained its academic rigor. In the 1920s and 1930s, A&T was an up-and-coming academic institution, quickly increasing and solidifying its academic reputation and becoming known to Black America as a place of excellence. A&T was also a hub for community gatherings, political dialogue, cultural events, and intellectual discussion, a place where Greensboro's African Americans, who were denied access to white institutions, could engage in and cultivate intelligent discourse.[43]

Elreta enrolled at A&T as a scholarship student in 1934. The school encouraged women like her to take a wide variety of courses even though professional options were limited for college-educated Black women. The interwar years saw expanding educational opportunities for Black women, and A&T's catalog stated that "all courses in the College are open to women on the same basis as men. There is a great demand for well-trained women not only as teachers but in practically all fields of endeavor." Despite this wording, college-educated Black women, who were expected to become leaders of their race, were generally steered toward teaching. Elreta did not have formal plans to stray far from what was expected of her. She majored in music, focusing heavily on cultivating her talents. She traveled around the state in plays "to show that decent kids could go to A&T college." At A&T she continued to apply the values of her childhood and embraced the notion of socially responsible individualism to use her talents and education for the betterment of her race.[44]

At A&T Elreta was both socially popular and academically successful. To earn extra money, she waited tables, while maintaining her grades and an active social life. She was consistently on the school's honor roll, earning a high grade point average, and was an active member of the Ivy Leaf Club, A&T's chapter of the Alpha Kappa Alpha sorority. Elreta also described herself as having many boyfriends, and she and her older sister, Etta, were regulars in the gossip section of the school's newspaper, the *Register*. In one edition, the columnist wrote, "A and T male students are sticking close to Home Sweet Home this year. . . . Motley has found a home at last with one of the Melton sisters," and later, "Wonder what Miss Elreta Melton will do now. Miss Loretta Bagwell and Miss Marion Leech are pulling straws over Mr. Richard Lewis. Whatta man!"[45] Elreta Alexander never divulged what happened with Richard Lewis, but she seemed to never have problems attracting the attention of men.

Elreta's older brother, Judson Melton, was also involved in the Greek system and served as president of the Alpha Phi Alpha fraternity at A&T. Alpha was a "high-brow, white-collar, light-skinned, high-achieving fraternity," as Elreta Alexander described it. Black fraternities were instrumental in forming what E. Franklin Frazier calls the "Black bourgeoisie." Frazier argues that membership in Greek letter societies for African American men indicated upward mobility: the ability to escape working-class roots and achieve middle-class status.[46] And like many fraternities, Alpha also provided social and recreational activities, like dances, for African American youth during Jim Crow.

Elreta claimed to have been the "official songstress" at A&T during the early 1930s. Her musical talent landed her several notable gigs, and she frequently sang solos at school events, such as dances, cantatas, and special programs.[47] It was her talent as a singer that led to her introduction to her first husband. During her last year at Dudley, at age fifteen, at the Alpha annual dance, Elreta had been invited to sing the 1933 Jerry Livingston hit, "Under a Blanket of Blue," during the intermission. After arriving at the dance with his sister and his girlfriend, Judson Melton put Girardeau "Tony" Alexander, a shy, innocent pledge, in charge of his little sister for the rest of the evening. Much to Elreta's dismay, Tony's dancing abilities were not up to her standards, and she left the party disappointed that she did not dance with other college men. From that night forward, however, Tony would always be a part of her life.

Tony Alexander's father, also named Girardeau, grew up in Brooklyn, and had been sent to attend college in North Carolina after impregnating a girl in New York. He became one of the first three engineering graduates from A&T, where he met and subsequently married Tony's mother, Lavinia Waugh. She was a Greensboro native and a graduate of Palmer Memorial Institute in Sedalia, North Carolina, which was founded by Dr. Charlotte Hawkins Brown. Tony was born on December 4, 1914, on East Market Street in Greensboro before the family returned to New York, where Tony grew up. Tony's father deserted the family when he was nine, so he was primarily raised by Lavinia. Tony returned to Greensboro at the behest of his maternal grandfather, Lee Waugh, who was a native of the area. It was common for young African

Americans with the ability to go to college to attend institutions where they or their parents had social, familial, or professional connections.[48]

It took a while for Tony to secure Elreta's affections. After she enrolled at A&T, however, he increasingly became a fixture in Elreta's life, even when she dated other young men. She later recalled, "I didn't want to get tied up with him, but gradually I began to date him. The first thing I did was teach him how to dance, in my father's living room." J. C. Melton kept a watchful eye over his youngest child's dating life. Frequently courting at the Melton house, Elreta stated that her father "was very jolly, and he would always come in and tell the fellows jokes. But he would never leave you in the living room but five or ten minutes, and you would hear him clear his throat." As Elreta and Tony became an exclusive couple, it became apparent that they had drastically different personalities. While Elreta was social and participated in school dances, Tony sat in the corner and watched. But Elreta grew to respect his intelligence and his work ethic. Despite their budding relationship, Elreta Alexander later admitted, "I'd still pull my antics. . . . He'd come in the front door and I'd run out the back . . . because I knew we were getting too close." Young Elreta was not in a hurry to be tied down, but despite her efforts she was linked with him in the A&T newspaper. In 1936, it was reported that "G. Alexand[er] is falling for the lovely Elrita [*sic*] Melton. Tony, she is plenty 'smart.'" Later that year in the column "Campus Chatter," the author stated, "If you'd stop mooning about Tony, Miss Melton, I'd tell you something. Perhaps he'd rather tell you."[49] The author was not specific as to what Tony would rather tell Elreta, but the statement foreshadowed the tempestuous bond the two formed.

As Tony's confidence grew, he began to exhibit some self-destructive behavior. He attended parties with another fraternity, the Omegas, known for their frequent drinking and carousing. Judson Melton even threatened to kick Tony out of Alpha. Elreta's best friend, Katharine Tynes, also grew weary of Tony, saying, "You know, I don't like him. He's so brilliant; [but] I don't like him."[50] After being put on probation by the fraternity, Tony cleaned up his act, but his hard drinking and erratic behavior returned several years later.

While Tony's behavior could be difficult to tolerate, it was the loss of her best friend that Elreta never overcame. Katharine Tynes, who was also the daughter of a minister in Greensboro, and Elreta both attended Dudley High and A&T. For years the friends were "almost like twins," and they encouraged each other through their academic endeavors. They pledged for a sorority together, double-dated, and went to school dances together. When Katharine died by suicide in July 1935 at the age of eighteen, Elreta, who was sixteen at the time, was devastated. As Elreta Alexander remembered forty-two years later:

> It changed my life; I began to look at people for what they were, and I was less concerned about just the good times: . . . I became determined to live out Katharine's life; . . . If I hadn't tried to live Katharine's life too, I think I would have just been a flirt. . . . After her death, I began taking up for the underdog. I talked to people on the street, which I hadn't done before.[51]

The death of her best friend haunted Elreta for years, and she stated that she felt Katharine's presence with her often.

After Katharine's death, Elreta began to feel sorry for Tony because "he could not communicate with such a brilliant mind." When Tony graduated from A&T, he gave Elreta his fraternity pin, and she promised to marry him "if I could grow up first; I was only 17 at the time." After she graduated from A&T in 1937 at age eighteen, Elreta Melton and Tony Alexander became engaged. Tony attended Meharry Medical College in Nashville, Tennessee, which was the first medical school for African Americans in the South, founded in 1876. Elreta went to Chester, South Carolina, for a year to teach history, math, and music. According to her, she did not necessarily want to become a teacher, but "I wanted to get free . . . hang loose."[52] After living under the strict guidance of her father, this teaching job was Elreta's first time on her own, in addition to being what was expected of her.

Teaching was a common profession among young, educated Black women, but it was not an easy job, with Black teachers earning less money and teaching more children than their white counterparts. A&T, like other historically Black colleges, trained women students in a variety of areas, which proved helpful for new teachers, who regularly found themselves faced with tasks requiring training outside their field, including raising money for the school and its students. The system of "double taxation" was even more prevalent in rural schools for African American children, where resources and opportunities were more limited than in urban areas such as Greensboro. Minimal funding came from local and state governments, while the community supported education by supplementing teachers' salaries or by supplying housing or providing food at a low cost. Elreta paid fifteen dollars a month for rent out of her fifty-seven-dollar monthly salary.[53]

At only nineteen years old, Elreta was not ready to settle down with one man. While in Chester, she became involved with a divorced man eighteen years her senior named Harold Crawford. Crawford was an engineering professor at South Carolina State University, a historically Black university approximately one hundred miles south of Chester. When Tony and Harold unexpectedly showed up to the same choral concert in Chester, Tony became so upset that he threatened to quit medical school and marry her right away. Elreta, however, did not want to marry while Tony was still in medical school. Reverend Melton also did not want her to get married yet and advised Elreta to think long and hard about her decision: "You could get pregnant, and then you couldn't work to send him through school, and you'd have to struggle."[54] Despite her father's advice and her own hesitations, Elreta reluctantly agreed to marry Tony.

Elreta Alexander later reflected that "at 19 years, one does not have the maturity of an adult." The seeming inevitability of the union, combined with immaturity and the guilt she felt due to Tony's emotional manipulation, ultimately overruled Elreta's doubts. On June 7, 1938, they were both in Greensboro, and with Reverend Melton out of town for a meeting, the couple eloped in a taxi to Asheboro, North Carolina, about thirty miles south. Elreta Alexander later remembered the clerk in the register of deeds office who issued their marriage license, "because she said she never will forget how scared I was."[55] Clearly, Elreta knew that marriage was not a wise decision. Her terror at getting married likely arose from some knowledge of the erratic nature of Tony's disposition. Time would prove that her fears were not unfounded.

The new Mrs. Alexander was nineteen years old; her husband was twenty-three. The couple returned to Greensboro, and the next day Tony left. He went to New York City where he worked during the summer before returning to Meharry in the fall. Elreta kept the marriage a secret from her family, which took its toll. She stated, "I stayed in my room for about a month, crying, and [my parents] thought I was sick and didn't know what was wrong with me. I was ashamed to tell them, I was scared of being married, I couldn't go out with fellows.... My parents were really concerned about my mental welfare." Elreta did not want to return to South Carolina, as the state did not allow married women to teach.[56] She later said she did not want to teach under false pretenses. Although jobs and money were scarce, Elreta was able to secure a position at Gates Training School in Sunbury, North Carolina, later in 1938.

In Sunbury, located in the Albemarle Sound region of northeastern North Carolina, Elreta Alexander quickly learned about the realities of Black families who did not have the benefit of a middle-class lifestyle or easy access to education. Sunbury is where Elreta's grandparents had married. She described the area and the children as "very poor ... farming country.... These kids, some of them would have to walk ten or twelve miles each way to go to school. And on rainy days, it was the first time I'd ever seen oxcarts, [they did] the best they could to get any education." Alexander taught the children of parents who worked in the agricultural or lumber industries, which were prominent in the area. At the time, Gates County had no paved roads, and citizens largely survived because they grew their own food. Earning $528 annually, Alexander taught English, math, and music, and under her direction the school choir began fundraising performances to raise money to bus children to school.[57]

The year after Sunbury, Elreta was in Taylorsville, North Carolina, approximately ninety miles west of Greensboro, where she taught math and music at Happy Plains School, the only school for Black students in Alexander County.[58] While Elreta taught in Taylorsville, Tony worked to complete medical school at Meharry. He had a small Model A Ford, which he drove over the Appalachian Mountains every two or three months to visit his wife. When Tony graduated from Meharry in 1940, he accepted an internship at Reynolds Hospital in Winston-Salem, North Carolina, before taking a two-year surgical residency at L. Richardson Hospital, the all-Black hospital in Greensboro.[59]

When Tony secured his residency, he demanded that Elreta stop teaching. While the male breadwinner model was never standard in African American families, middle-class Black men had difficulty escaping the ideal of a patriarchal family structure. The husband-as-provider model was especially important because it kept Black women out of the homes of white people, where they often performed degrading domestic labor. During the Great Depression, this family structure had been almost impossible to maintain. But as a doctor, Tony now had the financial ability to support himself and his wife. Elreta, playing the role of dutiful wife, returned to Greensboro, and the couple went public with their marriage.[60]

Even in these early years in Greensboro, Elreta already "realized [she] had made a very serious mistake" in marrying Tony. While Tony struggled with alcohol, he also had to face changing societal norms. Patriarchal and traditional family structures continued to change when the United States entered World War II. As more young women entered the job market and earned limited economic independence, assumptions based on the "man-as-provider model began to clash with reality." Elreta claimed later that Tony kept her on a tight leash financially, refusing to purchase items for their new house while bringing in $500 a month as a doctor. Many women wanted to assert their financial independence, and more married women began working for wages, further destabilizing older breadwinner models.[61] After much persuading, Tony gave Elreta permission to work as long as she was home by four o'clock in the afternoon when he returned for the day. A&T president F. D. Bluford offered Elreta a position as an assistant in the A&T library, where she earned $75 a month.[62]

It was in her new life as an unhappy, part-time housewife that Elreta made a formative decision about her career. In 1943, an African American Methodist minister, the Reverend Robert Sharp, ran for Greensboro City Council. Elreta later described him as "a perennial runner and a perennial loser, mainly to get [Black] people involved and to exercise their franchise." Sharp had certainly been a perennial loser. In his 1933 race for Greensboro City Council, only about 12 percent of the voters citywide had supported him. In the next two elections, white candidates polled higher than Sharp even in Black areas, and he never received more than 15 percent of the ballots cast.[63] With little work to do at home, as she was not yet a mother and only worked part time, Elreta decided to volunteer for Sharp's 1943 campaign and learn a little bit about politics. According to Elreta, workers for African American politicians in Greensboro "more or less" paid African Americans for their votes. Reverend Sharp, however, did not pay and subsequently lost the election, coming in ninth out of twelve candidates. It was, however, his best showing in a Greensboro City Council election.[64]

Alexander was distraught. She was consoled by Sharp, however, who said, "Elreta, I didn't run to win. . . . In your lifetime, you'll see something change; you'll see us marching to the polls and being a part of citizenship. . . . Don't cry about it; do something about it." The next day, Sharp brought her a copy of *Blackstone's Commentaries on the Law* and told her she would make a good lawyer. Alexander initially laughed at the suggestion, and her father thought it was absurd and suggested she work on her master's degree and go back into teaching. But she instead decided to take back some of the agency she had given up early in her marriage and tell Tony she would be going back to school. According to Elreta, "The tables had turned. No longer was he the sniveling lover; he was the big man, the pretty little doctor . . . and he had the women running after him . . . and he'd been as poor as Joe's turkey." Tony, with his newfound confidence and large paycheck, had no problems with his wife returning to school. He responded, "Go to any school you want to, but you have to live with my mother in New York. I'm glad to get you out of town." After marrying young and while still in school, Tony was perhaps eager to discover himself on his own terms as well. Elreta agreed to Tony's condition but not without making him hurt. She "looked at every school in New York that taught law: Fordham, New York U, St. John's, Columbia. And I looked and I said, all right, which one is the most expensive? That bastard, I'm gonna take care of him. I'm gonna make him spend some of his money." Elreta only applied to Columbia University Law School, and after the admissions staff reviewed her character and credentials, she was accepted to its summer program.[65]

What started out as a part-time housewife's attempt to stay active put Elreta Alexander on the path to a groundbreaking legal career. Because of Sharp's loss in the city council election, Alexander tapped into her sense of justice and began to pursue a career seeking justice for others. She later stated that the excuses she gave for going to law school was that Tony was registered for the draft, she wanted to find her career, and "you couldn't tell what was going to happen and we didn't have children." Men were leaving to fight in the war, and women were taking on new responsibilities on the home front. The U.S. involvement in World War II therefore provided a way to explain Elreta's failed effort at middle-class and gender conformity. She decided to join the waves of women leaving the home and embarking on professional careers, while still carrying with her to New York the lessons of her childhood.[66]

CHAPTER 2

Between Two Worlds

THE LIFE OF A HOUSEWIFE and part-time library worker was not for Elreta Alexander. Attending Columbia Law School was her way out of the traditional domestic role her husband wanted from her. Alexander's time in New York was formative not only because it marked the beginning of her impressive legal career, but because her experiences serve as a lens through which one can examine the increasing integration of the legal profession, regional understandings of race, the nature of activism, and how women navigated new worlds opening up to them because of World War II. Before she was a precursor to other Black women legal scholars, she had to learn how to operate in a nearly all-white environment as the first African American woman at Columbia Law. She was accepted into the university's summer program in 1943 and continued to pursue her degree in the fall. While at Columbia and after returning to Greensboro, Alexander made formative decisions about her identity, her career, and her personal life. New York presented Alexander with decisions she would have never faced had she remained in Greensboro, such as consciously embracing her identity as a Black woman, leaving the Harlem legal scene and returning home, and what kind of activism she would embrace.

Alexander's pursuit of a legal career set her on a path where she would break down career barriers for other African American women, even though it initially started as a way to seek revenge on her husband, Dr. Tony Alexander. Her decision to attend Columbia was not based on the school's stellar reputation, but rather was a furious and determined choice to spend some of her husband's new salary. Further, she thought that if she left town, her husband would miss her and eventually beg her to come home. Tony, however, never asked her to come home but demanded that Alexander live with his mother, Lavinia, who lived half an hour away from Columbia by subway.[1]

Elreta Alexander had nervously prepared for her new life in New York. She recalled, "My sister made me some beautiful clothes so I could be decent going to Columbia Law School." Part of attending Columbia was fitting in with her classmates, whom the professors "expected to become Senators." She could not help standing out, however. After growing up in an environment somewhat shielded from racial struggles, Alexander for the first time was singled out because of her race. Yet it was not the typical scrutiny that most African Americans of the time experienced. The dean of the law school, Young B. Smith, warmly greeted Alexander: "We welcome you Ms. Alexander. You know, you're the first woman of your race we've ever accepted in this school. We've had women here since 1927." Dean Smith emphasized that the law school had hoped to admit an African American woman, and that Alexander's performance could determine whether the faculty would be open to admitting others. Smith's greeting unnerved Alexander. She later said that she felt trapped: "they put the weight of a whole race of people on me," so much that she could not even hear the lectures during the first six weeks of classes. But when Alexander's mother-in-law told her to go home because she should be with her husband instead of in law school, the comment strengthened Alexander's resolve and made her determined to continue.[2]

World War II affected the operation of Columbia Law School. The number of law students drastically decreased during the war years as young men went off to fight, bringing enrollment down to 118 in October 1943, from 505 in October 1940, a drop of 77 percent. With fewer students, seminars were canceled, the moot court halted operations, and the *Columbia Law Review* ran with a reduced staff and cut the number of yearly issues from eight to six. In an attempt to mitigate the effects of lower enrollment, Columbia Law had introduced in December 1941 an accelerated program whose aim was to help male students subject to the draft complete as much of their coursework as possible before being called to war. Many other students, including Alexander, took advantage of the program, attending additional fourteen-week summer sessions, which allowed law students to complete a three-year program in two. Despite fewer students, Columbia Law professors saw their workloads increase, as year-round teaching responsibilities were spread among a faculty reduced by one-third. Many had been granted leaves of absence to participate in military or government service. By 1943, the student body included ambitious women able to earn slots in the law school due to the lack of young men, as well as men who were physically disqualified from service. When Alexander entered the program, one-half of the law school's student body were first-year students, and of those, 43 percent were women.[3]

As in other occupations, the high number of men fighting overseas created opportunities not previously available to women, including married women. While Columbia Law's accelerated program was originally designed to help young men finish their law degrees before entering the armed services, it also produced women attorneys of "first-rate ability" who could help fill a demand for young lawyers. One of those was Bella Abzug, who would later become a member of Congress. In 1976, Abzug stated, "When I was at Columbia Law School, America was involved in World War II. As terrible as the war was, it opened many doors to American women that might otherwise have remained shut. . . . Suddenly woman power was perceived as a national resource." Elreta Alexander's admittance into Columbia also opened doors for other African American women. Constance Baker Motley entered Columbia Law in February 1944, just a few months after Alexander. Motley too was a light-skinned, middle-class African American. Raised in New Haven, Connecticut, her family also placed emphasis on the importance of an education. Motley went on to become the first African American woman to be appointed to the federal judiciary.[4]

The North offered more opportunities to Black women than the rural South did, and Black women such as Ella Baker, Pauli Murray, and Elreta Alexander took advantage of opportunities in New York.[5] While Alexander was undoubtedly academically gifted, her admittance to Columbia may not have been based solely on grades. Years later she expressed her belief that Columbia had selected her because she was a married woman with light skin and therefore a "safe" choice.[6] Alexander's start at Columbia was rocky. Because of the pressure put on her immediately upon arrival, her mind was disoriented, and she could not answer the questions in class. She was sure the faculty felt they had selected the wrong Black woman, but she made it through the first summer session before going to talk to Dean Smith. She explained that her husband needed her at home. Tony Alexander had been made a draft board physician, which kept him in Greensboro and out of World War II, despite having registered for the draft. Smith was not happy with Alexander's decision. He told her, "You're making a serious mistake. The South is going to need a person like you. . . . You can communicate with anybody." The day after Elreta Alexander arrived back in Greensboro, a letter arrived from Smith, asking Tony if he could spare her for the semester, stating that it was best for her to remain in law school. Tony, who still enjoyed the financial and social perks of being a young, handsome doctor, said to his wife, "What the hell are you doing here? Get yourself back on up there!" Alexander returned to Columbia and never considered leaving the school again.[7] From then until she finished her degree, Alexander thrived at Columbia Law.

Several professors and fellow students at Columbia had a major influence on Alexander. Professor Jerome Michael taught criminal law and the philosophy of law. During World War II, Michael served as a special assistant to the attorney general of the United States while remaining at Columbia. According to Alexander, Michael was "an attractive Jewish man with monocles." Uncharacteristically timid while at Columbia, Alexander rarely spoke up in class. That did not stop her, however, from apparently making an impression on the married Michael. Alexander believed that "Prof. Michael had an interest in me that wasn't academic, because he was always inviting me into his office to confer on this nice sofa he had there. . . . He made his intentions known. He had a hard crush on me." Michael was also particularly hard on Herman Taylor, another African American student, because the professor had observed the close friendship Taylor had with Alexander.[8] For Michael, who was a professor at one of the most prestigious law schools in the country, pursuing Elreta Alexander took advantage of the hierarchy of the professor-student relationship. Sexual harassment of women by white-collar professionals was common, and it was also justified by the myth that Black women were sexually voracious and indiscriminate.[9] Alexander, to her credit, did not succumb to Michael's advances. But given her timidity at Columbia and the disproportionate power dynamic, it is unlikely that she offered a strong rebuke. Regardless of the inappropriateness of Professor Michael's feelings or actions toward Alexander, he was known for preparing his students for the rigors of practicing law. Michael developed students' abilities to think clearly and provided them with opportunities to develop applicable skills in preparation for their profession, which would serve Alexander in later courtroom battles.[10]

Professor Paul R. Hays also influenced Alexander. According to Constance Baker Motley, Hays was regarded as the most liberal professor in the law school. During Alexander's time at Columbia, Hays was a young, successful lawyer for Pepsi-Cola, very popular with the students, and known for taking an interest in their careers even after they graduated.[11] When Alexander took his course on labor law, he made her argue on the side of management—he knew she leaned toward the labor side—which provided her with balance and perspective. Hays later made her paper on international labor law required reading for his course. "A Student's Plan for Peace" shows a future attorney dedicated to human and civil rights. Written in April 1944, Alexander's plan was built on the assumption that the Allied nations would establish some sort of international association and utilize the International Labour Organization in global labor relations.[12] Obviously closely following world events and evolving global discussions, Alexander proposed a world organization consisting of three major divisions: an assembly, a security council, and a world court, all designed to "increase men's happiness in socioeconomic fields . . . [and] to aid in the preservation of peace." Alexander also addressed the plight of oppressed peoples in the United States and throughout the world: "The exploitation of racial, religious and minority groups is another dark spot in our national and international history. The thirst for economic power which has made the peoples of the world half slave and half free has sought its justification in the *a priori* development of a psychology of innate superiority, or condescending benevolence, or what have you."[13] Professor Hays's course, and law school in general, gave Alexander the opportunity to develop and articulate broad beliefs and ideas on race in the United States and throughout the world. Decades later, when Alexander contacted Hays for a reference for a fellowship, he told her, "Nobody who ever met you failed to remember you."[14] Alexander's skill as a litigator, along with her personality, made an impression on the Columbia Law faculty.

Like during her time at A&T, Alexander balanced rigorous coursework with an active social life. Meetings with friends at Chock Full o' Nuts, dinner parties, and strolls down Broadway frequently filled her social calendar. Herman Taylor, one of the few other African American students at Columbia Law, became a close friend. Because "Herman" sounded like "German," Alexander opted to call him "Fritz." Taylor was from Richmond, Virginia, and had graduated in 1938 from Virginia Union University, another historically Black university. While the two shared a somewhat similar background, Taylor did not come from a middle-class family. Growing up, Taylor had made money by completing tasks for Black doctors, but they had adopted "white man's ways" and forced Taylor to come in the back door. According to Alexander, Taylor was bitter. But he persevered and had received a master's in business administration at Columbia before attending law school. At Columbia he worked at the faculty club and provided Alexander with turkey sandwiches. Taylor also worked for the National Association for the Advancement of Colored People (NAACP), keeping records for Thurgood Marshall. In fact, it was through Herman Taylor that Constance Baker Motley secured her first job at the NAACP's Legal Defense and Educational Fund, replacing Taylor as a clerk to Marshall.[15] Despite having a small number of African American students, Columbia Law produced some of the most groundbreaking Black attorneys in the nation.

Alexander's New York social life also presented the opportunity to embrace her identity as a Black woman. Alexander's race seemed to be more of an issue in New York City than it had been in Greensboro, where she primarily spent time with other African Americans. Issues of colorism continued to be prominent in Alexander's relationships, and Taylor was significantly darker than she was. While northern states did not adopt the strict Jim Crow policies that permeated the South, the issue of colorism was just as pervasive at Columbia as it was at Dudley High School. Alexander was cognizant of the issue and was willing to point out that people treated two individuals of the same race differently because of their skin tone. When Alexander received invitations to parties, she insisted Taylor be invited as well. "The white students would invite me to all their parties; I was invisible and didn't shock their mores.... I always took Herman with me when I'd go with my white friends, and sometimes sitting on the subway, Herman would be the only dark person in the group." Having attended all-Black schools until Columbia, Alexander became acutely aware that her light skin afforded her opportunities not open to Taylor. It was when walking down Broadway with white friends that Alexander first realized she could "pass" without trying.[16]

Over the years many African Americans with light complexions, such as Alexander, "passed" as white. In the antebellum South, those who could "pass" did so to avoid not their Blackness, but the confines of slavery. After emancipation, "passing" as white helped some African Americans avoid the horrors of the Jim Crow era, but it could also be seen as a traitorous move against their own race, and often meant denying their family and community. As Alexander increasingly became part of a predominately white legal community, her ability to "pass" as white taught her about the power of racial privilege. She realized that her light skin gave her the ability to walk down Broadway without pause, while Herman Taylor did not have the same opportunity. For Alexander, this was an unexpected foray into the white world outside the segregated South she grew up in. She stated, "In New York, my Negro blood was hidden.... I was thrown into this white world, but I did have two sets of friends. Some weekends I'd be with the black lawyers and their friends.... But most of the time it was in a white world." Alexander later used her ability to "pass" as an effective weapon against racial discrimination, as a method of exposing the hypocrisy of supremacist thinking on the part of most whites.[17]

In her oral history, Alexander stated that many of the white students at Columbia Law had limited experience interacting with Black people, so "the only image they had of Negros was what they read in the paper or riding through Harlem." Other light-skinned African Americans had used their time at Columbia Law to reinvent themselves as white. After graduation in 1902, Theophilus John Minton Syphax legally changed his last name to McKee and started living as a white man, ultimately becoming a prominent Wall Street attorney. While the pressure of being an African American at an elite school such as Columbia might have been too much for some, Alexander met it head on.[18]

At Columbia, Alexander confronted her white friend, Mildred Preen, a member of the New Jersey state legislature while still a student, about avoiding Herman Taylor and other African Americans, but not her. She said, "You love me in spite of the fact that I am a Negro. But I want you to know that I will be a Negro all of my life, and I will never disclaim this. You must see me as I am.... I'm not going to live on the other side." Alexander said her white friends "just couldn't seem to understand how this girl with so many talents and with such fair skin, how she could be identified with Negros." Determined to show white society just how talented a Black woman could be, Alexander made the conscious decision to embrace her Blackness at Columbia Law and use her professional standing to advocate for other African Americans.[19]

Not only did Alexander openly embrace her Blackness at Columbia, she leveraged it to her advantage, using family connections to make herself known among prominent African Americans in Harlem. During the war many African Americans migrating north relied on family for contacts, employment information, and housing.[20] Middle-class professionals were no exception. Judge Miles Page mentored Alexander, served as one of her sponsors for the New York bar, and encouraged her to stay in New York to practice law. He even took her to meet Mayor Fiorello La Guardia, who had appointed Page to his position on the special sessions court. Alexander also later discussed her friendship with Judge Hubert Delany, who was a La Guardia–appointed judge in domestic relations court.[21] She even studied for the New York bar in the ten-room apartment of artist Romare Bearden, who was the nephew of Alexander's godmother, Anna Stuart.[22]

Alexander graduated from Columbia Law School on June 5, 1945. Returning to North Carolina after graduation had always been her plan. She had wanted to go home, work for the NAACP, and do civil rights litigation. The state of North Carolina, however, thwarted those plans. In 1945, North Carolina still did not want to admit African Americans into the state's white law schools. In 1940, a law school had been set up for African Americans at North Carolina Central University, then known as North Carolina College for Negroes. North Carolina would also pay to send African Americans out of state to law school.[23] Alexander, however, had not applied for state funding to attend Columbia because she was determined to use Tony's money. The statute also stated that North Carolina residents who attended law school had to register with the state within six months of beginning their studies in order to become eligible to take the bar exam. The only other ways for African Americans to become eligible to take the North Carolina bar was to prove they were "exceptional and meritorious" or to practice law in another state for five years.[24]

Alexander enlisted the aid of Professor Richard Powell, who taught property law at Columbia and during the summer taught at the University of North Carolina (UNC) Law School. He advised her that the law was a segregation statute: North Carolina did not want Black lawyers in the state. Powell and the dean of the UNC Law School, Robert Wettach, met with the law faculty at UNC, who designated her as "exceptional and meritorious" so she could practice in North Carolina. Other Columbia law school professors and Dean Smith submitted affidavits and attempted to contact the North Carolina bar on Alexander's behalf. With no response from the state, Alexander began studying for the New York bar exam, which was offered three times a year. North Carolina only offered it once a year, and so she proceeded with her application to take it, which prompted her hometown newspaper, the *Greensboro Record*, to publish a story in July 1945 under the heading "Negro Woman Applies to Take Bar."[25]

In addition to the obstacles to taking the North Carolina bar, Alexander found herself with yet another barrier to overcome. She woke up one Saturday morning in July 1945 with plans to study. She and her husband had purchased their first house in Greensboro, which had a partial basement with a heater room. She described in 1977 what occurred: "I went down to turn on the heater to heat the water so I could take a bath. The furnace was off. I went back to sleep.... The heater had been on maybe an hour and a half or two hours." They had just installed insulation in their little nine-by-ten-foot basement. When Alexander went back down, a slow gas leak caused an explosion and trapped her in the basement. She said, "It was butane gas, five times as hot as city gas. It worked the hell out of my legs, second- and third-degree burns. I was burned, as my late aunt said, 'from amazing grace to floating opportunity.'" Tony heard the blast and ran down to his wife. He went back to the phone where he had been speaking with another doctor and told him, "Elreta's been burned very badly.... Get over here as quick as you can and call the hospital."[26] Alexander's injuries left her bedridden for weeks, and Tony Alexander took time off and treated his wife's burns. The difficult situation, however, created some tense moments in the Alexander house. Etta Melton frequently argued with Tony over what she viewed as his rough treatment of her sister.

The week after Alexander's accident, she received a letter from the North Carolina Board of Examiners that she had been deemed "exceptional and meritorious," and she could sit for the bar exam. But Alexander was still too injured to take it. She cried and cried and was consoled by her father, who said, "Baby, God is trying to teach you a lesson. You can't walk, so you have to be still and know. In five years, you'll understand." After recovering enough to travel again, Alexander returned to New York and passed that bar exam in October 1945. She then took a position in Harlem at the Black law firm of Dyer and Stevens.[27]

Although Alexander's first job as an attorney was unpaid, it introduced her to activism in the Harlem community. Hope Stevens, a Harlem legal pioneer and partner in the firm, was one of Alexander's mentors. Originally from the Caribbean islands of St. Kitts and Nevis, Stevens migrated to New York in 1924 during the Harlem Renaissance. After graduating from City College in 1933 and Brooklyn Law School in 1936, he represented the former British colony in its fight for self-determination. In 1941, Stevens served as president of the Manhattan chapter of the National Negro Congress and helped negotiate an agreement with private bus companies in Harlem to hire Black drivers. He was also one of the Black lawyers and businessmen in Harlem who created the United Mutual Life Insurance Company, and in 1948 he helped found the Carver Federal Savings and Loan Association, which "set an example for other banks in lending money to Negroes to purchase property."[28] Together, Stevens and his partner Joe Dyer would give Alexander a crash course on how to be a trial attorney.

Alexander's early legal experience came with some successes and some embarrassing mishaps. Her first duty at Dyer and Stevens was to go down to Chambers Street to answer the calendar, which established what time and at what location each case would be tried. All she had to do was respond with "Ready" or "For the motion" when the firm's cases came up so they would be assigned to the proper division. When her time came, Alexander recalled, she opened her mouth, but nothing came out. Fortunately, Dyer, feeling she might get nervous, was there to call "Ready."[29] Alexander was able to preserve some of her dignity and keep working. It would not be long before she found her voice.

Alexander also quickly gained experience by working on high-profile cases. Having done the research for Stevens in a lawsuit against the Delaware-Lackawanna Railroad, in which Stevens represented porters and waiters in a salary dispute, Alexander prepared the appellate brief in the case to be argued before the U.S. Court of Appeals for the Second Circuit. At the time of the hearing, however, Stevens was still in the Caribbean representing another client. The firm could not afford to have the case thrown out, but Alexander was not yet able to appear before the court. Even though she had passed the New York bar exam, she had not yet received her license nor been sworn in. With the help of a former Columbia Law classmate, Alexander was able to get the court's permission to proceed. Despite her inexperience and the five attorneys representing the Delaware-Lackawanna Railroad, Alexander won the case. Her presence was memorable to the judges but not because of her skills as a litigator. To argue the case, Alexander had bought a new suit, complete with a brown hat with a feather. As she made her argument, the feather waved at the justices, who were apparently amused by the young attorney's outfit. While the trial marked the first of many wins, it also marked the first time Alexander was remembered for her fashion sense.[30]

Alexander continued to practice her courtroom skills. In a landlord-tenant case in which she represented a landlord suing a tenant for "possession of contraband," she later said she was so nervous that she bumbled her entire argument and left her boss, Hope Stevens, embarrassed, the judge laughing behind his hands, and the jury totally confused. Alexander, however, won the case. After the trial, the judge asked Alexander to approach the bench and said, "Little lady, you have a good stance before the jury. Don't be discouraged. Just keep on. Keep on trying cases."[31] Alexander took the judge's words to heart and kept navigating her way through the legal system. As a young attorney, Alexander argued assault, driving under the influence, and divorce cases. She won some and lost some, but she gained valuable experience and honed her trial technique.

While Alexander worked in Harlem, she was determined to practice law in her home state. In the spring of 1946, she returned to Raleigh, North Carolina, to apply again to take the bar exam. The secretary who gave her the application said, "Them damn Yankees got too upset about you. We're damn sick about them damn Yankees trying to run our business down here."[32] The secretary told Alexander she had to be a resident of North Carolina for twelve months before taking the exam and was not allowed to file because she had been practicing in New York. While waiting to reestablish her North Carolina residency, Alexander continued to work in Harlem with Dyer and Stevens but remained unpaid other than the costs of traveling back and forth so as not to compromise her residency.[33]

The struggle to take the North Carolina bar at times left Alexander discouraged. She lamented the fact that in North Carolina she did not have any "big white people" to speak for her, as she did in New York. One evening in 1947, Alexander sat on the porch of her parents' home discussing her options with her father. As they talked, Fannie White walked past the house. White was a former parishioner of Reverend Melton's church and the longtime cook for Pierce Rucker, a prominent white businessman in Greensboro and chair of the North Carolina Democratic Party. Melton stopped White and asked her to put in a good word with Rucker on behalf of his daughter. White mentioned that North Carolina governor Gregg Cherry would be dining with the Ruckers the following evening, and she agreed to bring it up. Two days later Rucker asked to meet with Alexander. He told her to apply for the bar again, without emphasizing her membership in the New York bar, and assured her that she would not have any more problems. Alexander reapplied for the North Carolina bar, passed, was accepted, and became the first African American woman to practice law in the state.[34]

For any African American—man or woman—it took a tremendous amount of perseverance and networking to be accepted in the North Carolina bar. In many cases Black applicants to southern bars had to have the recommendation of practicing attorneys, who were typically white men hesitant to recommend an African American. Many of these men had entered the profession through an informal network of camaraderie, to which African Americans—let alone African American women—were not privy.³⁵ Many Black lawyers in the South had difficulty taking or passing the bar. For example, the Georgia bar exam became known as the "graveyard for the aspirations of many blacks." Even African Americans who graduated from the most elite law schools would frequently fail the Georgia bar.³⁶ It had taken Alexander a year of driving between New York and North Carolina on weekends to establish her North Carolina residency. But in 1947, Alexander was finally able to practice law in her home state. Even after she passed the North Carolina bar, Ed Cannon, the executive director of the state bar, apparently watched closely to make sure she did not take on civil rights cases.³⁷ Despite the struggle, being the first African American woman to join the North Carolina bar was no small feat and obviously one in which Alexander took pride. Almost fifty years later she still had the *Greensboro Record* clipping reporting her accomplishment and recalled in detail the difficulty she had in reaching that achievement.³⁸

Alexander had been forced to rely on the "vouching system" that Jim Crow society required for many African Americans to get ahead professionally or socially. Black individuals often had to have a white patron testify to their integrity and honesty. Because Fannie White vouched for Alexander, and because Pierce Rucker thought of Alexander as "an educated Aunt Jane who would come home and keep the Black folks in their place," she was able to take the exam.³⁹ This networking also extended to voting rights, as some southern states would not allow an African American to even take a literacy test to vote unless an already registered voter would vouch for them. Few southern whites, however, would vouch for a potential Black voter.⁴⁰ While Alexander had to navigate the complexities of Jim Crow society in order to join the bar, this system of networking ultimately allowed her to take her place in North Carolina history.

After becoming licensed, Alexander set up her law practice in her hometown of Greensboro, where her husband practiced medicine. Greensboro was a town that often attracted ambitious young African Americans. North Carolina had long been thought of as the most progressive state in the South, and the status of African Americans in Greensboro exceeded that of African Americans in other North Carolina cities. By the 1950s, African Americans in Greensboro had a higher median education than those in other North Carolina cities, largely due to schools such as Bennett College and Alexander's alma mater, North Carolina Agricultural and Technical University.⁴¹ In 1951, Dr. William Hampton became the first African American to serve on the Greensboro City Council, and he also served as president of the Greensboro Citizens Association, an organization of African American leaders who wanted to get rid of "those political parasites . . . who were selling the vote."[42] Greensboro's Black citizens took great pride in their community organizations and their churches.[43]

Black professionals, however, still could not gain acceptance from many white organizations. According to her former law partner, Alexander was denied membership in the Greensboro Bar Association when she gained entry to the North Carolina bar in 1947.[44] In the mid-1950s, Welch Jordan, Alexander's personal attorney, informed her that the Greensboro bar was finally ready to accept her, but she replied, "I'm not ready to accept them. . . . I've made it without them. I don't need them." She went on to prove that she did not need the Greensboro bar, and she refused to join the organization for the rest of her career.[45]

From the inception of her law practice, Alexander made a mark in the Greensboro community as the only African American woman attorney in town. She did not become an NAACP attorney, but became an in-demand speaker in African American communities around the state, giving encouraging talks on family, citizenship, and self-reliance.[46] Her new status as an inspiring woman helped Alexander transition from nervous law student to self-assured attorney. The fact that the Black community wanted to hear her story increased her confidence. The speeches also helped to cultivate her courtroom style, which became a hallmark of her advocacy. "I had many speaking engagements soon after I became a lawyer. Most of the invitations, I believe, were made because of the novelty of a Negro woman lawyer. Most of the groups were Negro, and they wanted to give hope to the people in their church, or school. . . . I developed a style and after years became an adept public speaker; but the early invitations had nothing to do with my ability as a speaker. . . . I was a bit stiff."[47] As Alexander found her voice, the increasingly tumultuous civil rights movement gave her a chance to help Greensboro's Black citizens in and out of the courtroom.

In the 1950s the turmoil over school desegregation gave Black leaders in Greensboro a chance to be heard. The June 18, 1955, edition of the *Greensboro Record* featured Alexander's views on school integration one year after the *Brown v. Board of Education* decision was handed down. Alexander stated, "I believe that we, as good citizens, will accept the law and earnestly seek to comply therewith," and she suggested formulating interscholastic teacher-student exchanges and integrating parent-teacher associations, adding that "any practicable program must be based on achieving understanding leading to mutual respect." Alexander was very active during the school integration period in Greensboro, particularly in the initial stages during the 1950s. She worked to organize parents and to make the transition for students as easy as possible.[48] Although the rhetoric around Greensboro's attempts to integrate schools seemed more progressive than what was heard in many other southern cities, it actually was one of the last southern cities to integrate. Alexander and fellow advocates faced opposition from the Guilford County School Board and political leaders in Raleigh. School board superintendent Benjamin Smith was eager to start the integration process, while others felt the *Brown* decision simply meant segregation would no longer be strictly enforced. Meanwhile, the state legislature enacted the Pupil Assignment Plan, which gave local school districts authority over school assignments in an attempt to delay integration. Although some limited desegregation occurred in Greensboro schools in 1957, like most of the South, the city's schools were not fully integrated until the early 1970s.[49]

Alexander was personally dedicated to overcoming the barriers of segregation. Greensboro was a heavily segregated city in the 1950s, with African American citizens expected to live and work in the southeastern quadrant of the city. Alexander's first office was in East Greensboro. She recalled that "anytime I'd go to speak anyplace ... and I didn't know where I was going, I'd look for the railroad tracks. If you'd go south and east of the railroad tracks, there you'd find the brothers." She wanted, however, to make her presence known throughout the entire city. "I was determined that I was going to move west of the railroad tracks." And in 1957, she did just that. Alexander was able to rent a house from some friends on East Gaston Street near downtown Greensboro. The house had been converted to office space and also provided Alexander with an apartment; she was "half separated" from her husband at the time.[50]

Alexander also showed her views on segregation through performance, which became her unique form of activism. Performance was used following World War I and during the Russian Revolution, as well as in Weimar Germany and in the U.S.S.R. as a way to support communism. Called agitprop (agitation and propaganda) plays, these performances were often created by ordinary people on the streets or at political rallies. Alexander used performance in legal settings as a method to foster social change. This method of activism came easily for Alexander, as she always considered herself a "showman," and she stated that "it always seemed kind of stupid to me for people to treat people as second-class citizens and expect a first-class performance."⁵¹ Not only did Alexander give a first-class performance, but she also used that performance to demonstrate that she was a first-class citizen.

In the 1950s, many of the courtrooms where Alexander tried her cases were segregated. On the days when she appeared in a segregated courtroom, Alexander would "wear a mink coat into the courtroom and instead of sitting with whites, I would sit behind the bar next to the dirtiest, blackest, Negro working man.... It would upset the court." She was never held in contempt of court, but she was told several times by judges to sit inside the bar with the other attorneys. Alexander would respond, "If my people have to sit on one side, I want to be with my people." She effectively used performance to point out the hypocrisy and injustice of segregation. Alexander's performance extended to water fountains as well. She would approach white judges, saying she wanted to "see what the difference is in this white water and this colored water."⁵² Alexander was never penalized for breaking the customs of segregation, but she surely shocked whites in power with her behavior.

Alexander particularly called attention to the attitudes and behaviors of white male attorneys. While male lawyers in North Carolina respectfully referred to each other as "Mr." or "Attorney," most of them simply referred to Alexander as "Elreta." When she was trying a case once in eastern North Carolina, the other attorney called her "Alexander." She responded, "If you want to communicate with me, sir, if you'll just write it on a piece of paper, I'll answer you on a piece of paper.... Other than that, if you'll just grunt like a pig, then I'll respond. But if you call me anything, you call me '*Mrs*. Alexander' or 'Lawyer Alexander.'"⁵³ Alexander turned demanding respect into a creatively articulated performance and used it to change the attitudes of individuals in North Carolina.

While Alexander used performance as a method of activism, all African Americans in the Jim Crow South had to "perform race" for white spectators. African Americans were expected to adhere to certain behavioral norms around whites and obey the social and racial hierarchy. Daily interactions between Black and white people became what historian Stephen A. Berrey calls the "Jim Crow routine." Breaking the rules of the routine could have dangerous consequences for African Americans.⁵⁴ Alexander had been taught how to navigate Jim Crow performances. The notions of respectability stressed to her as a child were based on performing in a certain manner and living up to certain expectations. But because of her time at Columbia, Alexander had seen how the role of performance varied outside the South. Living in New

York allowed her to come back to North Carolina and see these interactions with a new perspective. With an Ivy League law degree in hand, Alexander was no longer willing to perform deference to whites. As a Black woman, Alexander refused to conform to any routine and instead shook those in power by giving an alternative performance than what was expected of her. With increased confidence, Alexander did not tolerate disrespect and used performance to prove her point.

Alexander was not the only African American woman attorney who challenged expected performances when disrespected. When Constance Baker Motley served as counsel for James Meredith in his attempt to enroll at the University of Mississippi, local newspapers referred to her as "the Motley woman." In the courtroom, "opposition lawyers called her either 'Constance' or 'Motley.'" But like Alexander, Motley did not let discrimination go without pointing out its absurdity. In one instance, Motley attempted to shake hands with Dugas Shands, the assistant attorney general of Mississippi. Shands would not shake her extended hand, prompting Motley to say, "Oh, that's right, Mr. Shands. You don't shake hands with Negroes, do you?" Surely Shands did not expect his behavior to be called out by a Black woman. As African American women in a white- and male-dominated profession, Alexander and Motley had to prove repeatedly that their race and gender did not hamper their ability and intelligence. They set out to demonstrate they were more able and more intelligent than most of the white men in the field.[55]

In 1950, Alexander made that point quite clearly. Her clients, a group of prominent African American professionals led by Dr. George Simkins Jr., had petitioned for African American residents to be allowed to use the Gillespie Park Golf Course and then sued the city of Greensboro in 1949. John Hughes, a white city council member, stated that he did not want any "Nigra men out there" while his wife played golf. In her determination to prove that brains were not color-coded, Alexander responded, "Isn't your wife a secretary? [I am] . . . a lawyer, a graduate of one of the finest schools in the world. . . . I don't believe we have anything to communicate about. We wouldn't be on the same level. . . . The same thing with these men. Can you think of any reason why these men would want to be fresh with your wife when you've got a woman like Elreta Alexander here? In my race, we got any kind they want to pick. From Elreta Alexander on up and on down." The Gillespie Park Golf Course remained segregated for several more years, despite Alexander's attempt. Instead, the city of Greensboro built a separate golf course for African Americans, Nocho Park, for which Alexander wrote the charter. While she did not win the case for integration, she did take credit for setting up the first African American golf course in Greensboro, although the course reeked from the smells coming from the adjacent sewage treatment facility.[56]

Alexander believed that "every case ... was a civil rights case; if I'd been a 'civil rights lawyer' I couldn't have done anything else." Even if every case did not result in integration or change discriminatory laws, Alexander succeeded if she improved the lives of her clients. In her budding law career, most of Alexander's cases involved mundane problems. Many dealt with issues between renters and landlords, liquor sales, driving infractions, and small criminal charges, and she stood up for underprivileged African Americans. One of her first cases on returning to Greensboro involved prosecuting a husband for nonsupport of his wife and child. The husband sold ice and coal from his truck, making more than his estranged wife, and as Alexander said, "At the time money was still scarce in this area even though the war was just over." Alexander was hired to prosecute the case against the husband and won; however, at the time, the rate of support was set at five dollars for an African American child, while it was ten dollars for a white child. She asked the judge to "consider the fact that milk and baby food, diapers [all cost the same] to a Negro mother as ... to a white mother." She "wanted [the] court to go on record for the rights of children." The judge agreed, and from then on allotments were based on the ability of the father to pay, regardless of race.[57] While this was not a civil rights victory in the larger sense, Alexander was able to change laws to drastically improve the lives of many Black citizens.

In May 1955 Elreta Alexander jumped over another civil rights hurdle, when she became the first Black woman to argue a case before the North Carolina Supreme Court. She represented two teenage boys convicted of robbery, and she argued that the judge presiding over the initial trial did not inform the jury of lesser degrees of the crime. This position was accepted by the court, and a new trial was ordered for the two defendants.[58]

By 1956 there were other African American attorneys in Greensboro: Herbert Parks, who was Alexander's associate; Major S. High; and J. Kenneth Lee.[59] As the only woman, and one of the few female trial lawyers in the state, Alexander became a well-respected and in-demand Greensboro figure and continued as a popular public speaker throughout North Carolina. She received invitations from the Woman's Baptist Home and Foreign Ministry Convention, the New Homemakers of America national meeting in Washington, D.C., and various churches around North Carolina.[60] Alexander also began to make news across the state. The *High Point Enterprise* listed one of her speaking events in its "News of Interest to Colored People" section.[61] In 1957, a Winton, North Carolina, headline read, "Negro Woman Lawyer at Hertford Court." Alexander was representing the defendant in a case over damages in a car accident, and according to the newspaper, "Negro lawyers have been rare in appearance in Hertford Court and this is the first woman lawyer of either race to appear." The newspaper also noted that Alexander "appeared in a black dress, with high spike heels and with a tan briefcase."[62] During this time Alexander began to become known for her fashion sense. Three years after the Winton newspaper noted her outfit, on March 18, 1960, she was selected as "one of the better dressed women" in her part of the country by the *Pittsburgh Courier*.[63]

Because she was the only African American woman attorney in her area, her appearance drew attention to, and sometimes distracted from, her skill as a litigator. Her style reflected her middle-class status, which could exacerbate class tensions in the African American community. On the other hand, in a white-dominated profession, a certain amount of conformity with white standards of beauty seemed to be necessary.[64] As historian Robin D. G. Kelley has claimed, clothes and appearance "carried a great deal of social meaning and were often signifiers of power (or lack thereof)." For Alexander and other Black professional women, clothing could be a powerful political statement. The fact that Alexander bought her clothes at upscale retailers, such as Lord & Taylor, signified that African Americans could be affluent and sophisticated, and it also helped dispel common stereotypes about Black women regarding sexual licentiousness and their capabilities beyond domestic wage work. A stylish, well-dressed Black woman "personified racial uplift and racial progress."[65] Alexander's wardrobe was a part of the politics of respectability that had been ingrained in her as a child.

Alexander also knew how to have fun with fashion. Not only were her outfits well coordinated, but she made use of her accessories in the courtroom. Taking her cue from Clarence Darrow, who placed a fine wire in his cigars to distract jurors with the length of the ash, Alexander would remove her hatpin and twirl it close to the defendant's head, which distracted the jury from the prosecutor's arguments. Beyond that performance, Alexander stated, "Style makes people feel important, to you, to me, and to other people too."[66] Alexander's style bolstered her sense of power in the courtroom.

Alexander also participated in club work, particularly with the Links, an organization of Black professional women. The Links focused on "racial uplift for socially disadvantaged members of their race." The founders embraced the

Du Boisian concept of socially responsible individualism that Alexander had grown up with—the belief that with privilege came the responsibility to help others. Often accused of elitism, members of the Links generally came from the Black middle and upper classes, which allowed the group to provide substantial support to organizations, such as the NAACP and the United Negro College Fund, in addition to providing educational opportunities for Black youth. Membership was through invitation only and was restricted to women who had a record of service in the community. Among her fellow Links members was Coretta Scott King, who helped charter the Montgomery, Alabama, chapter of the Links in 1959. Alexander described the Greensboro chapter as "not a segregated group, although only one or two white women were members; they were married to Black men. The women in the Links were overachievers, or else their husbands were." Alexander became an overachiever in the Links, serving on committees and giving speeches on both the local and national levels on behalf of the organization.[67]

In Greensboro, she addressed many student groups, encouraging the next generation of young Black leaders to embrace social responsibility and use their education to uplift their race. She frequently spoke at Dudley High School, alongside men like John Tarpley, who had been instrumental in her early education.[68] In 1958, she received an outstanding alumnus award from her alma mater, North Carolina Agricultural and Technical State University, and in 1961, she was added to the Who's Who of American Women list.[69] Career success was also accompanied by financial security. By the early 1960s, Alexander was a successful attorney, and her husband was a successful surgeon. They were able to afford a nice country home and a housekeeper. Their success and money, however, did not make the Alexanders impervious to racial discrimination, as Greensboro increasingly became the focus of the civil rights movement.

On February 1, 1960, four Black male students from NC A&T sat down at the Woolworth's lunch counter in downtown Greensboro after purchasing small items in the store. They were not served food nor did they expect to be served. But until the store closed that evening, the four men sat. Inspired by these actions, the sit-in movement took hold among African American students in North Carolina and throughout the South. In Greensboro, negotiations between the city, white business leaders, and African American leaders over desegregation created a tense environment. Negotiations frequently broke down, leading to increases in the number of Black students sitting-in at lunch counters in protest. Picketers in favor of or against segregation were frequently seen with their signs marching up and down Elm Street. Greensboro, which had been known for its racial progressiveness, suddenly did not seem so progressive to the rest of the nation.[70]

In an interview seventeen years after the first sit-in, Alexander staked her claim to the historical moment. According to her account, prior to the first sit-in, one of the four men called her office asking "what would happen if they went into one of the eating establishments where Negroes were not allowed to sit.... The fellows were having a rap session, because I could hear them arguing over what to do on the phone." She told them that she could not predict the outcome, but in her legal opinion, the U.S. Supreme Court would ultimately declare the segregated lunch counter to be unconstitutional. She also advised them that the easier route would be to collect a little money and file a civil lawsuit. The four men did not take Alexander's advice. The next thing she knew, the sit-ins began, and the city of Greensboro went wild.[71] African American professionals stood with the young men and marched with the picketers in front of the Woolworth's. While Alexander might have had a small role in the sit-in, she did not march with them because her young son, Girardeau, was frightened by the events and rising community tension. She did, however, support behind the scenes the Black professionals of Greensboro who stood by the students.

Even though Alexander was not a demonstrator, she did not completely stay on the sidelines. Those who knew her never questioned her stance on civil rights. A week after the initial sit-in, she received a letter from Arnold S. Lott with the Department of the Navy: "My wife and I have been following with great interest the boycott of the local stores there in Greensboro. I thought you might like to know that my daughter, Marilyn, was one of the three students from Women's College named in the press for having supported the boycott.... They're ... on your side, as we are." Alexander also made sure the whole city knew her position. On April 7, 1960, she wrote a letter to an editor partly in rhyme: "So here's a little ditty / To my fair city / Where a man's no fool / 'Til he wants a stool." Alexander worked closely with Cleo M. McCoy, the director of religious activities at NC A&T. In a letter to Poindexter Orr, chair of the Social Action Council at the Congregational Church of Park Manor in Chicago, McCoy stated, "I am sure that you will not be surprised to learn that your friend, Mrs. Elreta Alexander, is making a marvelous contribution as a leader across racial lines during this immediate period of social stress. Of course, this situation did not have to develop to bring out her capacity for clear vision and fruitful expression of ideas. She occupies an enviable position in the legal profession as well as the civic life of the state." Because of his friendship with Alexander, Orr donated $100 to support the sit-in efforts.[72] Using her professional status, Alexander found ways to advocate on behalf of civil rights.

While Black students in Greensboro fought to integrate public spaces, Black professionals fought for full work rights. They were often denied membership in professional societies. In addition to Elreta Alexander being denied membership in the Greensboro bar, in 1960 Dr. Tony Alexander and thirteen other African American surgeons from Greensboro and High Point were denied full membership in the Guilford County Medical Society. Tony eventually withdrew his bid, calling the organization "Un American."[73] In 1962, Dr. Alexander was involved in a discrimination lawsuit, *Simkins v. Cone*, against Moses Cone and Wesley Long Hospitals, the white hospitals in Greensboro, over their hiring policies.[74] When Moses Cone Hospital had opened in 1953, its administrator, Dr. Joseph Lichty, stated he wanted to have a completely integrated hospital with Black and white doctors, nurses, and patients. When the hospital took some tentative steps toward a desegregated patient population, however, the white elites in Greensboro protested to the board of trustees and the hospital director. Applications by Black doctors to work at Cone were turned down, and the hospital ultimately only hired one Black technician.[75] Dentist George Simkins, who had previously worked to integrate the Gillespie Park Golf Course, along with Dr. Alexander and nine other doctors filed suit on behalf of themselves and Black patients, "alleging that the defendants have discriminated against them because of their race, in violation of the Fifth [*sic*] and Fourteenth Amendments to the United States Constitution." The two hospitals had received approximately $3.2 million in federal and state monies under the 1946 Hill-Burton Hospital Survey and Construction Act, which the plaintiffs argued made the facilities subject to the equal protection clause of the Constitution. On December 5, 1962, the Middle District Court of North Carolina ruled against the plaintiffs. In a move that shocked both the plaintiffs and the defendants, Attorney General Robert F. Kennedy appealed as a friend of the court, and the case went to the Fourth Circuit Court of Appeals, where the plaintiffs won in a three-to-two decision. Because of the use of federal funds in the construction of the hospitals, the equal protection clause of the Fourteenth Amendment was applied for the first time to a private entity to ban racial discrimination.[76] Tony and Elreta shared a similar social conscience, and both used their professional standing to promote racial equality, which likely helped maintain the bond and admiration they shared early in their relationship.

Elreta Alexander also faced de facto segregation with her speaking engagements. The first statewide integrated group she spoke to was the North Carolina Nurses Association; she talked about law and the nursing profession. According to Alexander, the usual arrangement was that Black nurses would only join after dinner, and they would enter through a back door. Alexander recalled, "I was determined I wouldn't embarrass any of my friends, but I would not go in that back door. I'd stand in the window first and give my speech. I do not go in anybody's back door, AS A RULE." Despite being nervous, Alexander arrived at the Irving Park Delicatessen, walked right in the front door, and went to the speaker's table. During her speech Alexander made sure the nurses association knew that its "speaker does not choose to use the back door to come and teach." According to Alexander, her position received more complaints from other African Americans than it did from whites, as many Black waiters thought, "that woman don't have no better sense than to go in the front door."[77]

By the mid-1960s, Elreta Alexander was an established attorney in North Carolina. After embracing her Blackness at Columbia University, she honed her unique form of activism as the civil rights movement arrived in Greensboro. Through performance and everyday acts of resistance, she used her career as a platform to create change for African Americans within the law. Her career would soon expand beyond golf courses and child support cases. The summer of 1964 would change the trajectory of her legal work, as an interracial rape case forced her to confront head on the racial inequities in the southern criminal justice system.

CHAPTER 3
Changing the System

ELRETA MELTON ALEXANDER had experienced several life-changing moments: the death of her friend Katharine Tynes, her marriage to Girardeau "Tony" Alexander, and the loss of the Reverend Robert Sharp in the city council race, which convinced her to go to law school. All of these events were part of her path to becoming a pioneering attorney. But in 1964 she took on an interracial rape case that would again change the trajectory of her life and put the entire North Carolina justice system on trial. In a case where racial and gender stereotypes collided, Alexander confronted the obstacles facing African American men in the criminal justice system, basing her defense of them on a flawed jury system and the historical bias and disproportionately harsh sentences Black men received. Ultimately, Alexander exposed the discriminatory jury selection process in Guilford County, which had been used against African Americans.

This trial is important when examining Alexander's career and tactics as an attorney, but it also shows how she used her position to advocate for civil rights. Trial details show the depth of discrimination Alexander faced regularly in her career. But like other early Black legal pioneers, she did not set out to change the legal system. She instead sought to force the system to follow its own rules. Doing so did not ensure that she would win her case, but her actions helped other African Americans receive fairer trials in the future and secured the basic guarantees of due process. While she worked on this trial, racial tensions in the South reached a boiling point. As a Black woman challenging the procedures of a white court system, Alexander willingly put her own life at risk. And rather than relying on her performative activism in the courtroom, Alexander focused on keeping her clients alive. The long, complicated case brought out her commitment to helping African Americans access a more equitable justice system.

On June 21, 1964, four young Black men and two Black women went to Horney Place, an old, rundown mansion off Penny Road in High Point, North Carolina, to drink some beers and do some target shooting. Beyond Horney Place was an area in the woods known as a "lovers' lane," and on that evening, twenty-year-old Mary Lue Marion and her married boyfriend, Mick Wilson, sat in his car. Charles Donald Yoes and the three other young men, Leroy Davis, Julian Hairston, and Willie Hale, all drunk, decided to play a prank on the white couple. Running down there with a rifle, they banged on the car, telling the couple they were with the sheriff's department. The incident moved beyond a mere prank, however, when the men allegedly beat Wilson and raped Marion. The two women in the group, Janice Dockerty and Alberta Lyles, then stole Marion's purse. After the incident, Yoes fled to Norfolk, Virginia. Dockerty and Lyles became scared and turned in the entire group to the police. Yoes was apprehended in Virginia on July 3 and brought back to North Carolina. The four men were all charged with "successive rapes of the same woman in Guilford County."[1]

Eighteen miles away from the crime scene, Alexander had just returned to work following a Links conference in Nassau, Bahamas, when Charles Yoes's mother came to see her. Distraught, Mrs. Yoes had been unable to find an attorney willing to take her son's case, and she asked Alexander to represent him at the preliminary hearing concerning his rape charge. Initially, Alexander was reluctant. "[I] didn't want to get involved in anything this complicated," she later said.[2] After looking at the evidence, however, Alexander felt that Charles Yoes was not guilty of rape but was guilty of being an accessory after the fact. The Yoes family suffered from financial hardship, so Alexander agreed to represent Yoes at the preliminary hearing for a flat fee. It was the only money Alexander ever accepted from the Yoes family.

The ensuing trial brought out the worst types of segregationist behavior and eventually prompted her to run for district court judge to address the inequities faced by Black people in the Guilford County judicial system. For Alexander, an interracial rape case was difficult to defend. She was keenly aware of the possible consequences, including violence directed toward her by angry whites and a loss of clients. Additionally, decades before DNA testing, most of the case rested on the word of a white couple versus the word of young African Americans. Alexander knew winning was a long shot. The case, however, gave her the opportunity to address disparities in sentencing, bias in the jury selection process, and racial injustices in the judicial system. It ultimately led to a change in the way jury selection occurred in Guilford County.[3]

Charles D. Yoes was twenty-five years old and married; he and his wife had one child. The family lived with his mother in Jamestown, North Carolina, approximately six miles from High Point. On the night in question, Yoes's wife was out of town, so he had taken his girlfriend to spend time with his friends. Yoes admitted to hitting Mick Wilson, and Alexander believed he also had robbed him, probably after Wilson was beaten unconscious. Alexander and her co-counsels, Walter Johnson Jr. and Julius Chambers, knew they could not defend Yoes's involvement in the crime, even though he had no prior criminal record. Alexander's approach was to argue that Yoes was not one of the rapists, and she sought to lessen his punishment by focusing on the prevailing discrepancies in jury selection and sentencing based on race in the South.[4]

Just four years after the Woolworth's sit-ins, Greensboro, the Guilford County seat, was ground zero in the North Carolina civil rights movement, a movement further fueled by the Civil Rights Act of 1964, signed in early July by President Lyndon B. Johnson. The act, which banned segregation in public places and instituted equal employment opportunity measures, was a response to the violent attacks on nonviolent Black demonstrators by white law enforcement, which resulted in injury and death for many African Americans across the South. As Alexander prepared for trial, the Civil Rights Act led to increased violence and demonstrations.[5] According to Alexander, "The papers were full of racial news.... People could see every Negro jumping into every white woman's bedroom."[6] Fears of Black men's sexuality were still strong in the South. The southern rape complex, defined by the stereotype of Black men as sexual predators preying on virginal white women, did not die with the decline of ritualized mob lynching. The complex had long been used by white people as a means of racial and sexual suppression. With the increase of racial integration in schools and public facilities, white fears of Black rapists lusting after "innocent" white women were renewed with vigor.

Alexander claimed that the Guilford County sheriff, Clayton Jones, attempted to take advantage of these white fears and perhaps boost the importance of his own role in the case. "To give the public image that this was a high-flown trial and that somebody was going to lynch those boys... Sheriff Jones had sheriff's cars riding around and deputies marching in goose-step from the old courthouse to Elm and the Mayfair cafeteria.... This went on every day to heighten the passion of the people."[7] Even if Yoes and his codefendants were in no real danger of being lynched, it was easy to play on the fears of segregationist whites.

Stereotypes regarding race and sexuality had been reinforced since the slavery era. In the antebellum South, however, class often trumped race, with many slavers believing enslaved people over the accusations of rape by poor white women or preferring to deal with the punishment of the enslaved men themselves. Black women, of course, had long been the victims of rape by white men. After emancipation, the traditional southern class hierarchy fell apart. All white women, regardless of class, were protected from Black men and seen as symbols of white supremacy.[8] The rape of Black women by white men after the end of slavery was simply considered a "moral lapse" and better ignored, while the rape of a white woman by a Black man was a crime punishable by death.[9] Black women occupied the lowest rung in the social hierarchy. Even if they made it clear they were under no obligation to fulfill the white man's sexual desires, they were still violently raped and cast as loose women.[10] However, the rape of a white woman by an African American man (or even consensual interracial intimacy) was viewed as an affront to white superiority and masculinity; the issue served as a rallying cry for conservative male southerners and was yet another reason to deny suffrage and equal rights to Black men.[11] If Black men could vote and participate in politics, then they could also obtain forgiveness or leniency from Black politicians or sympathizing white liberals for their supposed crimes against white women, inciting more violence.[12]

Emancipation and the ensuing calls for political rights led to increased white violence and exploitation in an effort to maintain white supremacy. The oversexualized stereotype of African American men continued well into the twentieth century. Movies such as *The Birth of a Nation* (1915) depicted African American men as brutal sexual predators while the sexual violence endured by African American women for centuries was ignored. This promoted the idea that it was the virtue of white women that had to be protected. In the post-Reconstruction era, a white woman's accusation of rape could mean lynching without a trial for an African American man. Lynching could include public beatings, torture, forms of macabre sexual mutilation, primarily castration, and hanging by angry white mobs. While less than a quarter of lynching victims were accused of rape, a Black man did not have to actually engage in a sexual act to be perceived as a sexual threat to white women.[13]

Simply looking a white woman in the eye or making a friendly comment could put the safety of an African American man in jeopardy. If a Black man spent any time near a white female, many whites assumed he would try to sexually molest her. White women, who were treated as objects in the white man's quest to maintain racial dominance, could briefly experience a sense of control, determining the fate of a Black man with the pointing of a finger. In 1951, for example, in Yanceyville, North Carolina, approximately forty miles northeast of Greensboro, Mack Ingram simply looked at a white woman and was charged with attempted rape. He ultimately received a six-month sentence for assault, even with sworn testimony that he was never even close enough to touch the woman.[14]

In the 1960s a white woman's accusation of rape usually would lead to a trial for an African American man, but not necessarily a fair trial. All-white juries and white judges often led to skewed trials. Pervasive racism continued to distort the issue of sexual violence, as Black men were punished more harshly for the crime than white men were.[15] Increased racial integration led to white fears of increased miscegenation, which would lead to increased numbers of mixed-race individuals, threatening notions of white superiority that white southerners clung to desperately.[16] Feeling as though the federal government had imposed integration on them against their will, white southerners did everything in their power to maintain their segregated way of life, which indirectly led to a heated trial for Alexander. She later said, "It was right at the [height] of civil rights passion, and it's the worst trial I've ever been involved with." Defending a Black man accused of raping a white woman was a risky career move for Alexander. Her law practice was very profitable, and she served a mixed-race clientele who undoubtedly had differing opinions about the case. Alexander's own secretary commented, "If those boys did that, they ought to be hanged."[17] The stakes were high for Alexander as well as the defendant, and she faced a possible exodus of clients if Yoes was convicted of being a rapist.

Alexander's strategy was to go into the preliminary hearing ready to poke holes in the prosecution's argument. The three-hour hearing on July 13, 1964, was rife with conflicting evidence regarding Yoes's role in the assault on Marion. The testimony of Guilford County sheriff's deputy D. S. Lee was particularly damning. Lee said that after Yoes returned to town and turned himself in, Yoes led them to where he had disposed of a .22 rifle, which was recovered. Lee also testified that the four men and two women consumed two pints of whiskey during the day and had purchased beer on the way to Horney Place.

The group allegedly only left Horney Place to purchase more beer, and Yoes left once to retrieve a rifle for target practice. Yoes testified that he had killed a black snake with the rifle. Lee's testimony, however, stated that during the investigation police found seven empty beer cans, one full can, three .22 shells, and no dead black snake, indicating that Yoes had lied about his use of the rifle and establishing doubt about his credibility.[18] Yet Mary Lue Marion's testimony in that preliminary hearing cast doubt on Yoes's culpability. Marion testified that only two of the four men had touched her, and she was unable to identify Charles Yoes as one of her attackers. One of the two men, Marion claimed, raped her twice after dragging Wilson out of the car and badly beating him. She said that after the attack, the men threw Wilson back in the car, leaving him for dead while she stumbled up the road to the nearest house and called the police. Additionally, Wilson testified that he was unable to identify the men who had beaten him because he had been knocked unconscious.[19] Dockerty and Lyles also testified that Yoes and Davis never approached the crime scene. Despite the conflicting evidence, the grand jury returned bills of indictment against all four men on August 17, 1964. Janice Dockerty was later charged with rape based on her alleged role in the incident.[20]

Convinced that Yoes faced an unfair trial for a crime for which he was only an accessory, Alexander decided to stay on the case, hoping it would not last too long. After the preliminary hearing, the prosecuting attorney, solicitor Lonnie Herbin, was "determined the boys were going to sniff a little gas." She said, "Seeing that the boy was going to be railroaded and the feelings were so high, they talked me into it." She had tapes of the preliminary hearing, and Alexander felt her case was bolstered by a lack of evidence pointing to Yoes as one of the rapists. She also apparently felt tremendous empathy for Yoes's mother, saying, "I had promised only to set up the case in preliminary. Yoes's mother didn't have a lot of money." Alexander knew that since the family did not have the ability to afford proper legal counsel, she was the best hope of Yoes receiving a fair trial.[21]

Alexander also knew that if her client was convicted of this rape, he would undoubtedly face a harsher punishment than if he were white or if he were convicted of raping a Black woman. Yoes potentially faced the death penalty for his role in the crime, although white men accused of rape were rarely executed. Between 1930 and 1957, the state of North Carolina executed forty African American men, compared to four white men, convicted of rape.[22] Race-based inequality in the judicial system was not only a problem in North Carolina. Throughout the country, African Americans experienced a system of justice separate from that of whites and came to expect discrimination in all facets of the justice system.[23] Between 1945 and 1965, eleven southern states executed 13 percent of all convicted Black rapists. African American men were seven times more likely to receive the maximum penalty than were white men, and if convicted of raping a white woman, a Black man was eighteen times more likely to be executed than if he raped a Black woman or if a white man raped a white woman.[24] With these odds, it was imperative for Alexander to have a racially diverse jury. Alexander was not willing to accept the status quo, nor was she willing to abandon Yoes to the system of southern justice. For the sake of her client, whom she believed to be innocent, and having likely encountered many all-white juries during her years as a Greensboro attorney, Alexander investigated the county's jury selection procedures.

Alexander had a solid defense plan, but there were several factors that made her job difficult. The trial was moved from High Point to Greensboro on September 25, 1964, and each of the four men faced two charges of armed robbery and one charge of rape. While she had only received payment from Yoes's mother, Alexander led the defense for all four men. Alexander claimed that the court-appointed attorneys for the other defendants were ill prepared: "They came into court that first day with a clean yellow legal pad, not one bit of preparation. They'd never tried a capital case, or even a serious felony." Solicitor Herbin arranged for Alexander to cross-examine witnesses last, "so the other fellows could mess it up."[25] Despite the odds against them, she vigorously defended Charles Yoes and the other three suspects, attempting to lessen their sentences even if she could not establish their innocence.

On October 27, Alexander gave notice of her intention to challenge the constitutionality of the state's criminal assault statute, and she issued subpoenas to superior court clerks in seven nearby counties asking for court records of rape cases over the previous ten years to prove that Black men received harsher punishments.[26] Specifically, Alexander requested the name, age, and race of each person charged with rape as well as sentencing details and if the death sentence was imposed and carried out. In addition, she requested the name, age, and race of the victim in each case. Herbin asked for a recall of the subpoenas, which Robert M. Gambill, the presiding superior court judge, granted, stating he did not want to "bring all those records in here." When Alexander asked the judge what legal right Herbin had to recall the subpoenas, Gambill stated, "The Court will assume the solicitor is acting in good faith." Alexander was unable to make her case regarding the constitutionality of the state statute for Judge Gambill because he would only allow evidence of discrimination pertinent to this particular case.[27] This incident was the first of many times Alexander would face resistance from Robert Gambill.

On November 30, 1964, the same day that Alexander filed a motion for a separate trial for Yoes, solicitor Herbin filed a motion to consolidate the trials of the four men. Judge Gambill denied Alexander's motion, and the men were tried as a unit. If one man was convicted as a rapist, they would all be convicted and face the same punishment. Despite the setback, Alexander continued to base her defense strategy on the prevalent racist bias in the court system where Black men, particularly in cases where the rape victim was a white woman, received harsher sentences. Knowing that two of the men were likely guilty of raping Marion, Alexander had to try and lessen the punishments of all the defendants in order to spare Yoes's life.[28]

Alexander also filed a motion to quash Yoes's indictment on the basis that the grand jury had been "illegally constituted and composed" and had denied Yoes his right to due process and equal protection due to the lack of Black citizens on the jury. The motion stated that a smaller percentage of African Americans had been on grand juries in comparison to how many in Guilford County were qualified for jury duty. Alexander claimed that the grand jury was illegally comprised, rendering the indictment null and void and in violation of Yoes's rights under Article I, section 17, of the North Carolina Constitution and under the equal protection clause of the Fourteenth Amendment of the U.S. Constitution.[29]

Alexander also contested the constitutionality of North Carolina's rape statute by claiming that its enforcement and punishment were discriminatory against Black men. She stated that punishment had proven to be "unjust, cruel and inhumane" when African Americans were involved.[30] The motion claimed that the statute encouraging the death penalty in rape cases was unconstitutional, and it was used disproportionately against African American men accused of raping white women. Alexander included the following statistics to establish the disproportionate response to Black versus white criminals:

> Since 1930, 47 persons have been executed for the crime of rape in this State of which number 40 were Negroes, 2 were Indians and 5 were white men; that all of these persons were executed for having raped white women; that in those cases involving white defendants there were aggravating circumstances such as the extreme youth of the victim or the use of violence causing extreme injury or death; that the Negro population in the State of North Carolina and Guil-

ford County during the past 35 years has always been less than 26% and has never approached 90%, which the death sentence carried out on Negro males approximates 90% of such penalties exacted for the crime of rape, that for every white male suffering the death penalty for rape, some 8 Negroes have been executed which make the ratio in proportion to the adult male population of white males to Negro males approximately 24 Negro lives taken for rape to every 1 white male so convicted.[31]

Alexander and the rest of the defense team also argued that not only was the response to crime different based on race, but race was a discriminatory factor in jury selection. She questioned the selection process because it allowed for the "systematic exclusion of qualified jurors." This defense tactic was difficult since the grand jury selection process in Guilford County was a convoluted and antiquated procedure. Each person who paid property or poll taxes in the county had their name placed on a card, which was followed by a code number. If the code started with the number 1, the county resident was white; if it started with a 2, the resident was Black. Other numbers designated the school or fire district in which the person resided, whether they were in the military, and the last four digits of their Social Security number. These tax cards were also used to create a list for jury selection, creating the opportunity for bias based on key demographics.[32]

The county commissioners instructed that names be added from phone books and city directories so as to include individuals who were not property owners. The sheriff's department then examined the list and removed people who had died, who had been convicted of a crime, or who the sheriff felt was not mentally competent to serve on a jury. The list was then cut into pieces, with one individual's name and code on each piece; the pieces were then placed into a two-sided box. One side of the box had the names of jurors who could be used; the other had the names of jurors who would not be used, including those who had recently served on a jury and, according to Alexander, African Americans. Jurors were then selected in front of the county commissioners by a child, who picked names out of the side of the box with the people who could be used. The box of names was kept in the county commissioners' office, with one key in the possession of the sheriff and another in the possession of the chair of the county commissioners. This process was repeated every two years and had last occurred in 1963, over a year before the pretrial hearing.[33]

Alexander's assertion of discrimination against African Americans during this process was well founded. The codes, Alexander claimed, were knowingly used to identify race and keep African Americans off juries in the county, just as African Americans were systematically excluded from juries across the South. Proof of the discrimination, however, was often hard to accomplish by defense attorneys. Ensuring fairer representation meant placing more Black people on juries, but when they appeared for jury duty they were frequently eliminated, cited as underqualified, or used as tokens.[34]

Alexander subpoenaed the chair of the Guilford County commissioners, Dale Montgomery, to bring all county records pertaining to the selection of juries.[35] During the arraignment in the case, Guilford County officials had testified that race was not a factor in jury selection and that only tax officials knew the meaning of the code numbers 1 and 2. Alexander said she put Montgomery on the stand first "because I had an idea he didn't know any more about the selection of the grand or petit juries than a pig."[36] Indeed, Montgomery testified that he knew very little about the process. He stated that the county tax department prepared the list of possible jurors, the clerk of court determined whom to exclude from the list, and the sheriff's department determined the standards of qualification for jury members. Montgomery claimed that he did not know what those qualifications were. Other county commissioners also testified that no names were left out—or added to—the two-sided box after the preparation process, and there had been no exclusion of individuals from juries based on race.[37] When Alexander questioned county tax supervisor H. A. Wood in court as to why whites and African Americans were given distinctive codes on tax forms, Wood replied, "Because it's always been that way, I guess."[38] Alexander argued that the "deputy clerk could look right in the box and see whether she was putting whites or Negroes on the jury" if she knew what the codes meant.[39] Whether or not the codes were actually used in jury selection, racism and judging individuals based on race were so firmly entrenched in the southern psyche that few whites ever conceived of anything different.

While federal laws tried to remedy discrimination faced by African Americans, prejudice in the justice system hindered racial and gender equality throughout the country. Many juror selection lists, which often included tax records and voter registrations, already underrepresented African Americans due to exclusionary policies that historically made it difficult for them to vote. Requirements that jurors meet residency requirements and have no previous criminal records, together with exemptions based on economic and personal hardship, further led to the exclusion of Black and economically disadvantaged jurors. Attorneys and court officials also relied on their own personal biases and stereotypes in their acceptance or rejection of potential jurors. White women were said to be poor jurors because they were more biased against the defendants. African Americans, on the other hand, were believed to side with the defendants. The state of North Carolina did not require a litmus test for prospective jurors, leaving county officials—all white—to determine what qualified as a "good" juror.[40]

In Guilford County, Alexander argued, simply being Black made one a poor juror in the eyes of the court. On the same day, November 30, 1964, that Alexander filed to quash the bills of indictment based on the makeup of the grand jury, the motion was denied by Judge Gambill. He stated, "This matter of punishment is not to be proved with statistics . . . but is a matter of opinion," and the evidence proving that Black men received harsher punishments was "irrelevant and immaterial."[41] Further, Gambill ruled that the two-sided box from which the jury names were drawn was "properly constituted," and although codes demarcating race could be used to discriminate, there was no evidence supported by sworn testimony that county commissioners knew the meaning of the codes or that any name was left out of the two-sided box based on race.[42] Gambill was not going to rule in favor of anything that could benefit the defense. Jury selection for the trial began the next day.

Since Alexander could not convince Judge Gambill that the grand jury was unfairly comprised, then she would make sure the trial jury would be fair. On December 2, 1964, Alexander filed a challenge to the array, whereupon the court ordered that the two-sided box be brought into open court for the name selection.[43] Gambill ordered the sheriff to summon a specific number of competent individuals to serve as jurors. One hundred names were drawn from the box, and each potential juror was questioned by the prosecution and the defense. They were asked if they had any affiliation with any of the attorneys, how much they knew about the case, if they supported the death penalty in the case, and if they could approach the trial with an open mind. It took two weeks for the court to interview eight hundred people before finally establishing a jury and alternates. The jury of twelve was sworn in on December 14, 1964: ten white men, one white woman, and one Black man.

The beginning of the trial increased already high racial tensions in Greensboro, and some white southerners were ready to see the defendants—and the defense attorney—hang for the crime. Local reactions enhanced the need for security. Judge Gambill ordered additional deputies on duty in the courtroom to help maintain order. Sheriff's deputies surrounded the defendants with their hands on their guns.⁴⁴ Alexander started receiving threats from white men: "kill that bitch" in the courtroom. Her husband, Dr. Girardeau Alexander, sent a bodyguard to court with her.⁴⁵ Fortunately, Alexander had an ally in the sheriff's department. Deputy Hinson, one of the few African Americans on the force, told her that Guilford County sheriff Clayton Jones had ordered officers to shoot any defendant that moved—and to shoot Alexander along with them. None of the defendants moved during the trial; Charles Yoes actually fainted one day in court. Deputy Hinson also quietly informed Alexander that Sheriff Jones had bugged the defendants' jail cells in an attempt to hear one of the men confess. Throughout the trial, Alexander and her fellow defense attorneys communicated with their clients almost solely in writing. While the crimes Yoes and his friends were accused of were serious, the treatment they received was excessively harsh for young men whose most serious previous offense had been a traffic citation. The sheriff's department, however, was not the only entity that had ill will toward the defense.⁴⁶

Judge Robert Gambill, according to Alexander, "could not separate his prejudice from sitting fair and impartial on this case."⁴⁷ Gambill did not conceal his racist attitudes from the bench. He frequently referred to the defendants as "niggers" and allegedly would not allow evidence favorable to the defense to be considered by the jury. Alexander also stated that he quashed her motions to sequester the witnesses, refused to change the venue of the trial, and would not allow her to introduce into evidence the recordings of testimony from the preliminary hearing. When he called Alexander into his chambers, Gambill told her that "this is a bad case at a bad time, and those boys are going to get the death penalty anyway. You're not doing them any favors by dragging it out."⁴⁸ Encountering judges like Gambill was not uncommon, especially in the South. Also in 1964, a federal District Court judge in Mississippi, William Harold Cox, described African Americans as "chimpanzees" from the bench during a voter discrimination hearing. As in jury selection, the personal biases and beliefs of judges affected the trials and sentencing of accused individuals, especially poor and nonwhite defendants.⁴⁹ For the African American defendants in this case, getting a fair trial would prove to be extremely difficult.

With the twelve jury members in place, testimony began. On December 15 the first to testify on behalf of the prosecution was twenty-nine-year-old Mick Wilson. Wilson stated that he and Mary Lue Marion became turned around in High Point on their way back to Greensboro. After going down a dirt road, they stopped the car to talk, around 8:30–9:00 p.m. Their engine was turned

The Melton family, date unknown.
Martha Blakeney Hodges Special Collections and University Archives, University Libraries, University of North Carolina at Greensboro

Elreta Melton (*first row, seventh from right*) in class photo, date unknown.
Martha Blakeney Hodges Special Collections and University Archives, University Libraries, University of North Carolina at Greensboro

The Negro Citizens' Council
of the City of Wilmington

Observes

Citizenship Emphasis Day

PRESENTING

Champion of Human Rights

☆

First Negro Woman To Graduate From the School of Law of Columbia U.

Forceful Speaker

☆

Aggressive Civic And Political Leader

Mrs. Elreta Melton Alexander
Attorney-At-Law of Greensboro, N. C.

Tuesday, April 20, 1948
8:00 p. m.

Auditorium
John H. Shaw Boys' Club
9th & Nixon Sts.

═══════════ Emphasizing ═══════════

The Importance Of The Ballot

The Public Is Cordially Invited

"The only limit to our realization of to-morrow will be our doubts of today. Let us move forward with strong active faith."
—The Late President Roosevelt

R. S. JERVAY'S PRINT

Flyer for Elreta Melton Alexander speech, 1948.
Martha Blakeney Hodges Special Collections and University Archives, University Libraries, University of North Carolina at Greensboro

Elreta Melton Alexander head shot, circa 1968.
Martha Blakeney Hodges Special Collections and University Archives, University Libraries, University of North Carolina at Greensboro

The Symbol Of Justice Is A Woman

Elect A Living Symbol Of Justice

ELRETA MELTON ALEXANDER

The Only Woman Candidate
For District Judge In Guilford County

Campaign advertisement, 1968.
Martha Blakeney Hodges Special Collections and University Archives, University Libraries, University of North Carolina at Greensboro

Elreta Alexander playing the piano at home in Starmount Forest, Greensboro, 1968.
Martha Blakeney Hodges Special Collections and University Archives, University Libraries, University of North Carolina at Greensboro

Elreta Alexander at home in Starmount Forest, Greensboro, 1968.
Martha Blakeney Hodges Special Collections and University Archives, University Libraries, University of North Carolina at Greensboro

Elreta Melton Alexander presiding in court, date unknown.
Martha Blakeney Hodges Special Collections and University Archives, University Libraries, University of North Carolina at Greensboro

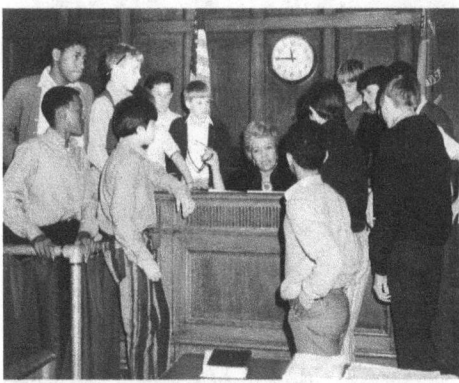

Elreta Melton Alexander with young people in court, date unknown.
Martha Blakeney Hodges Special Collections and University Archives, University Libraries, University of North Carolina at Greensboro

Elreta Melton Alexander in court, date unknown.
Martha Blakeney Hodges Special Collections and University Archives,
University Libraries, University of North Carolina at Greensboro

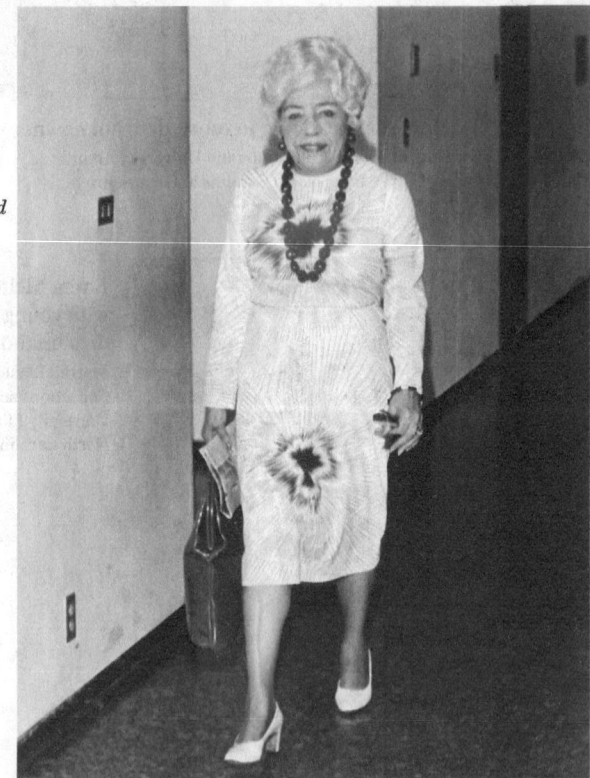

Elreta Melton
Alexander, 1979.
Photo by John Page,
Greensboro News and Record

off, and another car pulled up behind them. According to Wilson, "First thing I knowed two, four colored boys jumped out of the car and there was two on her side and two on mine.... I remember seeing two rifles—maybe there was just one—I was so scared maybe I thought they was two." The two on Marion's side opened the door and told her to pull up her dress. Wilson said he offered them money to leave the couple alone, but one of the Black men came around to his side, pointed a rifle at him, and told him to get out of the car. One of the men subsequently hit Wilson in the head with the butt of the rifle. Two allegedly beat up Wilson, while the other two raped Marion. Wilson lost consciousness and later awoke on the floor in the back seat of his car, with Marion nowhere to be found.[50]

Alexander knew the prosecution's strategy rested on playing up the "Black-male-as-rapist" trope for the jury. So during her cross-examination of Wilson she repeatedly attempted to poke holes in his story, asking him how they ended up so far down a secluded dirt road while trying to find their way back to Greensboro, implying that the couple went to have sex in an isolated area. She also tried to highlight discrepancies between his trial testimony and what he had testified in the preliminary hearing in order to establish what was actually going on in the car when Yoes and his friends approached. Years later, Alexander recalled that solicitor Lonnie Herbin revealed to her that he "almost fell out of his DA's chair at the Yoes trial [when Wilson] testified he hadn't had intercourse, because he told Lonnie in his office just before he came in to testify that he had had intercourse with her without using any prophylactic."[51] In all likelihood, Wilson perjured himself to protect the reputation of the white female victim in the eyes of the jury, thus reinforcing the stereotypes regarding Black men's sexuality and trying to prevent victim blaming by the defense.

Alexander did attempt to capitalize on the prevailing sexism that made victim blaming common in rape trials. Many times, the sexual history of a woman was used to determine her credibility. Indications that the victim was unchaste could be used to prove the probability of her consent in sexual intercourse. While a woman's sexual history could be put on display and called "evidence," the accused man's sexual history, including previous criminal charges against him, was rarely introduced to the jury.[52] In this case, the court's treatment of Mary Lue Marion was, at best, insensitive. Marion took the stand on December 16. Several times during her testimony the judge stated, "Now don't talk too fast, lady," or "Lady, tell us what he did." In one instance, Herbin asked Marion to "state whether or not they put their . . . fingers in your private parts." In another, the judge said, "Now, lady, intercourse means a number of things. Did he put his private parts in your private parts?"[53] When asked about the condition of her dress after the assault, Marion stated there was a "big spot in it." She was asked to stand and indicate where on herself the spot was located, and if she knew what the spot was. When asked by the prosecuting attorney what the spot was, Marion replied, "I can't say it in front of all these people."[54]

Alexander's cross-examination was just as uncomfortable as she attempted to cast doubt on Marion's credibility. Alexander had Marion repeat, for the third time, in detail the events of her evening leading up to the assault and reestablish her claim that she was not having sex with Wilson. Alexander focused on small variations in Wilson's and Marion's stories, reiterated Marion's testimony in questioning, and questioned her level of resistance after repeated rapes by the four men. Alexander reminded the jury of evidence that there were no tears in Marion's vaginal area, insinuating that Marion did not resist her attackers.[55]

Alexander used traditional, older ideals of morality against Marion. While women have always engaged in sexual activity, the twentieth century brought freer expressions of sexuality. As automobiles became common, the opportunity for sexual privacy increased as couples were able to spend time away from the watchful eyes of their parents. While more youths might have been having sex, attitudes about discussing sex in public remained largely unchanged through the mid-twentieth century. The responsibility to establish sexual limitations continued to fall on the woman, who was required to uphold notions of respectability, and talking openly about lewd sexual details in court would have assaulted traditional expectations of femininity. For Marion, the appearance of femininity was important. In order to convict in this case, the jury had to view her as a virginal victim ravished by the unrestrained sexual desires of Black men. Frankly discussing the large semen stain on her clothes, or that she had consensual premarital sex, would have marred the image Marion was likely trying to portray, a fact Alexander knew.[56]

Alexander's tough questioning led Marion to break down in tears on the stand. Alexander was convinced that intercourse had occurred between Marion and some of the defendants; however, she tried to determine whether or not the sexual encounter was actually rape. "I couldn't prove it, but I had information that her [Marion's] boyfriend [Wilson] had been using her for prostitution," Alexander claimed. "The neighbors had been complaining about cars going down this road, and white girls meeting Black boys down there.... I had heard that Mary Lue had been convicted of prostitution, but the courthouse records were clean." It was later revealed that Marion had been convicted of "occupying a room for immoral purposes," but the records were unable to be found during the trial. Whether Marion's previous record existed, or if it was intentionally hidden to aid the prosecution, was never established.[57] Had the records been found, Alexander undoubtedly would have used Marion's past to convince jurors that sex with two of the defendants was consensual.

If Marion did have consensual sex with two defendants, she had reason to lie about it. A white woman who had an intimate relationship with a Black man was considered damaged. White women sat on a pedestal of purity and goodness; exhibiting sexual freedom was the fastest way to be removed from that pedestal. While a white woman was not the legal property of white men, if she chose a relationship with a Black man, it was seen as a symbolic property loss. Other whites would exhibit vindictiveness toward a white woman who took a Black man as a lover, making her an outcast in white society.[58] If Alexander could prove that Marion had consented to intercourse with any of the defendants, she stood to lose her reputation and any place she held in white society. Marion maintained on the stand that she was raped, testifying that after being told to pull her dress up, one of the men ordered her to take off her underpants. After she refused to do so, Marion testified, "they cocked the gun so all they had to do was pull the trigger. I heard it click." Testifying that the rifle was pointed at her temple, Marion had no choice but to submit.[59]

Alexander was able to poke some holes in Marion's testimony. According to her later oral history, two of the defendants had confessed to having sex with Marion but testified she did not fight them. But in a southern rape trial, the word of a white woman still trumped the establishment of reasonable doubt through the testimony of a Black man or woman. From the stand, Marion identified defendant Julian Hairston as the first man to rape her, followed by Willie Hale. She pointed out both men from the stand but did not call them out by name. After Hairston and Hale allegedly raped Marion, she testified, the other two men, Yoes and Davis, also raped her. Then Hale and Hairston each raped her a second time. Marion stated she had intercourse six times that evening and that the rapes occurred in rapid succession. Alexander asked Marion if she specifically recalled defendant Yoes, to which Marion replied that she was so scared that evening that she did not remember Yoes specifically.[60] The whites in the community were inclined to accept Marion's testimony on the racist grounds that they would not want to believe that a white woman would have consensual sex with a Black man.[61] Even if Alexander had established credible doubt, most of the jury would have still believed Marion's account.

During Marion's testimony, Judge Gambill allowed a break for the jury. What occurred next was recorded by the court reporter:

> At this point in the reporter's notes the reporter was asked by each counsel for the defendant to record the fact that Sheriff Clayton Jones was seen by each to disappear out of sight having entered the jury room, being 4:20 PM; also that at 4:40 PM Sheriff Clayton Jones was next seen emerging from inside the jury room with the jurors as they returned to the jury box in open court. Reporter was also requested to record the fact that this entrance into the jury room by the Sheriff was called to the attention of the court (in the presence of the reporter) and the court made the statement, "Well, he has been sworn."[62]

The immediate perception was that Sheriff Jones spoke to the jurors about the case, raising issues of jury tampering. When Alexander pressed Judge Gambill about this breach of protocol, Gambill stated that Alexander would have to prove that Jones had "said something bad" while with the jury. Allegedly, Jones continued to interact with the jurors, even going so far as to accompany them inside their hotel rooms to talk with them.[63] There was little Alexander could do, however, as Gambill seemed intent that the four men would receive a guilty verdict.

On December 16 the prosecution called its final witnesses and asked for the death penalty for the defendants. A patrolman from the Guilford County Sheriff's Department, Frank Smith, testified that he had found Marion "crying and apparently hysterical" and Wilson "bleeding from the mouth and arm." Dr. Almon R. Cross, the gynecologist who examined Marion on the night of the alleged rapes, testified "there was no doubt" Marion had engaged in sex based on a physical examination that revealed swelling and a high volume of semen. Cross testified that there was a sore place on her mouth that "looked like her lips had been pressing her teeth," but there were no other injuries. Dr. Asa Parham, the general surgeon who treated Mick Wilson's wounds, testified that Wilson had multiple lacerations, but there was "no evidence of recent sexual intercourse."[64] This testimony undoubtedly hurt the defense's case even though it did not address whether any of the sex was consensual. In many interracial sexual crimes, the eagerness to find and punish a Black man overrode the logical need to thoroughly question any white men who might have been involved.[65] Before the emergence of DNA evidence, overt signs of physical harm were the primary evidentiary proof. Without physical evidence of rape, many juries had to determine whether they believed the story of the victim over that of her alleged rapist. In this case, the large amount of bodily fluids, the signs of obvious intercourse on Marion's body, and the testimony of Wilson and Marion overrode any reasonable doubt Alexander established.

Alexander gave her closing argument on Thursday, December 17. "I made one of the best jury speeches I ever have, proving how Yoes couldn't have had intercourse with this girl."[66] Alexander claimed that based on the height of the four defendants, forcible intercourse in the car with the doors closed would have been physically impossible. She pointed out that the doctor who examined Marion could only testify to the existence of semen, but not who that semen belonged to. Alexander argued that evidence that raises a "mere suspicion" is "an insufficient foundation for a verdict."[67] Alexander attempted to convey that enough reasonable doubt had been established as to whether or not rape actually occurred. The evidence showed that sex had happened, but the intent of the defendants could not be established.

After closing arguments, the jury left for deliberation on December 17 at 3:35 p.m. On Friday, December 18, 1964, at 7:13 p.m., in what had already become the longest criminal trial in Guilford County history, all four defendants were found guilty of rape. Alexander requested that the jury, which also recommended the punishment, be polled. Every white juror stated that guilty, no mercy, was the verdict, meaning they recommended the death penalty. Later, Alexander recalled that when the one Black juror was asked what his verdict was, he broke down in tears and said, "That's not my verdict. They made me say it." The *High Point Enterprise*, however, told a slightly different version of the story. John Siddle, "a Negro farmer and ex-boxer, was weeping in the jury box and appeared to lose control of his emotions entirely." When polled, according to the *Enterprise*, Siddle said, "Guilty, but I want to recommend mercy."[68] The official court transcript stated that "the jury returned into open court and announced it had reached a verdict, whereupon the foreman, speaking for the jury, announced as to the defendant Leroy Davis a verdict of 'guilty as charged' without a recommendation for mercy. Counsel for the defendant Davis then moved to have the jury polled, and one of the jurors, between sobs, stated that he recommended mercy."[69] Judge Gambill sent the jury back in order to come up with a unanimous verdict. At 8:00 p.m. the jury arrived at a sentence of life in prison.[70] Had it not been for the single African American man on the jury, who was there because of Alexander's questioning of jury selection procedures, Yoes and the other three defendants would have likely been put to death.

The reaction to the verdict in the community was swift. An editorial in the *High Point Enterprise* was not favorable toward the jury's decision. "If ever the death penalty were justified, it should seem to have been applicable in the case of those four sullen, brutish Negro men who slipped through the net of justice with their lives," the editorial stated. It went on to say that "we hope that Negroes . . . will recognize their high responsibility to deal justly rather than accept that duty as a way of coloring justice unjustifiedly." In an obvious jab at the lone African American on the jury, the editorial accused him of letting race influence his verdict.[71] Undoubtedly, in a southern state amid the civil rights movement, many other white Guilford County residents felt the ire reflected in the editorial.

Despite the loss, Alexander's defense argument had begun to change the justice system in Guilford County. At the beginning of January 1965, Judge Gambill ordered the codes distinguishing race to be removed from seventy thousand prospective juror slips. Gambill subsequently dismissed all jurors serving jury duty for that week until the issue was resolved, and he ruled that Guilford County commissioners knew about the racial codes on the juror slips, despite the fact that the commissioners had testified to the contrary in the case of Yoes and his codefendants. Soon after the verdict was handed down, Alexander began working on an appeal for Yoes. On January 12, 1965, the four men reappeared in court to appeal their conviction as paupers.[72] When Gambill denied the four defendants' request, Alexander objected and gave notice to the North Carolina Supreme Court.[73]

On January 12, 1965, Alexander filed fifty-two assignments of error, outlining the various mistakes made during and after the trial. Alexander cited the delivering of one verdict for all four men, Judge Gambill's denial of her frequent motions, numerous issues with the jury selection process, the expression of opinions by the court, possible jury tampering, and problems with the admission of evidence. On the same day she also filed a motion to obtain the trial transcript in order to prepare for the appeal. Meanwhile, Gambill allegedly kept the court reporter, Nellie Lovin, so busy she was unable to finish the trial transcript.[74] Despite Alexander's frequent appeals to the North Carolina Supreme Court for aid, it did not intervene in Gambill's delaying tactics.

On May 31, 1966, Alexander, her personal attorney Herbert Parks, and Charles Yoes appeared in superior court before Judge Walter E. Johnson Jr. Court reporter Lovin, solicitor Herbin, and assistant solicitor W. Edmund

Lowe also appeared. Alexander testified that she had only been furnished with an incomplete transcript of the trial, containing an incomplete account of the jury selection proceedings, including the comments and questions of the counsel and court. Alexander also sought evidence that Judge Gambill had violated § 1-180 of the North Carolina General Statutes, which required a judge not to express an opinion regarding the defendant's guilt or innocence. When Nellie Lovin took the stand, she testified that she had not supplied the complete testimony to Alexander; she was extremely busy and had no control over her court schedule. On July 7, 1966, the chief justice of the North Carolina Supreme Court, R. Hunt Parker, ordered Lovin to provide Alexander with a complete transcript.[75] Alexander later recalled that Lovin finally provided her with the transcript while Alexander sat at the hospital with her father, the Reverend J. C. Melton, who had suffered a stroke. For five days she sat with her father and prepared her report for the North Carolina Supreme Court.[76]

On October 26, 1966, the North Carolina Supreme Court agreed to hear the case.[77] Over the next months, both the defense and the prosecution worked on their briefs stating their cases. On November 1, 1967, North Carolina Supreme Court justice I. Beverly Lake issued his ruling, stating that there had been no error in the trial, and the sentence stood.[78] In his ruling, Justice Lake focused on the defense's allegations of racist misconduct on the part of the court. Regarding Alexander's evidence that Black men received harsher punishments, Lake wrote, "This contention of the defendants is clearly without merit." Concerning the allegations of racial bias in jury selection procedures, Lake wrote, "The record contains abundant evidence to support the finding by the trial judge that . . . there was no arbitrary or systematic exclusion of members of the Negro race. This alleged ground for the motion to quash the bills of indictment is, therefore, utterly without merit." Lake also stated that the right of the defendants to a fair trial was not infringed upon, and there was ample evidence to convict the men of rape.[79] That Justice Lake, an outspoken segregationist, would deny charges of racial bias in the judicial system is not surprising. Known in political circles throughout North Carolina, his reputation was that of the state's staunchest defender of segregation.[80] It is unlikely that Alexander could have convinced Lake of Yoes's innocence.

Alexander was unsurprised by the North Carolina Supreme Court ruling. She believed that the supreme court "didn't want this case" and that the court "issued a not-very-clear opinion, and affirmed, so it could get into federal court." In late 1967, claiming that she had spent $20,000 of her own money and three years working for Yoes on a one-week retainer, Alexander left the case. During those three years, her clientele had continued to grow, and now her father's health was declining. Alexander said, "I couldn't get involved any further. I told the boys to ask for court-appointed counsel and take the case to federal court, and that's finally what happened." Eventually all four men were declared indigent and given court-appointed attorneys who brought the case to federal court. While their convictions were never overturned, all four men were eventually put on work release after serving time in prison. Mary Lue Marion was apparently placed in a mental institution. Rumors of her mental condition had circulated around Greensboro and High Point before the case even started, including one that she had died in an institution. Alexander stated, "The papers say this [the rape] was the cause of her mental illness, but it's something else."[81] Alexander did not clarify what she believed to be the cause of Marion's mental illness, leaving lingering questions about what actually occurred on the evening of June 21, 1964.

Thirty years later, Alexander stood by her belief that Yoes was not one of the rapists. "Yoes should not have been in there, except guilt by association."[82] The fact that the four defendants did not spend the rest of their lives behind bars is extraordinary, especially given the lengths that the Guilford County Sheriff's Department went to in order to find the men guilty. In 1967, the *Greensboro Daily News* confirmed that Sheriff Clayton Jones had indeed bugged not just the cells of Yoes and his codefendants, but also the cells of other inmates. Jones stated that "to my knowledge no one's rights were ever violated by the use of the device." Lonnie Herbin, who had lost his reelection for solicitor in 1966, stated that he was appalled by the discovery and "had no knowledge at any time of any such device anywhere in the courthouse during my tenure as Solicitor."[83]

Elreta Alexander exposed the antiquated and prejudiced jury selection process in Guilford County, potentially helping many future African American defendants receive fairer trials. The case also had ripple effects beyond the lives of Charles Donald Yoes and the other defendants. In 1967, the North Carolina General Assembly enacted a law requiring each county to establish a jury commission tasked with preparing a master list of prospective jurors.[84] Alexander understood that this case "prompted the General Assembly to enact the Jury Commission the next session; the legislators had been working on it, but that case blew the lid off."[85] Alexander's defense of Yoes and his codefendants undoubtedly brought attention to the racism embedded in the North Carolina justice system.

Taking the case had been a calculated risk for Alexander, but it paid off. In the midst of the appeals process in 1966, Alexander became part of the first integrated law firm in the South. The Yoes case was taking up so much time that Alexander had to farm out her other cases. She began working with a young white attorney named Gerald "Jerry" Pell, and along with his brother Jim Pell and Ed Alston, they formed the law firm of Alston, Alexander, Pell, and Pell. The associates moved into the Southeastern Building in downtown Greensboro, making Alexander, the only woman and the only African American in the firm, the first Black tenant of the building. Alexander recalled that there "had been a clause in the building's lease that no Negros would be allowed to have professional offices in there. I knew that, so that's why Ed Alston and I decided to move up there." Alexander obviously saw this as another opportunity to integrate a professional space. After the firm was established, *Time* magazine called, but Alexander declined the interview. According to Jerry Pell, the firm did not publicize the partnership as the first integrated law firm in the South. They were not seeking publicity, but rather felt they were a good mix of attorneys. According to Pell, Alexander "did things for the right reason."[86] Even if Alexander in 1966 did not seek publicity for their integrated law firm or her other antiracism work, she certainly accepted credit at other times. In a 1977 interview, Alexander said, "The Yoes case was responsible for my getting into the partnership of a white law firm . . . the first integrated firm in the Southeast. One of the secretaries from the Pell firm (a white woman) had been with Julius Chambers and boast[ed] that Chambers' firm was the first integrated one, but *we* were the first."[87] Regardless of whether or not it was covered in *Time*, she was proud of yet another first.

When Alexander ran for district court judge in 1968, she stated that the Yoes case had made her decide to run. She said, "This is the kind of justice we've had in N.C. . . . This is the most repressive state in the Union."[88] Despite changing the jury selection process in Guilford County, Alexander still found overt oppression in the court system as an attorney, and she was determined to change that as a judge. She later said, "It was just in certain types of cases or when certain persons were on the bench some people were presumed guilty instead of innocent. . . . I told myself that one of these days I'd have a chance to do something about it."[89] Her chance came when she won a district court judgeship. From there, Alexander would continue to address inequities she found in the legal system, further solidifying her commitment to civil rights.

CHAPTER 4
Turbulence at Home

On July 9, 1950, Elreta Alexander sat down and typed a sixteen-page letter to her husband, Tony. In it she detailed twelve years of marital strife. Always the attorney, she wrote as if she was not only addressing her husband, but also outlining her potential court case in which her recollections could be admitted as evidence. She painstakingly recalled how the financial difficulties early in their marriage had led to Tony's bitterness, his numerous affairs, and eventually the physical, verbal, and mental abuse of his wife. She wrote: "You told me in the wee hours this morning—as you have so many times in the past—that you were tired . . . that you loved me but loved another better—that to continue under the yoke of our union was unbearable." According to Elreta, her husband stayed out until four and five o'clock in the morning, engaged in several extramarital affairs, and was physically and verbally abusive. Elreta recalled that Tony "nagged me, cursed me, in the presence of all the doctors and their wives." She was emotionally exhausted.[1]

By 1950 it seemed as though Elreta was ready to leave Tony: "I am heartily in favor of a speedy dissolution of our marriage on terms that I trust can be amicably adjusted." She also stated that she had not done so previously for four reasons: "Pride in my family, Pride in my race, and hating the social repercussions—and fear of bodily harm and death from you. For you have many times, while telling me to get the hell out, told me you would pursue me and kill me if I did leave you."[2] But despite the evidence she laid out against her husband in this letter, it would be another eighteen years before the Alexanders signed divorce papers.

In this chapter I explore the pressures Elreta Alexander faced in balancing a family and career as an African American woman. While the Alexanders were a professionally successful couple, their marriage was plagued with violence and infidelity. Elreta did not mention this in the available portions of her letter, but at the time she was approximately six months pregnant, which is perhaps one reason that she chose to remain in the toxic marriage. I argue that Elreta carefully compartmentalized her personal and professional lives so as to not jeopardize her pioneering accomplishments. As a prominent attorney, Elreta worried about what a divorce would do to her status in the Black community in Greensboro. She worried that the turmoil surrounding her marriage would hurt her reputation. Scholar Darlene Clark Hine describes the "culture of dissemblance," the secrecy practiced by Black women to protect their personal lives and their reputations.[3] In this case the dissemblance was more of a compartmentalization than a secret, as Elreta made few attempts to hide the problems in her marriage. Later, she discussed the violence extensively in her oral histories. An examination of her private life illuminates the morals and influences that guided her outside the courtroom and adds to her complexity, giving a fuller, more nuanced picture of her as a human being.[4] While she was powerful and tolerated no disrespect in her professional life, she was vulnerable and scared in her private life.

Many of the values Elreta took into her marriage came from being part of the close Melton family. In addition to being the bedrock social unit, family has been an important political concept for African Americans. In the 1950s, maintaining family integrity indicated respectability and morality to whites. Everyday acts of domesticity in African American households took on a different meaning as they were performed by families that strived to prove their worth in a white-dominated society.[5] Teaching respectability to young African Americans began at home, which is where young Elreta learned the ideals that would carry her through adulthood.

The bond between Elreta and her father, the Reverend J. C. Melton, was particularly tight. Melton was willing to sacrifice anything for his children to succeed. He made sure all three received college degrees—at the cost of his position at United Institutional Baptist—and he remained a pillar of support into their adulthoods. While he was close to all his children, the relationship between him and his youngest daughter was special. As an adult, Alexander stated that her father always put her on a pedestal.[6] Not wanting to disappoint him or create unwanted gossip surrounding her family weighed on Elreta.

A divorce would have certainly placed unwelcome attention on the Meltons. In some ways, Elreta and her siblings had always grown up in the spotlight. From their assigned front-row pew in church to their prominent standing in the community, many eyes were on them from the moment the family moved to Greensboro. While Elreta's mother, Alain, wanted to shield her children from the rigid expectations associated with being the "preacher's kids," it was impossible for young Elreta to not know that her family was expected to be extraordinary.[7]

Elreta was not alone in feeling the necessity of acting above the fray. During Jim Crow, the Black Baptist church placed more importance on the education of its ministers, and at the same time church women began to promote middle-class values in order to gain respectability for themselves and their church family.[8] As the head of the church, the minister and his family had to exemplify that respectability. While ministers had specific roles to fulfill in the community, these expectations also extended to his family. Mary Cook, a prominent Black Baptist woman in Kentucky and editor of the women's column in *American Baptist*, "pictured the ideal wife of a minister as a good homemaker, an intellectual, and at the forefront of social reform causes."[9] Alain Melton performed her assigned role well, but there were also high standards for her children.

Ministers' children learned to be well behaved with a focus on growing into respectable adults. One Georgia Baptist minister, Silas Xavier Floyd, compiled a book of stories for Black children entitled *Floyd's Flowers; or, Duty and Beauty for Colored Children* (1905). The book consisted of a hundred short stories that were essentially lessons in morality with examples of appropriate values for Black children. Specifically referring to marriage, he wrote, "In the olden times when folks got married they stayed married, but nowadays the courts are full of divorce cases.... Habits are great things— good habits or bad habits.... The same about loving and courting and getting married. Much depends upon training, upon habits."[10] Ministers like Floyd sought to provide direction and guidance for African American parents like the Meltons, who wished to raise their children with respectable, middle-class values. For Elreta, these lessons clearly took hold. In her letter to Tony, she stated, "I firmly believe in family life as the basis of all that is worthwhile," but a "reasonably compatible marriage is the foundation."[11] While a "reasonably compatible" marriage never materialized for the Alexanders, Elreta's belief in the importance of family remained.

Church and community expectations were only exceeded by the expectations J. C. Melton held for his children. While Elreta never specifically mentioned any use of *Floyd's Flowers* during her childhood, she certainly knew that her father set high academic, personal, and moral standards. As an adult, Elreta Alexander stated that if something "wasn't good enough for him to see, it wasn't good enough for me to do." While that might have been true during Elreta's childhood, her relationship with Tony changed her behavior around her father.[12] From the start, Elreta's marriage to Tony went against her father's wishes; the two eloped and kept their marriage secret for over a year. Elreta never elaborated on what her father's reaction was when they went public with their 1938 marriage, but her initial fear on her wedding day was that "Daddy'll skin me alive." Of course, it was shortly after the marriage became known that Elreta realized she had "made a very serious mistake." It was also early in the marriage that "Daddy kind of knew I was having trouble with my husband, even though I didn't talk about it."[13] The problems in the young marriage were part of the reason Elreta decided to go to law school. She hoped that in her absence Tony would have the opportunity to straighten out his own affairs and decide he wanted to be an active and attentive husband.[14] While law school certainly changed her life, it did not change her marriage.

Apparently Reverend Melton initially thought the young couple's marital problems would subside. But Elreta's father saw a different side of Tony after the accident that caused her burn injuries. After arguing with Elreta's sister, Etta, about her care, Tony insisted that he would be in charge of taking care of his wife at home. When Melton arrived to take his daughter to the hospital, Tony again insisted that he was taking care of his wife, but after Tony forced Elreta to get up and walk one day, reopening her wounds, Reverend Melton had had enough. "I'm gonna kill him. . . . I'll go down to prison. I cannot stand to see this." According to Elreta Alexander, this was the first time her father realized the problems in the marriage were serious.[15]

While pleasing her family was extremely important to Elreta, it is unlikely that J. C. and Alain Melton would have frowned on their daughter obtaining a divorce, given the deteriorating nature of her relationship with Tony. The situation, however, would have undoubtedly been disappointing and quite the story in the community, risking the reputation of the entire family. Having been raised with the concept of socially responsible individualism, Elreta likely felt she had to live with the consequences of her mistake not only for herself and her family, but also for her race. Having been raised with a keen sense of racial uplift, Elreta knew that African American marriages ending in divorce reflected badly on the community beyond the couple involved. In the 1950s, divorce created a stigma that affected not only the divorced woman, but also her family. Facing impending motherhood at a time when single Black mothers were increasingly vilified, Elreta Alexander actively tried to be better for her race.

Many African American women faced similar tribulations. The story of Septima Clark's marriage emphasizes the pressures placed on the private lives of Black women like Alexander. Septima Poinsette grew up in the early twentieth century in Charleston, South Carolina. While the Poinsette family did not enjoy the same middle-class comforts as the Meltons did, they still emphasized education and respectability. In 1919 Septima Poinsette first laid eyes on sailor Nerie Clark. Their subsequent elopement—much to the dismay of her strict mother—surprised her community in Charleston, where there were firm social hierarchies among African Americans. Several years into the marriage, she discovered that her husband had previously been married and was engaging in an affair. Septima left Nerie, but he died before a divorce was finalized. In marrying a sailor, Septima Clark had rejected the politics of respectability instilled in her as a child. Clark did not return to her native Charleston for another two years after Nerie's death.[16] Elreta Alexander, who did not want to face the same scrutiny as Septima Poinsette Clark, knew a divorce would not be seen as a respectable decision.

While the politics of respectability evolved from Elreta's childhood to adulthood, many stereotypes remained pervasive. "New middle-class Black people," like the Alexanders, worked to counter tropes that historically associated hypersexuality with Blackness.[17] During the first part of the twentieth century, African American women took great pains to avoid the appearance of sexual promiscuity. Having been subjected to unwanted sexual advances from white men since the slavery era, Black women wanted to dispel the Jezebel stereotype: the sexual Black woman who felt "virtue was something that could be traded for food."[18] For example, Septima Poinsette Clark dealt with her mounting marital issues by remaining quiet about her personal life in an attempt not to be seen as sexually irresponsible.[19] As an accomplished young African American woman, Elreta had to balance self-care, pride in her race and in her gender, and her personal and professional life. By remaining in a dysfunctional marriage, Alexander sought to avoid the erroneous stereotypes that had plagued Black women since the slavery era.

The emphasis on racial uplift likely contributed to Alexander's decision to remain in her marriage. Marriage was a key component of the politics of respectability. After the Civil War, white missionaries often compared the Christian value of monogamy with the "heathen" behavior of nonwhite, non-Christians who did not practice fidelity within a marriage. Adopting Eurocentric, Christian values increasingly became a marker of "civilization." For African Americans, adopting "white" marriage ideals indicated racial progress and signaled they were not inferior to whites.[20] What for whites was a personal part of life, for African Americans was political, "a testimony to capability as piercing white eyes peered through domesticity, searching for degeneracy."[21] Particularly for middle-class African Americans, such as the Alexanders, marriage was an opportunity for racial uplift. By showing that African Americans were capable of successful domestic lives, they also proved to whites their worth in other areas.[22] While marriage could provide financial stability, it also linked to status, respectability, and moral superiority.[23] It dispelled persistent myths of the Black woman as Jezebel and of violent Black men.

During the mid-twentieth century, African Americans like Tony were also under pressure to portray the image of the "best black man." The concept of the best black man had emerged to describe men who were well educated, married virtuous women, and raised children to follow in their accomplished footsteps.[24] J. C. Melton, for example, performed the role of best black man to a tee. The well-educated Meltons were paradigms of the Black middle class. Having been raised without a father at home, Tony Alexander lacked that example growing up.

Even if Tony had grown up in a household like the Meltons', the African American middle class was not a monolithic group. Tony was a well-educated and successful man but did not subscribe to the best black man concept like his father-in-law did. Many men of Tony's generation felt the concept to be out of date. As historian Glenda Gilmore states, "A new assertive generation of middle-class African Americans believed that the only way to guarantee rights was to exercise them in daily actions. Some in the rising generation demanded instantly the same level of respect that the Best Men had so carefully earned over a lifetime."[25] Indeed, Tony's level of success had drastically changed him. He was no longer the shy college student whom Elreta Melton met at the dance when she was fifteen. He had become an arrogant, demanding, and violent husband and father. While Tony certainly earned respect because of his educational and career achievements, at home he behaved in anything but a respectable manner.

Elreta knew that if Tony's abuse became public, it could perpetuate stereotypes of Black men as unprepared for the responsibilities of citizenhood. Since Reconstruction, white portrayals of Black men as lustful predators seeking out white women had served as justification for political disenfranchisement. Black men were also represented as "lacking the civic virtue necessary to be responsible citizens ... incapable of domestic virtue, of fulfilling the role of patriarchs who responsibly rule over households and provide for their families."[26] Elreta was concerned about how Tony represented not just himself, but also their race. In her mind, Tony perpetuated the negative stereotypes. In her 1950 letter, she recalled Tony's visits to New York while she was at Columbia Law. While Tony accused her of having a "white complex," Elreta wrote, "as a doctor you represented the highest in our race, and if you didn't show respect for your wife, what could the whites think when the only opportunity they had for observation was a crude, ill-mannered, prude, who could sport a[n] M.D."[27] Elreta had grown up surrounded by men who portrayed the "best" role exceptionally. Yet despite the numerous Black men who were pillars of their community, most whites would not differentiate between Tony's bad behavior and the actions of other Black men.

To those unfamiliar with the details of Tony and Elreta Alexander's marriage, they seemed to be the perfect representation of Black middle-class respectability. A surgeon and an attorney, both possessed the benefits of light skin, advanced education, and increasing wealth. Elreta was keenly aware of that paradigm in 1950, when she wrote that the potential social repercussions were one reason that she remained in her marriage. For upwardly mobile Black couples like the Alexanders, marriage was fraught with pressures both public and private, which influenced the internal workings of the marriage and how they presented themselves to the outside world.[28]

While time would prove that Elreta had close friends willing to help protect her from her husband's abuse, she was also aware that if she divorced him she would have to endure the judgment of the respectability-minded, middle-class Black community. Divorce was rare, and it was not until the 1950s that marital counseling became a popular option for couples experiencing difficulties.[29] Domestic violence, such as Alexander experienced, transcended race and class, but most women refused to admit they were victims of abuse at the hands of their husbands.[30] In many cases, blame was placed on the woman for her own abuse because it was seen as the wife's responsibility to keep her husband happy.[31] Unmarried women in the 1940s and 1950s were considered to be deviants, as marriage and motherhood were believed to be the ultimate aspirations of most American women. If she initiated a divorce, Elreta likely would have been seen as immoral or selfish, which was yet another stigma that could affect her legal career.[32] A woman such as Elreta Alexander in a white- and male-dominated profession could show little weakness professionally, which meant keeping the tribulations of her personal life hidden. Further, Elreta now had a child to consider. The need for stability overrode her desire to get a divorce.

Despite the violence and Tony's infidelity, their son, Girardeau Alexander III, was born on October 4, 1950, when Elreta was thirty-one. She doted on her only child, buying him expensive clothes and making sure he always received excellent care when she worked. Alexander recalled, "He wore the little sailor collars and Eton collars and all these things. I . . . wanted to make him Little Lord Fauntleroy. . . . He never crawled. I was working and he had so many people care for him that one day he got up and started running." Like his mother, Girardeau was an academically gifted child, with his primary school teachers describing him as "more advanced than the average student his age."[33] Elreta and Girardeau formed a close parent-child relationship, and she worked to shield him from his parents' turbulent relationship. Perhaps in an attempt to compensate for his relationship with his father, or perhaps to instill ideals of respectability, Elreta gave her child the best of everything.

With Elreta's attention focused on her career and Girardeau, she became less concerned about her husband's philandering and more worried about the safety of herself and her son. Tony's increasing dependence on alcohol often caused violent outbursts, prompting Elreta to leave the family home with Girardeau for weeks at a time. Alexander later remembered, "I was definitely afraid Tony would try to hurt me. . . . You have no idea what it's like to be tortured day and night, for the phone to ring at all hours; you're scared for it to ring, you're scared for it not to ring. No rest, no anything."[34]

Elreta's fears were justified. On April 30, 1957, "after having been cruelly subjected to almost daily abuse, drunken attacks," Tony attacked Elreta in his office, wielding a gun in an attempt to kill her. Tony's office was across the street from J. C. and Alain Melton's house. Reverend Melton, hearing his daughter's screams, grabbed his shotgun and marched over, saving Elreta's life. Immediately after the incident, Elreta took out a warrant against Tony and filed an emergency order for child custody. Elreta stated that some of the Black officers at the municipal court urged her not to end her marriage; they "begged me, 'Don't do it. My God, it's going to be the worst thing for your race' and blah blah blah. I said 'I've got to get my child out.'"[35] Despite this incident, by August of that year the Alexanders had reconciled.[36]

In the late 1950s and '60s, the Alexanders were increasingly an off-again, on-again couple; the patterns of separation and reconciliation became more frequent. The 1957 reconciliation, for example, did not last long. By 1959, Elreta and young Girardeau were living in a small apartment above Elreta's office to avoid Tony's violent behavior. One evening in December 1959 or 1960, Tony broke in and nearly beat Elreta to death in her bed as their son watched. Once again, Tony used his medical skills to repair the physical damage he had done to his wife. He took his family to their country home for several days where he tried "to get her brutally misfigured [sic] face reasonably acceptable."[37]

The 1960s brought increased scrutiny for single Black women. In 1965 the assistant secretary of labor, Daniel Patrick Moynihan, published a report entitled *The Negro Family: The Case for National Action*. The purpose of the Moynihan report was to address poverty in African American families. Arguing that a deteriorating family structure and female-headed homes were the "fundamental source of weakness of the Negro community," Moynihan contributed to the stigmatization of single Black mothers.[38] By then, the prospect of being a single mother likely did not daunt Elreta, as she had operated in that capacity for much of the time since her son's birth. However, this did not reduce the stigma that single motherhood through divorce would bring, nor would it ameliorate juggling a busy career with single parenthood.

The reasons Elreta outlined for staying in her marriage—pride in her family, pride in her race, and pride in her social status—were all justified for the times. However, the most tangible reason she stayed in the abusive marriage was fear of bodily harm or death. She had a valid basis to be afraid of Tony. When drunk, he could be extremely violent. For example, shortly after her burn trauma, while she was still bedridden, Tony realized she had developed an infection. In an angry rage, he dumped her bedpan all over her bed.[39] Once, when Elreta caught Tony with another woman, Tony grabbed his wife and dragged her across the street, screaming, "Goddammit, I'm going to get my gun and kill you!"[40] She eventually resorted to carrying a gun in her purse at all times.[41] Elreta, like many women, remained with her husband because the possible consequences of leaving were too risky.

Starting in the late nineteenth century, more and more women used abuse as a justification for divorce. Between 1867 and 1906, 218,520 divorces were granted in the United States on the grounds of spousal abuse.[42] Yet spousal abuse remained so common that some states just attempted to regulate it.[43] Prior to the 1970s domestic violence was not seen as a widespread phenomenon, affecting all classes and races. The term "battered woman" did not yet exist. Abuse was also seen as limited to physical altercations and did not necessarily include verbal and emotional damage. The common assumption was that the wife acted in a manner to provoke her husband into abusing her. Elreta, a strong, intelligent, and powerful career woman, would likely have been blamed for her own abuse because she did not conform to traditional gender roles. Furthermore, husbands have historically held the authority to chastise, discipline, or beat their wives based on socially constructed ideas of household structure.[44] Until 1958, coverture laws still prevented women from bringing suit against their husbands, treating domestic violence as a minor issue.[45] Elreta carried a gun in her purse for protection, yet few people at the time understood the reality of what it was like to live with an abusive spouse. Until the late 1960s women had few places to discuss domestic violence. It was not until the rise of consciousness-raising groups during the feminist movements of the 1960s and 1970s that women could verbalize their pain without any sense of shame.[46]

Tony Alexander followed the patterns of many men who abuse their wife. He would lash out violently, but rarely blamed himself for his lack of self-control. For men like Tony, a great deal of value was placed on the idea of manhood. After emancipation, marriage was seen as a means to promote citizenship and prove that a Black man could now be the head of his own household.[47] At the same time, white resentment about the new social presence of African Americans led to depictions of Black men as unwilling and unable to fulfill domestic obligations toward their wives and children, as well as incapable of fulfilling the duties of citizenship.[48] While this rhetoric was an attempt to keep social and political power in the hands of white men, many in the African American community felt that one way to combat these stereotypes was to adhere to and maintain prescribed gender roles in the family. For a Black man, the ability to head his family and maintain a domestic relationship signaled responsibility and a preparedness for citizenship.[49] Thus, the patriarchal family became a key component of Black middle-class status. Expectations dictated that women should be dutiful wives, while men should provide financial stability and leadership for the family.

Elreta and Tony Alexander initially sought to adhere to these social norms while at the same time defining themselves on their own terms.[50] But as Elreta's ambition and success grew, so did the discord in the marriage, pushing Tony's attitude regarding gender roles to the extreme. According to Elreta, "[Tony stated that] the only thing a man owed his wife was support. If she didn't have to worry about the economic[s] of living, she [should] be ready, willing, and able to function as a wife. You [Tony] have insisted on this attitude even to the point of asking me to secure women with which you could have intercourse in my presence. This is to say nothing about the numerous and sundry times you have tried to have affairs with my family, friends, and any attractive woman who came in the house."[51]

As was clearly the case in the Alexander household, the defined gender roles did not always play out as expected. Most Black women worked to provide much-needed income. Many labored as domestics for white families, taking care of children or doing laundry. Work looked different for educated, middle-class Black women though. For example, Alain Melton was a teacher, which was a respectable job for a middle-class Black woman. Her work, however, did not disrupt the patriarchal ideals or upstage J. C. Melton's work as a pastor—a very public position. Elreta Melton Alexander, however, did not take the traditional middle-class path. Had she remained a teacher, even if she had earned her master's degree in education as her father initially suggested, she would have been a successful wife reflecting Black middle-class respectability, in no way upstaging Tony's lucrative career as a surgeon. The Alexanders would have still been a prominent couple in Greensboro's Black community. Conjecture as to whether or not this route would have saved their marriage or tamed Tony's violent temper, however, is unnecessary. Tony Alexander had married a woman destined to break barriers.

In the Alexanders' marriage, Elreta's star shone brightest. While Tony was a plaintiff in the landmark case of *Simkins v. Cone*, he was not known for integrating white spaces at the level of his wife. Elreta, who regularly was written about in local newspapers for her numerous accomplishments, speeches, and legal cases, eclipsed Tony's visibility in the community. Additionally, her law practice eventually became very lucrative, making her wealthy in her own right without needing financial support from her husband. Yet despite the dysfunction, there were some levels of emotional attachment between Tony and Elreta. "He wanted me to succeed, but he didn't because he was afraid he would lose me. Which he would have, but for the fact that I knew that man needed me. That man could not do his work without knowing I was still with him." Tony was proud of his wife, but he was also jealous. Despite his numerous affairs, Elreta was always Tony's confidante. In that respect, she stayed true to her expected duties as a wife.⁵²

The nature of Elreta's high-powered career certainly altered the spousal roles and how Tony and Elreta approached their marriage. Scholars such as Barbara Ehrenreich have commented on the reactions of men who find themselves in marriages with strong, independent career women. The probability of divorce increases with the wife's level of success and financial independence. While this situation threatens traditional gender roles, it also becomes easier for men to leave if their wives are capable of financially talking care of themselves.⁵³ If Elreta had divorced Tony sooner, or if Tony had left with one of his mistresses, by the 1960s Elreta would have been capable of providing a comfortable life on her own for herself and her son. But that was certainly not the case in 1950 when she penned her letter.

Other middle-class Black marriages also suffered when the husband felt eclipsed by his wife. Anastasia Curwood uses the marriage of her paternal grandparents, Sarah and James Curwood, to analyze middle-class Black marriages in the interwar years. Like Tony Alexander, James Curwood often lived in his wife's shadow. James's "insecurity, combined with mental illness and alcoholism, translated into jealousy, infidelity, and violence."⁵⁴ Like James, Tony's insecurity could have been one reason for his infidelity. In an interview, Elreta Alexander commented that Tony would "get less intelligent women so that his inferiority complex wouldn't get the best of him. Women will take any kind of abuse to be associated with a big man."⁵⁵ Tony's abuse apparently extended to women other than his wife, and he undoubtedly had other issues beyond his wife's success. In 1977 Elreta commented that Tony had shown signs of schizophrenia, and his dependence on alcohol caused increasing health problems as he aged.⁵⁶ Unfortunately, mental health issues were a constant theme for Elreta, as her son later dealt with severe mental illness.

While Elreta was not ready to divorce Tony, her increasing financial independence allowed her to physically distance herself from him, which became easier as her son grew older. In 1958, she sent Girardeau to summer camp in Wareham, Massachusetts, and rented a home for six weeks in nearby Cape Cod. As a Black woman of means, Elreta claimed she received so much attention on her trip that she returned to Greensboro more exhausted than when she left. On returning home, Elreta decided that a career in international law would be a good excuse to leave the country with her son. In 1959, she applied for and received a fellowship to study international law in Geneva, Switzerland. In December 1959 or 1960, after Tony's severe beating of his wife in her apartment, Elreta and Girardeau left for Europe, vacationing in Spain, Italy, and the Middle East before going to Switzerland.[57]

For Elreta, the stress of her career, the state of race relations in the United States, and the violence of her marriage all had made her want to leave the country. She later said that although many of her clients and close friends were white, "by the same token Girardeau was getting to the age when he would have to realize he would always be a Negro, and that meant he would be a second-class citizen all his life." Life in a different country meant avoiding the "great pangs of discrimination, having to spend twice as much money to keep from being discriminated against, nowhere to eat downtown, you had to stand up—your dignity was assailed." So, she tried "to put an ocean between Tony and me."[58] Unfortunately, family circumstances kept her and Girardeau close to Tony.

After arriving home from their trip to Europe and the Middle East, Alexander and her son began to make financial arrangements to move to Switzerland for the duration of the international law course, which would take about three years. The plan was delayed, however, when the city of Greensboro began proceedings to acquire property, which included her parents' home and Tony's office, to construct Lindsay Street east of downtown. Elreta received an extension from the school in Geneva to attend at a later date; however, her family did not settle with the city until the end of 1963, at which point her parents' home was torn down to make way for the new street. While the Meltons' new house was being built, Elreta Alexander's mother went into cardiac arrest. Tony was able to save Alain, but Elreta knew that she could not leave the country for three years. While she gave up on her plans to return to Europe, Elreta still tried to distance herself from Tony, continuing to seek employment opportunities outside Greensboro. In 1963, she pursued a job with the United Nations, and she frequently applied to boarding schools on her son's behalf to get the increasingly troubled boy away from his abusive father.[59] Alain Alexander died in 1964. Elreta sought opportunities for herself and Girardeau in the Northeast, trying to get her son into schools, including Groton in Massachusetts and the Tilton School in New Hampshire.[60] Girardeau eventually was enrolled at Cornwall Academy in Great Barrington, Massachusetts, in the fall of 1966.[61]

Tony continued his affairs, and in 1966 began a relationship with a woman working in his office named Yvonne "Vonny" Waller. Elreta described Vonny as "brown-skinned" and having "a little class . . . but always kept something going on in the neighborhood." Vonny was also in an unstable marriage. In August 1966, Elreta described Tony as becoming "increasingly nasty at home." She had a detective follow Tony and Vonny to New York City, where they checked into a hotel as "Dr. and Mrs. Alexander." Also in 1966, she inquired about a job at Harvard Law School, which did not pan out.[62] Finally, Elreta had had enough. She said, "Tony, you go your way and I'll go mine. I just have to take care of Girardeau."[63] In February 1967 Elreta requested another separation from Tony. Tony left, but he and Vonny began intensely harassing Elreta. In one of several violent incidents, a drunk Tony showed up at the Alexander home in June 1967. Tony demanded to talk to Elreta, but Girardeau, who was home for the summer, blocked him. Tony lunged at his son, but "Girardeau gave him a single uppercut and knocked him six feet over in the corner." Knowing that Tony frequently kept guns close by, Elreta and Girardeau fled the house, with Tony screaming that he would kill them both. Elreta later said she heard rumors that Tony and Vonny had devised a plan to kill her with a hypodermic needle.[64]

The situation became so dire that Elreta sought refuge at her friend Nell's house in the fall of 1967. On October 30, 1967, she wrote to Tony, "I have asked Colonel [Walter] Burch to personally deliver my request that you permit my personal belongings to be removed from the house. With all of our problems, I do not believe you would deny me this request. A personal meeting at this time would not help our situation, and, could possibly make it beyond repair. They say time heals wounds. I trust that this will prove true in our case."[65] For her safety, her law partners Jim and Jerry Pell, along with her secretary, Anne, packed up Elreta's clothing and personal belongings when Tony was at work. Friendly police officers also kept watch over Elreta, taking Tony's death threats very seriously.[66] As the Alexanders' marriage reached new lows of dysfunction and violence, societal factors also changed, making a divorce seem like less of a threat to Elreta's pride in her family and race, easing the social repercussions.

Elreta Alexander came of age in a time and a culture that frequently devalued women in general; domestic violence was a problem that transcended racial and class lines. Elreta, however, was never one to be devalued. She continued with her career, carefully compartmentalizing her tumultuous personal life and her successful professional life. As mentioned, many Black women were accustomed to practicing what Hine calls the "culture of dissemblance," the need to protect one's personal life from outside intrusion.[67] While her safety and personal problems undoubtedly weighed heavily on her mind, she hid her feelings from public view. Keeping one's private life guarded is a survival strategy for many marginalized people, particularly Black women, who have historically lacked access to privacy.[68]

As an attorney, Elreta Alexander helped other Black women and men secure their own divorces. Anastasia Curwood discusses the "new Negro feminists" who worried about their personal autonomy, but knew that when it came to social justice their fate was intertwined with those of other marginalized women.[69] While many of the women Curwood places in the category of "new Negro feminist," like Amy Jacques Garvey and Zora Neale Hurston, predate Elreta Alexander, the premise holds true. Like Alexander, many of these women did not expressly describe themselves as feminists, but they began to blend their family lives with their lives outside the home. They felt that their work, community service, and roles as wife and mother could not be disentangled and that women should seek to be more independent.[70] While Elreta had been a practitioner of dissemblance, eighteen years after she wrote to Tony telling him the reasons that she had remained married to him, the situation was no longer tenable. In order to stand up for other marginalized people, Elreta had to legally end their marriage.

On January 15, 1968, the Reverend J. C. Melton died at the age of eighty-six after years of declining health.[71] As with the death of her mother in 1964, Elreta never elaborated on her father's death or the emotional impact of losing a parent whom she adored and wanted to please. But two months after the death of her father, another period of Elreta's life came to a close. She filed for divorce from her husband in March 1968. Although Tony and Elreta were separated in January 1968, it is significant that J. C. Melton died before the official end of his daughter's marriage. While Melton would have supported his daughter through a divorce from Tony, Elreta also no longer had to deal with any possible feelings of disappointing him.

By the 1960s many of the ideals of respectability that the Meltons had instilled in Elreta fell away as women began to more actively and openly pursue their own best interests. Elreta had grown up with the idea that if Black women raised strong families and subscribed to respectability politics, then assimilation into U.S. society was possible. Time, however, had shown otherwise. As the Moynihan report proved, the hard work of Black women to maintain family structures was not recognized by the white establishment. Regardless of how respectably African Americans performed, U.S. society and institutions still denied them the full benefits of citizenship.[72] For Black women like Alexander, it was increasingly clear that respectability politics did nothing to help women in violent marriages. In the 1960s the divorce rate skyrocketed as more women, whether or not they identified as feminists, increasingly identified with the women's movement.[73] As gender roles changed and evolved, many African Americans altered their views on marriage. The ideal of self-sacrifice in marriage for the sake of respectability gave way to personal satisfaction emotionally, economically, and professionally.[74] While Alexander held on to the idea of respectability in her career, it was no longer sustainable in her marriage.

Legal changes in the 1960s also made it easier for Alexander to finally obtain a divorce. In 1965 the state of North Carolina passed a no-fault divorce law. Prior to this law, a couple could only obtain a divorce if one of the parties was deemed to be at "fault," such as because of adultery or cruelty, while the other was seen as "innocent." Fault-based laws created a barrier to obtaining a divorce for any couple, but in a no-fault divorce, neither party is assigned blame; the law recognizes that the couple can no longer exist as a married unit. Additionally, only one spouse is needed to obtain a divorce, making the process significantly easier. The passage of the no-fault divorce law was followed by an increase in the divorce rate in North Carolina as more couples were able to end their marriages.[75] Among them were Tony and Elreta Alexander.

While their dramatic marriage had come to an end, their relationship did not, and Elreta continued to care for Tony for the rest of his life. At the beginning of their relationship, despite early warning flags, Elreta had stated that she "began to feel sorry for Tony, that he could not communicate with such a brilliant mind."[76] Despite everything Tony put his family through, there was always some level of mutual affection and understanding. Tony and Elreta's relationship did not end with the signing of divorce papers.

CHAPTER 5

A Reluctant Pioneer?

IN DECEMBER 1968 THE *Greensboro Daily News* profiled Judge Elreta Alexander, dubbing her a "reluctant pioneer": "The role of pioneer is not one Elreta Melton Alexander chose for herself. But when circumstances thrust it upon her, she did not run away."[1] While Alexander was undoubtedly a pioneer, reluctant she was not. She never ran away from difficult circumstances, but met them head on. During the last half of the 1960s, Alexander published a book of poetry, ran for office, integrated an all-white neighborhood, and made the controversial decision to defend members of the Ku Klux Klan. None of these accomplishments are those of a reluctant pioneer. These are the actions of an unconventional activist.

Despite her tumultuous personal life, Elreta Alexander was an extremely successful and popular attorney in Greensboro. Although she had already changed the landscape of the legal system in North Carolina, her foray into politics after the Yoes case solidified her place in the state and in legal history. After the legal injustices she witnessed and after over twenty years as an attorney in Greensboro, Alexander decided to run for a district court judgeship in Guilford County. Her entry into the political arena revealed the contradictory nature of this complicated pragmatist. The cases she accepted prior to running and her choice of party affiliation during the campaign show that Elreta Alexander's approach to racial justice was unique. As a judge, Alexander would change policies concerning juvenile sentencing. Her personal and professional lives, as well as the intersections of class, race, and gender, would continue to shape and influence her brand of activism.

Alexander's style of activism typically pointed out racial injustices through performance. Known for her bravado, she created scenes when she drank out of "whites-only" water fountains or sat in the Black sections of segregated courtrooms. In 1967, Alexander continued to highlight the injustice of segregation and the treatment of African Americans through performance, but also through her poetry when she published a collection titled *When Is a Man Free?* Alexander first had delivered the poems in 1966 at the Emancipation Anniversary in New Britain, Connecticut, and at the Fifteenth General Assembly of the Links, Inc. There is little doubt that Alexander's delivery of her work was fiery, and the performance of her poetry was an extension of her professional activism.

The book made a small splash in Greensboro, with the *Greensboro Daily News* saying that Alexander "writes with deep feeling, and not inconsiderable poetic ability."[2] Alexander dedicated the book to "the realization by men of the nature of their being, common to all, that makes them one." While her dedication calls for unity, her poetry contains some fierce rhetoric directed at whites.

> You say we are lazy, ill-mannered, half-crazy
>   Ungrateful, immoral, unprepared;
>
> Yet we have climbed your ladders round by round,
> In spite of your attempts to push us down.
>
> Your statistics show we commit more crimes—
> Oh, I wish I had the dimes
> For the cases I have tried:
> Verdict—"guilty"—when simply justice was denied.[3]

Her words reflect not only her personal and professional frustration, but also the frustration of many African Americans in the twentieth century who struggled because of the racism they experienced in institutional and social structures.

Alexander's poetry also displays her extensive knowledge of history and religion. Her words highlight the entrenched racism in the United States, discussing the country's history from the Atlantic slave trade to the Revolutionary War, from the Hayes-Tilden Compromise of 1877 to urban redevelopment and the Federal Housing Administration. In the eponymous poem "When Is a Man Free?" she writes:

> In Africa, the black man we tracked
> Shackled him, and brought him back
>
>> To a life of misery,
>> And tortures that have no rivalry.
>> When he cried out to be free
>> His body hung, dying, from a tree;
>> His children, we auctioned for pay;
>> Our chance for decency, thrown away

She goes on:

> But then came the year 1876—
> The Hayes-Tilden compromise was the big fix
>
>> That opened Pandora's lid of hate,
>> Chasing freed men outside the gate
>>> of liberty
>
>> In exchange for votes for the Presidency,
>> Rule was restored to the Confederacy;
>> And men of color were disfranchised,
>> Tortured, intimidated, outlawed, ostracized.

Man is not free.[4]

The poem "What Men Will Be Freed?" draws from chapters 4–8 of the book of Revelation, with which she undoubtedly was familiar because of her father, the Reverend J. C. Melton. While her first poem is pointed and angry, this one is dark, ominous, and full of symbolism. She describes it as "visions of a vision of John the Divine" and sections the poem with reference to the Four Horsemen of the apocalypse. In the section "The Rider and the White Horse," she writes:

> No sooner had God let him loose
> Than his blessings he did misuse
>> For his own vanity.
> From ancient lands, to cross the Mediterranean,
>> Friend and foe, he overran;
> Mighty kingdoms fell under the weight
>> Of the rider, who became a symbol of hate.

Through Europe, Africa, Asia, he ran,
No continent escaped the weight of his hand,
Followed by men lusting for power, wealth and fame.
 Ravished humanity, to HIS eternal shame.

Across the ocean, he discovered new places,
 Dispersed the natives who had bronze faces,
 Labeled them savages, their wealth to steal,
 Declared them outlaws, an excuse to kill.

Kidnapped black men in a primitive land,
 Who had never against him turned a hand,
  Transported them to distant shores,
   In chains, to do his chores.

When he could not justify the use of his might,
He asserted it was based on divine right,
 Whereby he was ordained to be ruler of men,
  Using Scriptures to verify his sins
   of
    Colonization
    Desecration
    Exploitation[5]

 Her book, published in Philadelphia, likely would have made more news had it been published in the South, that is, if a publisher of racial poetry could have been found in the 1960s South. Instead, Alexander used the self-publishing company Dorrance. The book revealed her true feelings about the treatment of African Americans in the United States, which were much angrier than she relayed in her professional life. Alexander could not give judges and juries lectures on oppression throughout U.S. history, so she found another way to express her anger. Obviously she was image-conscious in the Greensboro community, and her poetry provided an outlet through which she could truly share her feelings on race without compromising the reputation she had built as an attorney accepted by the white community.

 Five months after her book of poetry appeared in print, Alexander lost the most important intellectual, spiritual, and emotional driving force in her life: her father. In addition to Reverend Melton's death, her son, Girardeau's, mental health began to deteriorate. As he got older it had become apparent that something was wrong, and young Girardeau was eventually diagnosed with paranoid schizophrenia. Alexander frequently corresponded with schools and summer camps in the Northeast where his needs could be met. She attempted to give her son everything, but despite her best intentions, she could not control Girardeau's illness. He graduated from Cornwall Academy in 1968 with high marks, but on his return to Greensboro he became sicker. His mother recalled that he would "sit by the window, withdrawing. He was retreating from me, thinking about all these things that were scrambled up in his head.... I could see Girardeau was going downhill fast. Schizophrenia was rapidly overtaking him." The quick progression of Girardeau's schizophrenia in his late teens is consistent with the hallmarks of the disease. As a mother, Alexander did everything she could to protect her child from his volatile father, but the tumult exacerbated his condition.[6]

Needing to find a safe home for herself and her son, Alexander pulled everything she had out of the bank and placed a down payment on a home on West Friendly Avenue in an affluent, historically white neighborhood. She found the house through a neighbor, who told her that living in that neighborhood might be a good move for her safety, insinuating that Tony would be less likely to attack her in a rich, white area. She thus became the first Black resident of Starmount Forest, an area that had previously used restrictive racial covenants to keep African Americans from living there. The 1968 Civil Rights Act had passed in April of that year, with Title VIII, known as the Fair Housing Act (FHA), protecting home buyers from racial discrimination and outlawing restrictive racial covenants. Soon after the passing of the FHA, the president of the Greensboro Realtors Association stated he did not think it was a good time for an African American to buy a home in an all-white neighborhood. Of course, that did not deter Alexander, whose prominent career and wealth made her move to Starmount possible. While Alexander had experience and was comfortable in a white world, her housekeeper, Lucille, disapproved of the move. When asked if she would continue to work for Alexander in her new home, Lucille stated that the white residents would run her out. While the FHA made violence against African Americans who integrated white neighborhoods a federal crime, violence nonetheless continued into the 1980s. But ultimately, Alexander's purchase of the home was less of a political statement regarding integration than it was a move to provide her son with stability and safety.[7]

Alexander had good cause to fear for their safety not only because of her husband, but also because of the controversial cases she continued to take on. As a shrewd and brilliant attorney, Alexander did not avoid challenges. In perhaps her most controversial move, Alexander defended members of the Ku Klux Klan on a variety of charges. During this time the Klan had a significant presence in Greensboro. The Klansmen wanted a good lawyer regardless of race or religion, and they found one in Elreta Alexander. While Alexander was undoubtedly a skilled litigator, it still seems unlikely the Klan would have accepted the skills of a Black woman without an additional motive. Internal control of the local Klan was in dispute, leading to assaults among members. Additionally, the Klan had an internal court system in which they disciplined members who were caught cheating on their wives, not paying child support, and other moral or social violations. Several Klan members hired Alexander to represent them in individual assault cases, not related to their Klan activities. On booking, police would find Klan membership cards in the wallets of Alexander's clients and ask her if she knew whom she was there to represent. "Money's green," she would quip. How could the same woman who wrote about the "nation with racial hate" defend the perpetrators of that abhorrence? Her commitment to the law and to the Sixth Amendment likely provided a justification for her representation of Ku Klux Klan members. As an attorney with white clients, she might have gone too far, however, to show her objectivity and unwillingness to back down from a challenge. On the other hand, Alexander had recently become the single mother of a son with severe mental illness. Although she had a comfortable lifestyle, she also needed to ensure a stable income.[8]

Regardless of her motivations, Alexander also saw her representation of Klan members as a form of civil rights activism. In what might have been the height of her performance activism, she took the opportunity to try to change Klansmen's views on race. She later credited herself with convincing some clients to leave the Klan. It is unknown exactly how many Klan members she represented, but she later said, "We don't have a viable KKK here now, and they'll tell you it's mainly because of my representing them and being so fair." She knew that one of the reasons she was sought by Klansmen for representation was because they did not want judges to know they were KKK members. If they were defended by a Black woman attorney for simple assault cases, they thought no one would suspect their extracurricular hateful activity.[9]

The incongruity of a Black woman attorney representing members of the Ku Klux Klan is one of many racial contradictions in Greensboro during the late 1960s. Despite the city being home of the sit-in movement, Greensboro hid its racial strife behind what historian William Chafe calls the "progressive mystique." Greensboro's attempts to project itself as a modern New South city covered up political conservatism and the racial tensions that simmered among the city's residents. In response to the 1964 Civil Rights Act and increasing civil rights demonstrations, the Klan provided an outlet for white supremacists to vent their anxieties and frustrations. Additionally, with two historically Black colleges, the Black population of Greensboro had a higher average level of education than in most other southern cities, creating racial competition for manufacturing jobs with the city's blue-collar, white population by the late 1960s. These factors led to Greensboro becoming a hotbed for the KKK.[10]

With Greensboro's large white supremacist population, Alexander found herself with plenty of KKK members to "convert" to the side of racial open-mindedness. Alexander recalled one white man whom she had represented on several cases coming to her office one day and admitting he was a member of the Klan. He said, "You know, you've made a believer out of me. You didn't know it, but I belonged to the Ku Klux Klan. After the way you've treated me, though, been so nice, I quit. I don't believe colored people and Jews are inferior anymore." Alexander responded that she had known about her client's affiliation with the Klan and pointed to a bust of Abraham Lincoln in her office, commenting that the spirit of Lincoln must have rubbed off on him. It is unlikely that Lincoln influenced a Klan member, but Alexander also credited herself: "I do have a charisma that attracts people regardless of age, race, sex or creed."[11] For Alexander, that ability to attract was part of her activism.

Alexander's charisma also proved useful as she made her first foray into electoral politics. In early 1968 there was speculation that Alexander would make herself a candidate for a judgeship. She added to the speculation when in February of that year she changed her party affiliation from Democratic to Republican.[12] That move made Alexander a political anomaly. In the decades after the Civil War, the Democrats had been the defenders of white supremacy. Prior to 1948, most African Americans in North Carolina associated themselves with the Republican Party. But as Democrats slowly started to adopt more racially inclusive policies in the twentieth century, white southerners left the party, sparking what political scientists Merle Black and Earl Black call the "great white switch." President Lyndon B. Johnson signed the Civil Rights Act of 1964 and the Voting Rights Act of 1965, and the old Democratic South disappeared. In 1964, for example, South Carolina senator Strom Thurmond left the Democratic Party to become the first Republican senator from the Deep South in the twentieth century. Additionally, when civil rights opponent Barry Goldwater secured the Republican Party's presidential nomination in 1964, his party alienated Black voters and provided a new political home for southern white racists. The Republican Party that emerged from the South had little to do with the principles of Lincoln and was much more in tune with the views of Goldwater.[13]

By 1968, most African Americans had left the Republican Party, but Alexander might have found some ideological commonalities with other Black Republicans. Although there was no longer a solid Democratic South, a solid Republican South had not yet emerged.[14] In North Carolina—in particular in Guilford County—Democrats were still firmly in control. While Alexander was initially part of the Black Democratic electorate, she saw an opportunity as a Black woman in the Republican Party. She was not unfamiliar with Republican insiders. Ten years prior to running for district court judge, Alexander had been in regular correspondence and enjoyed a friendship with Val J. Washington, the director of minorities for the Republican National Committee.[15] But Alexander did not really associate herself with either party: "I'm not a party person. I think we've lost the whole perspective of what constitutional government is about. . . . I've never felt [like a] dyed-in-the-wool Republican, [or] dyed-in-the-wool Democrat."[16] She stated explicitly that she was not a conservative and believed that "integration was the only way for Black people to succeed."[17] Alexander's change of party affiliation was yet another example of her determination to integrate formerly all-white spaces. At the same time, simply aligning with a political party with which she did not have strong ideological ties for the sake of integration seems hollow.

While Alexander was in the political minority among African Americans, she was not the only Black Republican who used party affiliation as a method of achieving political equality. Other African Americans, such as Tennessee business leader George W. Lee, who remained or joined the Republican Party during this time were rooted in the politics of respectability in which Alexander had been raised, and they did not want to see the GOP become solely a party for white men. Morality, personal responsibility, and a strong work ethic were traditional conservative values that were undoubtedly important to Alexander, based on her upbringing. She was also accustomed to working within conservative institutional and power networks, having made a career in the North Carolina justice system. Alexander, who integrated southern courtrooms in the 1950s and 1960s, was likely undaunted by the challenges of being a Black woman in the Republican Party.[18]

Alexander might have also sensed the political winds shifting. As became apparent several years later, Alexander's ambitions at the time went beyond Guilford County. Knowing she likely had the Black vote secured, her change of party affiliation might have been a calculated career move designed to secure bipartisan support and place her ahead of the changing political climate. Regardless of her intentions, Alexander's shift of party brought attention to herself, her career, and her unique approach to practicing law.

Shortly after switching her party affiliation, Alexander held a press conference and announced her intention to run for district court judge. She stated:

> The jurisdiction of the District Court and the duties of the judges elected to that bench require dedicated persons who are legally trained and skilled as experienced practicing attorneys. I believe I possess the requisite qualifications. When elected to this high office, I shall discharge my responsibilities in accordance with law and ever mindful of my oath to do "... equal law and right to all persons, rich and poor, without having regard to any persons" ... "and faithfully, truly and justly, according to the best of my skill and judgement do equal justice to the public and to individuals."[19]

During the race Alexander did not do much active campaigning but placed several ads in Guilford County newspapers. The ads featured a picture of Alexander, dressed in a dark suit with pearls, and encouraged voters to "elect a living symbol of justice." A campaign brochure featured a head shot of Alexander with the line "The symbol of justice is a woman" and a picture of a Lady Justice statue.[20] Alexander had principled reasons for not campaigning for the judgeship. She told her alma mater's newspaper, the *Register*, that conducting a partisan political campaign could potentially skew her ability to maintain neutrality under the law.[21] Her integrity was noted by local newspapers, one of which said Alexander was an "attorney of proven skill and courage."[22] Alexander's reputation was firmly established in Guilford County.

Close to Election Day, however, her son's mental health took another turn for the worse. Girardeau began to hallucinate, waking his mother up one night screaming that his father was outside their house with a machine gun. Alexander called the police. When they arrived, they found Girardeau running around outside with a large butcher knife. He screamed, "Don't you see my Daddy? There he is! Don't you hear the machine gun?" Girardeau's father, Tony, was not there. Girardeau was taken to the psychiatric ward of Cone Hospital, and Alexander considered having her name removed from the ballot. Her son came first. She consulted with her former high school principal, Dr. John Tarpley, who had known Alexander most of her life. He said,

"Leave your name on. You may not get elected. But if you're not, at least you won't [have] put your personal things ahead of yourself. Don't cop out." After talking with Tarpley, she decided to stay in the race.[23]

On Election Day 1968, with the southern backlash to Johnson's civil rights policies and increasing frustration over the Vietnam War, Republican Richard Nixon received 39,152 votes in Guilford County, winning the local presidential vote over Democrat Hubert Humphrey. Republicans Howard Coble and Odell Payne both won seats in the North Carolina House of Representatives, and High Point Republican Calvin Coolidge Murrow won a seat in the North Carolina Senate.[24] Alexander came in third in her twelve-candidate race, garnering 33,968 votes to win one of the six judge vacancies. Her victory made her the first African American woman judge in North Carolina and likely the nation's first African American woman to be elected to a district court judgeship. In Guilford County, she was the only woman, the only African American, and the only Republican to earn a judgeship. Her win was partially attributed to single-shot voting in majority-Black precincts, meaning that many African American citizens only voted for the Black candidates, leaving the rest of the ballot blank.[25] Voter registration among African Americans had increased significantly in 1968. Largely due to reforms after the 1965 Voting Rights Act, in Greensboro alone 2,000 African Americans had newly registered to vote, bringing the total in the city to 13,500.[26]

The well-publicized campaigns of two prominent African Americans in Guilford County also brought many first-time voters to the polls that year. In addition to Alexander, another popular African American attorney in Greensboro, Henry Frye, ran as a Democrat and became the first African American to be elected to the North Carolina legislature in the twentieth century.[27] The headline of the *Carolina Peacemaker*, an African American newspaper, read, "A New Day Has Dawned: Frye to Legislature; Alexander to District Court." The article explained, "Observers of the local scene commented that they had never before seen the polling places so crowded by Black Greensburghers [sic] who were seeking to cast their vote."[28] Local Black organizations endorsed both Frye and Alexander, although they were running from different political parties. Decades later, Frye stated that Alexander's Republican status was a real anomaly among African Americans, but her outgoing personality and qualifications secured her enough white votes to win the judgeship.[29]

When Alexander was elected, only 1.3 percent of the nation's attorneys were Black, and only 314 out of an estimated 16,700 full-time judges were Black.[30] Not only was there a severe lack of African Americans in the legal profession, but there was also a lack of women. In 1970, out of those 16,700 judges in state courts, only 183 were women.[31] Alexander joined a small but highly accomplished group of legal scholars, and running as a Republican had made her unique. While in this instance, integrating the Republican Party worked out in her favor, she would find being a member of the GOP problematic later in her career.

According to Alexander, the whites in power in Raleigh were not thrilled with her victory. As part of Nixon's southern strategy, Republicans played on the racial fears of white social conservatives in order to gain political power. Having an elected African American judge in their midst was not part of that plan. "When my election was heard about in Raleigh, the power structure said, 'My God, this is opening doors; maybe we're going too fast,'" stated Alexander. After her win, the state board of elections changed the way local elections were held. Instead of the system where the top vote-getting candidates won a seat and then were assigned to a district, North Carolina created a numbered seating plan in which judges had to run for a specific seat against another candidate. "I believe the numbered seat system was instituted just because I won the election," said Alexander. She undoubtedly had benefited from single-shot voting in 1968 since she received most of her votes from predominately Black precincts in Greensboro and High Point. It was noted, however, that she also ran well in predominately white precincts throughout Guilford County. The numbered seat plan became particularly popular among Republicans and African Americans though, because it allowed enough of their votes to elect at least one of their candidates even in heavily white Democratic areas.[32] In 1970, however, a suit was filed in the federal Eastern District Court, arguing that the numbered seat system was "enacted with the intent, and [has] had the purpose and effect of diluting, minimizing, and canceling out the voting strength of Negro and Republican minorities in North Carolina." In 1972 the three-judge panel ruled against the state, striking down the numbered seat system.[33]

Alexander largely credited her father, the Reverend J. C. Melton, with her early achievements, such as her graduation from Dudley High at fifteen and her graduation from NC A&T at eighteen. She also credited her unhappy marriage with her success, stating that she might have "settled into a pattern of normal domesticity" had her marriage worked well. But her famous firsts, from Columbia to her integration of the Starmount Forest neighborhood, show that her pioneering accomplishments were hardly thrust upon her. Instead they show a Black woman who embraced her own agency and deliberately worked toward change. But in 1968, Alexander likely recognized the need to appear to be a "reluctant pioneer" so as not to scare the establishment that she was quickly changing.[34]

Alexander's election provided her with a larger platform to discuss the barriers of race and gender. She stated her belief that "the number one illness in American is prejudice based on color." But she also found something optimistic to say about the ardent white supremacists who dominated southern politics. "[Mississippi politicians Theodore G.] Bilbo and [John E.] Rankin did more good than harm... because they embarrassed the good conservative southern white persons and provoked them into action.... Unless there [was] a catalytic agent you wouldn't get any action."[35] Alexander certainly saw her career as a positive reaction to white supremacist forces.

Alexander provided some insight into her life as a career-oriented woman in the 1960s. She said she did not choose to be a pioneer but accepted the title: "That is the burden of life... and without a burden life can be meaningless." That burden, however, sometimes left Alexander feeling isolated. As she later reflected, "It's lonely. You have to be with the people, but not of them. You can't participate with them." Alexander grew up as part of what W. E. B. Du Bois called the "talented tenth," focusing on education, career, and racial uplift. They would be the paradigms of Black success. But like Alexander, other Black women in this elite category felt the weight of loneliness. For Walteen Grady-Truely, who grew up in the 1950s, shouldering the responsibilities she had as a Black woman affected her career choices: "I wanted to be a lawyer. It was always with an eye towards creating a world where there would be more people like me... who had the advantage of having access to the whole world." Her endeavors, however, left her lonely: "There's a sense that if you're African American and on the cutting edge economically and educationally, there are not going to be other people like you. There are so few of us."[36] In addition to there being few women like Alexander or Grady-Truely, their respectability-based approach was increasingly seen as conservative, and younger civil rights activists adopted more confrontational approaches. Alexander was again between two worlds. She did not fit into the white Starmount Forest neighborhood in Greensboro, but she also had few African Americans she could relate to.

Alexander's closest friend was Sally Pell, the mother of her former law partners Jim and Jerry Pell. (Alexander had left the firm when she became a judge.) The two women frequently traveled together and made regular shopping excursions. The Pells were Jewish, and the two women bonded over their shared minority status. Sally Pell was born in 1912 and reared in Cleveland, Ohio, in the 1920s and 1930s during the high point of anti-Semitism in the United States. In the post–World War II nation, however, the racial component of anti-Semitism fell out of favor as Jews became increasingly viewed as white. Despite that shift, Jews who were accepted into the white mainstream remained cognizant of ethnic differences and attempted to not disrupt the sense of homogeneity clung to by Christian whites. If Jews like the Pells embraced civil rights for African Americans, they could draw the ire of their white Christian neighbors. When Jim and Jerry Pell formed a law firm with Alexander, they received calls warning them that they would never work in Greensboro, but they went ahead anyway. Sally Pell and Elreta Alexander, who shared the same upper-class status and sense of injustice, had much more in common than they had differences, and the friendship lasted until Pell's death in 1995.[37]

Judge Alexander's heavy workload also likely contributed to her isolation. Alexander's responsibilities as a district court judge involved hearing misdemeanor cases, criminal traffic cases, and preliminary hearings in felony cases. The six district court judges in Guilford County rotated their assignments. One week, Judge Alexander would be in domestic court, the next in criminal court, and the next in juvenile court.[38] When Alexander took the oath, she stated that she "didn't have an agenda in mind . . . except I knew where justice was supposed to be. And each case stands on its own and gives account of its own merit."[39]

Alexander became best known for her work in juvenile court, where she created in 1969 the Judgment Day program, an accomplishment of which she was particularly proud. At the time, there were few programs in the North Carolina judicial system for troubled youth, a fact with which Judge Alexander would have been familiar based on her experiences with her son, Girardeau. So she took matters into her own hands. Alexander later stated, "I felt that sentencing should take into consideration protection, deterrence, and rehabilitation, that you didn't want . . . just [to] be harsh because you had a right to give people time."[40] Her Judgment Day program incorporated everything she felt sentencing should take into consideration. It was well intentioned, groundbreaking, and by most accounts, successful. But it was not without controversy.

The Judgment Day program was established specifically for young first-time offenders. It was modeled after deferred-sentencing programs, in which convictions are cleared from offenders' records if they do not commit any more transgressions within a certain period of time. In Alexander's program, after hearing a guilty plea, the judge would refrain from entering a judgment and instead give the young offender various tasks to perform. These generally consisted of community service, writing reports on the dangers of crime, and actions to rehabilitate themselves. The reports had to be presented before churches, schools, youth-based societies, and the judge.[41] On a preset date, the young person would read their report and make their case for rehabilitation to the court. If the report satisfied the judge, then the conviction would be dropped from the offender's record.

Alexander's philosophy was that the bench should be used for something other than punishment. The idea that courts could treat rather than punish, also known as rehabilitative justice, came from the Progressive movement of the early twentieth century. The goal of rehabilitative justice is to find the cause of the crime and treat the accused accordingly. From this idea, pioneered by Progressive Era sociologists such as Julia Lathrop, came juvenile courts, probation programs, parole programs, and reformatories. It widened judicial discretion and created options within the existing penal process. Judge Alexander took these ideas and created a program unique to Guilford County, treating each person who went through the program on a case-by-case basis.[42]

For decades before the creation of the Judgment Day program, women had taken a leading role in juvenile justice matters. In 1899, the first separate court for juveniles was established in Cook County, Illinois. Chicago and Milwaukee both pioneered the juvenile court movement in the early twentieth century, and well-to-do, Progressive women led the way.[43] Despite the good intentions of Progressive reformers, however, the nature of juvenile crime changed with the arrival of urbanization and industrialization. With both parents working outside the home, poor children were left to fend for themselves.

The training school model for delinquent girls was initiated in Chicago by professional maternalists, those who worked in roles such as probation officer, social worker, and judge. These maternalists focused on the specific problems of wayward girls and included Progressive reformers such as Jane Addams, Julia Lathrop, and Florence Kelley. They argued that women were best able to help rehabilitate delinquent girls and that juvenile crime should be treated on an individual basis.[44] The creation of Hull House by Addams gave these women a place to cultivate "social motherhood," and they worked at Hull House's kindergarten, children's clubs, and mothering classes.[45] But the model created by these Progressive reformers did not keep up with the changing nature of juvenile crimes.⁴⁶

Judge Alexander attempted to carry on that reformist tradition, but enthusiasm for the Progressive model of rehabilitation had significantly declined by the time she created the Judgment Day program. Soon after their inception, juvenile courts were most frequently used by working-class and immigrant parents as a means of controlling their troubled children.⁴⁷ By the 1960s, changing cultural and political dynamics undermined support for the rehabilitative model. Postwar rises in juvenile delinquency convinced many that the juvenile justice system needed an overhaul.⁴⁸ Liberals criticized judicial discretion, arguing that it led to unequal punishment, while conservatives advocated for a "crackdown" on crime and cited civil rights marches and civil disobedience for the erosion of legal and moral values.⁴⁹ As a result, there were fewer programs for juvenile offenders. Juvenile courts also varied, depending on the makeup of the courts and the statutes of each state.⁵⁰ In North Carolina, Judgment Day was unique and innovative. Another former law partner of Alexander's stated, "I couldn't speak for any other state, but as far as the state of North Carolina, she was the first one to do this."⁵¹

Judge Alexander touted the achievements of the program and how it changed the lives of the young people who went through it. An overweight young woman who pled guilty to writing bad checks reported to the court that she had gone to Weight Watchers, got a job, and found legal means of shopping. In another instance, Alexander sent a young man to jail when he would not give his final speech. When he finally did give his report, he realized he had found his calling in speaking to the public, eventually received his Ph.D., and became a minister. Alexander noted that many who went through the program became lawyers and business professionals, all because she gave them another chance, which they would not have received from a different judge.⁵²

Judges and attorneys, however, attacked the program. In North Carolina, judges already used their own discretion in sentencing, and postponing judgment was not unusual. Debate arose around the Judgment Day program over the length of postponement and if judges should be allowed to dismiss a case based on meeting certain conditions. Judge Alexander felt that incarcerating youthful offenders would not provide the structure and guidance they needed. She believed that punishment did not solve the root of the problem and argued that many young people could reform their lives because the program provided them with a support system. The young offenders went on to succeed "because somebody cared and they didn't have to stand up there alone."⁵³

Alexander's program coincided with a rise in heavy policing tactics, which was of concern to many African Americans because the incarceration rates of men of color skyrocketed. During the civil rights movement and the period Manning Marable calls the "Second Reconstruction," African Americans increasingly challenged the status quo, making increased demands for opportunity and equality. As they did during the Reconstruction period of the late nineteenth century, whites felt increased anxiety at the changing social norms and responded by hardening laws and increasing law enforcement. On the streets and even in schools, officials embraced more punitive policies. Petty crimes and violations of social norms began to warrant harsher punishments, and the trumped-up enforcement largely came, once again, at the expense of Black men's freedom.⁵⁴

Judge Alexander played a crucial role in determining the sentences of young Black offenders and used the Judgment Day program to push back against the increasing incarceration of young Black men and others. As an attorney, Alexander had witnessed firsthand the bias Black men faced in the justice system when she represented Charles Yoes and his codefendants. The program, however, helped more than just young Black men. A local newspaper described the young offenders going through the Judgment Day program as coming from a "myriad of lifestyles, personalities and backgrounds." Another stated that "these people aren't ignoramuses, and they aren't from poverty homes. A number have been good students, school and church leaders, who just had to try [drugs] out."⁵⁵ Newspapers also reported the large number of participants. On one scheduled Judgment Day, Judge Alexander heard 437 cases.⁵⁶ While many nonminority offenders benefited from the program, young African American men were undoubtedly helped, and many went on to have successful careers because of it. For example, Joe Williams, an African American man, testified later to the impact of Judge Alexander's influence. When Williams himself became a judge, he stated, "This judge has had many chances. . . . Judge Elreta Alexander gave me a chance by encouraging me to go to college and to stop doing some of the foolish things I was doing."⁵⁷ His testimony reaffirmed Alexander's commitment to seeing youth succeed.

While the Judgment Day program was groundbreaking, it was not suitable for every offender. Judge Alexander did not always use the program for nonviolent juveniles. Several years after the creation of Judgment Day, a fourteen-year-old girl stood before the judge. Alexander had sent her to training school because she was "getting to be a habitual thief." When asked what she was going to do about her situation, the girl responded, "I'm not going to steal no more . . . stealin' don't get you nowhere." Judge Alexander then allowed the girl to go home as long as she reported to her caseworker every thirty days. She warned the girl, however, that "if you come back here, you're going to be in training school for a long time."[58] Judgment Day demonstrated that a rigid justice system does not meet the needs of all citizens, especially juveniles.

Alexander created the Judgment Day program during a transitional time in the juvenile justice system. In a 1964 case, fifteen-year-old Gerald Gault was sentenced to six years at a state industrial school for making a lewd phone call to his neighbor. After the disproportionately harsh sentence, the U.S. Supreme Court formalized procedures for juvenile courts, requiring all states to provide the same due process to juveniles as they did to adults. While the goal of juvenile courts was intended to be rehabilitation, in some cases broad judicial discretion led to extreme punishments for minor criminal offenses, especially in cases where the sociocultural inequalities between court officials and the young offenders were extreme. The implementation of procedural reforms was not designed to remove the rehabilitative aspect of the juvenile system, but rather to provide more suitable services and minimize the role of the state in the intervention into minors' lives. While Judge Alexander's intentions were pure, the Judgment Day program became caught up in these systemic changes.[59]

Less than ten years after Alexander created Judgment Day, she was forced to change the procedure after a fellow district court judge attacked the program. Republican judge John B. Hatfield, also of Guilford County, said the program was being abused, that "Judgement Day is totally unjustified by the rules of procedure," and that judges cannot impose rehabilitation or punishment before they have decided a case.[60] In 1978, judicial discretion was under attack. In the Judgment Day program, a defendant admitted guilt, but whether the juvenile received a deferred sentence, or what the conditions of the sentence were, was purely up to the presiding judge. Further attacks on judicial discretion prompted state and federal policy makers to impose tougher sanctions on juvenile offenders and to ease the movement of young people into the adult justice system. By 1998 the federal Office of Juvenile Justice and Delinquency Prevention authorized states to get tough on offending juveniles, offering financial incentives to states that enabled more children to be prosecuted in criminal courts. Those tougher sanctions gave the judge less latitude to consider basic adolescent developmental issues and other factors, such as the defendant's family background and educational history, in adjudicating juvenile cases.[61]

When Alexander created the Judgement Day program, she did not yet have to worry about such attacks on sentencing discretion. The state of North Carolina gave judges nearly unlimited discretion, dating back to the 1777 North Carolina legislature, which "imposed no limitations whatever upon the trial judge's power to determine the length of an offender's confinement."[62] Judge Alexander rarely sent a Judgment Day participant to jail, and she was able to impose sentences that she saw as prudent and necessary given the offense. Her favorite quote—and her primary judicial philosophy—was "the truth shall set you free."[63] She built the Judgment Day program on that philosophy. If a young person committed a crime, but then told the truth and worked toward their own rehabilitation and self-improvement, they were free.

But in October 1979, the assistant attorney general of North Carolina ruled that Judgment Day, while worthwhile, had no statutory authority.[64] By 1980, the future of the program was uncertain after Guilford County district attorney Mike Schlosser, backed by state law, said that it was the job of the prosecutor—not the judge—to dismiss or reduce charges. He prevented Judge Joe Williams and Judge Alexander—the only two judges implementing the program—from proceeding by insisting he had the sole prerogative to dismiss cases.[65]

The attack on Judgment Day was in line with the rollback of rehab-focused approaches to justice that accompanied the rise of conservatism in the later twentieth century. Federal and state legislatures began to pass mandatory-sentencing laws, taking away judicial discretion and giving the power to prosecutors. The result was drastic increases in the number of individuals incarcerated and in the length of their sentences. The "war on crime" and the "war on drugs" during the 1980s and later ultimately resulted in disproportionately high rates of incarceration for Black men and other marginalized people—the exact issue Judge Alexander was likely addressing when she created the Judgment Day program.[66]

Alexander has not been described as an "activist judge." She managed to transcend the racial divide in Greensboro with her election, and thus would not have wanted to be known as an activist at the time, even though her poetry and the Judgment Day program could qualify her as such. In her public comments, she attempted to strike a neutral tone, likely for the same reasons she accepted the term "reluctant pioneer." As an elected judge, she had to be careful not to alienate the white people who voted for her. In 1969 she commented, "I want to make each decision in accordance with the law and my own conscience."[67] When directly asked about civil rights, she took a conciliatory tone. In a televised interview with Greensboro's CBS affiliate, she stated that love—not force—was the long-term solution to the nation's civil rights unrest. "You can bring an adversary to terms (by force)... but he will arise again." But she followed that statement by saying that "you cannot bring order out of chaos," and unruliness cannot be sanctioned.[68] But while she was careful to keep her public comments impartial, she spoke freely in the courtroom. She frequently encouraged young Black defendants to get an education, believing that prison and fines did not help the individual.

Judge Alexander also was known for other courtroom innovations. She became an advocate for mental health from the bench. Surely drawing from her own experiences with her son, she created headlines for ordering a Vietnam War veteran to receive mental health therapy. Alexander believed that the United States was not preparing its veterans for civilian life: "These boys are coming back (from Vietnam) and they are reacting to peacetime situations as if they are still at war.... Wartime reactions are obviously the cause of some of the trouble many have gotten into at home."[69] Alexander's innovative approach to dispensing justice certainly drew attention to causes she was passionate about.

When Alexander became a district court judge, she shook up more than just the racial and gender makeup of the judiciary. She also altered her unique performance style to fit her new position as judge. Peering down from the bench and wearing a huge string of pearls, she "easily lapsed into sermons" and spoke in a "rich, melodious voice that glid[ed] up and down the scale."[70] When she had announced her candidacy for the judgeship, a newspaper article stated that "her striking headgear has become her courtroom trademark: Her sometimes flamboyant hats have livened up the scenery at a lot of otherwise dull trials."[71] But on the bench, she lost the hats and began to sport more daring wigs. According to her former law partner Jerry Pell, wigs were always a part of Alexander's style. Pell recalled seeing Alexander only once without a wig, and early in her career they were always brown. The pictures of Alexander used for her 1968 district court judge race featured well-coiffed dark hair; her appearance is that of a strong, confident African American woman. As she approached middle age and faced the challenge of accessorizing a judge's robe, the wigs became blonder. The *Greensboro Daily News* dubbed Alexander "easily the champion wig wearer."⁷² Blonde wigs became a staple of Alexander's wardrobe on the bench.

The embrace of blonde wigs likely reflected Alexander's own perception of her race and gender. For Black women, hair has always been an important aspect of how they are perceived by society. The rise of the Black Power movement coincided with Judge Alexander's prominence on the bench. Many women in the Black Power movement embraced natural hair as a valorization of their Blackness and a rejection of white conceptions of beauty. But wigs also grew in popularity at this time among African American women. While Afro wigs sold well among younger Black women, Alexander could not don a politically divisive hairstyle. Many Black women saw blonde wigs as a reflection of culturally enforced European notions of beauty, but other Black professional women sought feminine hairstyles that were not associated with radical political positions, such as Afros. As a woman who had a reputation for being fashion-forward, Alexander's wigs also added a bit of flair without alienating the largely white electorate who had voted for her. And practically speaking, they were an alternative to heavily processing her hair in order to be respectable in professional settings.⁷³

Judge Alexander also became known for her rhetoric. A 1969 profile of Alexander described her as slipping "easily into the language of the people who appear before her in court." The reporter noted one memorable case in which she admonished a young woman in the middle of a love triangle; the two men were defendants in her courtroom. Alexander said to the young woman, "Listen here, Sweet Mama. You'd better cool yourself down, Sugar Lips, and find yourself something other than men to hustle. Or I'll have you up here pretty soon. You find something else to do other than sit around and have illegitimate children and pick up your welfare checks."⁷⁴ While her words clearly were rooted in respectability politics, she adapted her language in order to reach individual offenders. Alexander rarely minced words with those who appeared in her courtroom.

Alexander's civil rights rhetoric was most on display when she spoke in front of Black audiences. She was the commencement speaker at her alma mater, North Carolina Agricultural and Technical State University, in 1969. The title of her speech was "The Commencement and Conquest of Freedom," and she quoted directly from her book of poetry, *When Is a Man Free?* stating, "A man is free when he can see that his brother is none other than he." Alexander emphasized her own brand of activism, which focused on the notions of respectability and racial uplift. Eschewing violence as a means of activism, she stated, "Hate, jealousy, and revenge are self-defeating in the discovery and utilization of God-given talents." While obviously promoting her own view of achievement, she also lauded the virtues of awareness, appreciation, and accommodation, and she made concessions for those who took an alternative path. Alexander noted in her speech, "Everybody ha[s] got to do his thing. . . . Some persons like to associate this popular theme with the vulgar, the uncouth, the odd balls and the hippies. But I saw that each can do his own thing, with due respect for the other's thing."[75] Alexander recognized that her form of activism was not everybody's form of activism.

Alexander was recognized for her contributions not just by Greensboro's African American community but also by women's organizations. In 1969, the Greensboro Chamber of Commerce gave her the Dolley Madison Award for her "outstanding contribution of womanpower for the better[ment] of the community."[76] Alexander increasingly was a vocal proponent of women in the workplace. In March 1970, she was invited to speak at an event hosted by the faculty wives of the University of North Carolina at Greensboro. She delivered a speech entitled "Women as Engineers of New Educational Domains."[77] Alexander was also a regular speaker at the North Carolina Girls State conventions throughout the 1970s. In 1972, when Sylvia Allen became the first Black teen to be elected as governor during the Tar Heel Girls State conference, she cited Judge Alexander as one of the most inspiring speakers of the week.[78]

Alexander was embraced by both Black and white women and was a popular speaker for groups of both races. When she addressed Black women's groups, such as the Links, her audience understood how the intersection of race and gender shaped her career experiences. But when speaking to largely white audiences, such as the group at North Carolina Girls State, Alexander likely had to separate her experience as a woman from her Black experience. But even though the burgeoning white feminist movement underemphasized race in order to promote gender issues, Alexander remained a strong example of a powerful Black woman who embraced both parts of herself.[79]

Because of her high-profile position, Judge Alexander began to be known throughout North Carolina. In 1971, a profile of Alexander was run on the same day by the *Robesonian* in Lumberton and by the *Gastonia Gazette* in Gastonia, small towns 150 miles apart. The article, "North Carolina's First Negro Jurist Has Originality," credited her with blazing "trails for her sex and race in the legal field, all the while keeping her own identity without becoming a symbol instead of a person." She was quoted saying that racism was an illness: "You treat an ill person with compassion, and the antidote of love."[80] Following in the civil rights tradition of Martin Luther King Jr. and his embrace of agape, the unconditional love Jesus practiced, Alexander demonstrated her radical form of love by defending Klan members and in her Judgment Day program.

In 1972, Judge Alexander's originality brought her national attention, as she was frequently mentioned as a possible presidential appointee to the federal Middle District Court seat, which would have made her the first African American to hold a southern federal judgeship. Alexander was initially brought to the attention of White House assistants Harry Dent and Fred Malek by Bob Brown. Brown was a native of High Point, North Carolina, and served as a special assistant to the president. He was Richard Nixon's first major Black appointee. Dent in particular championed Judge Alexander, suggesting to Attorney General Richard Kleindienst that he name Alexander to fill a vacancy on the Fourth Circuit (potentially to succeed Thurgood Marshall on the Supreme Court), or appoint her to the Middle District seat and let the North Carolina Republican Party name her successor, which he noted was the best political option.[81]

Lack of party loyalty, however, became an issue for the potential Nixon appointee despite the fact Alexander had won her election as a Republican. The chair of the Sixth District of the North Carolina Republican Party stated, "I think Mrs. Alexander is a very capable person and highly qualified for the job, but she is a relative newcomer to the party." Others questioned whether appointing a Black woman would be a hindrance to Nixon's southern strategy, where Nixon courted white votes and deliberately elicited fears of racial equality. Attorney General Kleindienst was hesitant to name Judge Alexander because of the potential political backlash among white conservatives in North Carolina. Observers noted, on the other hand, that if Nixon did appoint an African American and "if that Black person who is also a woman turns out to be a jurist of Mrs. Alexander's ability, not only the Republican Party but the Middle District will have gained tremendously."[82]

In a letter to Nixon's chief of staff, Bob Haldeman, Malek stated that Brown and Dent "both are convinced [Alexander] is a reasonable, able, and deserving person. They agree there would be some adverse repercussions, perhaps mostly from North Carolina Republicans. However, quite a few people have written letters in her behalf, and her credentials cannot be successfully challenged." Malek also argued that the potential gain of Black support for Nixon could be worth the white backlash. Alexander certainly had the support of

Republican voters, as evidenced in a letter to the editor of the *Greensboro Record*. The writer stated, "I am white, male (and Republican) and it is my sincere opinion, and the opinion of many acquaintants, Mrs. Alexander is the finest jurist in our area." But one source in the GOP said, "Her problems lie not with the Nixon administration but with the approval of the state Republican executive committee.... If she can just get on the list of nominees for Washington to consider, I feel she's got the job." While the Nixon administration received overwhelmingly glowing reviews of Alexander, the head of the North Carolina Republican Party simply said, "She's okay."[83] Ultimately, Hiram Ward was appointed by Nixon to the position. Alexander did not receive a nomination, nor did any other African American during the Nixon administration. It would not be the last time the North Carolina Republican Party failed to support her.

While not receiving the endorsement of her fellow Republicans likely stung, Judge Alexander was busy presiding over a high-profile case involving a theft ring in the High Point Police Department. In addition, the support she had from many in her hometown was shown to be solid when she won another term as district court judge in November 1972. In that election, Alexander ran unopposed and did not make a single campaign speech or post a single billboard, saying it demeaned the office. Her achievements began to attract national attention, and a profile of Alexander was included in the *Miami Herald*, which marveled at her accomplishments as a Black Republican woman.[84]

Judge Alexander had amassed financial wealth, and she was an in-demand speaker throughout the East Coast, a published poet, and a leader in the city of Greensboro. She had divorced Tony in March 1968, and their previously troubled relationship became a warm friendship. In 1971 she had told him, "Tony, if I had known I could get along with you so well, I'd have divorced you the day I married you."[85] She commented that sometimes Tony would call her when he was drunk, but for the most part, their relationship was amicable. Their son, Girardeau, however, continued to be troubled, especially in his relationship with his father.

In March 1973, Tony had an American Medical Association convention in Honolulu, Hawaii, and requested that Girardeau accompany him. Even though Tony and his son had spent an increasing amount of time together, Girardeau was hesitant. His father promised that he would remain sober throughout the trip, and they would spend time together sightseeing. Before leaving, Tony kissed Elreta, telling her that he would always love her. She later said, "I felt something very strange, but I didn't have time to think about it. I had a speech to get ready for the DAR [Daughters of the American Revolution]." Tony and Girardeau called Elreta when they arrived in Honolulu and one other time to check in. The next thing she heard was on the night of March 18, 1973, when Girardeau called and said, "Momma, I think I've killed my father." According to Girardeau, Tony had gotten very drunk. When Girardeau announced he was going to get a soda from the vending machine, Tony said, "Goddammit, you spend too much money! You and your goddamn momma spend too much money!" Girardeau warned his father not to talk about his mother, and when Tony started hitting him, Girardeau grabbed a scalpel lying on a table. According to Elreta, in his drunken stupor Tony stumbled into Girardeau, and the scalpel penetrated his chest. Girardeau immediately called the hotel management, asking for an ambulance, and was soon taken into police custody. His mother, with the help of Sally Pell, immediately flew to Honolulu.[86]

When Elreta Alexander arrived in Hawaii, she went directly to the police station to be with her son. Tony was still unconscious, and two weeks later he came down with pneumonia and had to have an emergency tracheotomy. He survived the procedure but remained unconscious. After three weeks, Judge Alexander had used up all her vacation days. After four weeks, she was concerned about her place on the bench: "I knew Chief District Judge [Edward] Kuykendall really didn't like me at all. . . . He didn't like the publicity and all that I got, and all the people writing saying what a fine judge I was; that's been the hard part being a woman, a double dose of it." Desperate to get back to work but unwilling to leave her former husband in Hawaii, Elreta secured an air force transport to get Tony back to North Carolina, where he was admitted to Wesley Long Hospital. After several weeks in Greensboro, Tony regained consciousness, but his health, which had probably been compromised by his heavy drinking, never fully recovered. No charges were filed against Girardeau, and for the rest of Tony's life, Elreta was his primary caretaker, even though they never lived together after their divorce.[87]

Between 1968 and 1973, Elreta Alexander's judgeship increased her visibility and her ability to make meaningful change in the community. Alexander always claimed that she did not set out to be a pioneer. But when given the opportunity to challenge the status quo, Alexander never shirked. She pursued some of her most meaningful and most controversial career decisions during this time. Despite her unique approach, Alexander was very engaged in racial issues and contemplated matters of justice, as evidenced by her poetry and her concern for the Black community. Judge Alexander had managed to overcome all the obstacles put in her way in her professional life, but in 1974 she would discover the limits to her influence. That year, she experienced her most significant career loss and had to examine the hurdles of race and gender that remained. In a 1993 interview, Alexander stated, "You have fear. You just don't show it. You know, you've got to walk through it, or else you're going to drop dead."[88] This perspective continued to drive her through the difficult years ahead.

CHAPTER 6

Attempting the Impossible

MAY 7, 1974, WAS A BAD DAY for Judge Elreta Melton Alexander. Having run in the Republican primary for chief justice of the North Carolina Supreme Court, she lost to a white male fire extinguisher salesman, James Newcomb, who boasted only a high school degree. It was a stunning loss that reflected poorly on the North Carolina Republican Party and brought up the issues of sexism and racism that still permeated North Carolina politics. Her electoral success in Guilford County had not translated into statewide success. Playing the role of "reluctant pioneer," she was hesitant to attribute the defeat to racism, and she later said that she had only experienced racial discrimination a couple of times in her life without mentioning this loss.[1] But a well-known Columbia Law graduate does not lose a judgeship to someone with no legal training without some sort of bias at play. In a defeat that could be attributed to "racism, sexism, or gross ignorance," it became apparent that the best candidate does not always win.[2]

The primary loss marked the beginning of a difficult time in Alexander's career, as she found herself stymied by the institutional structures that held back so many women of color. Throughout her career, her successes and failures demonstrated both the possibilities and the limitations confronting African American women in the post–civil rights era. The early 1970s were the pinnacle of Judge Alexander's professional success; people showed up in court just to see her in action. At the time of the 1974 election, her achievements had received statewide and national recognition. Her electability, however, had never been tested outside Guilford County. Alexander had not publicly discussed seeking a higher office. Therefore, it came as a surprise to many when she filed as a Republican candidate for the position of chief justice of the North Carolina Supreme Court in February 1974. Judge Alexander released a statement: "In filing for election to the Office of Chief Justice of the Supreme Court of North Carolina . . . I do so in full awareness of this high office. In asking the voters of this state to favorably consider my candidacy, it is in appreciation for their judgement and in respect for their constitutional right to nominate and elect eligible, competent and dedicated representatives to elective public office." She touted her education, her qualifications, her "temperament, judgement, maturity, courage and character," and her experiences as an attorney and judge in Guilford County.[3]

As an African American woman, Judge Alexander faced an uphill battle running for a statewide seat in North Carolina. Nineteen seventy-four was a midterm election year, so press coverage was not as extensive as it would have been in a presidential election year. Additionally, the supreme court contest typically received little attention. At least one newspaper, however, covered the upcoming campaign: "Her candidacy will mean that an all-woman battle is looming for the state's highest judicial post. Democrat Susie Sharp of Reidsville, a long-time associate justice on the Supreme Court, has filed for chief justice."[4] Sharp ran unopposed for the Democratic nomination, and it seemed like the historic Alexander-Sharp race was set.

When Judge Alexander filed to be the Republican candidate she knew she faced a difficult run. While she was well known in her native Guilford County, she did not have the same level of name recognition throughout the rest of the state, especially in the predominately white areas of Appalachia and western North Carolina. This statewide campaign would require more money and more travel than her previous two campaigns. Susie Sharp, the white Democratic nominee, was the state's first woman superior court judge and the state's first woman associate of the North Carolina Supreme Court.[5] Sharp was arguably better known across the state.

Alexander never mentioned any particular inspiration for her run for supreme court chief justice. When asked why she decided to campaign for the position, she stated, "I am qualified and it is my duty to offer my services to the people of North Carolina."[6] It was claimed that Alexander did not consult with or give notice to the state Republican Party before she filed, leaving many to speculate about her motives. Some, including Susie Sharp, believed she ran to increase her name recognition and her chances of being appointed to a higher court after the election.[7] But Alexander had been in contact with the North Carolina Republican Party regarding the 1974 chief justice campaign. She had written to North Carolina GOP chair Thomas Bennett in January 1974 declining his invitation to serve on a judicial election committee. She had cited the North Carolina Code of Judicial Conduct, canon 7, stating, "(1) A judge or candidate for election to judicial office should not... (b) publicly endorse a candidate for public office." The North Carolina Supreme Court, however, endorsed Susie Sharp, a justice on the court. Alexander asked Bennett if the state supreme court's endorsement of Sharp established "a legal precedent affording immunity to other judges for similar public endorsements."[8] Alexander was likely mulling her run for the supreme court, and whether or not she could seek the endorsement of her fellow justices in light of similar endorsements was a reasonable question. Bennett, however, apparently forgot about Alexander's letter, as he stated in May 1974 that the Republican judicial candidates committee could not recruit anyone to run for chief justice against Sharp because "no attorney was interested in filing due to the fact it would require a statewide race and an expensive campaign with the odds stacked against him."[9] The Republican judicial candidates committee was obviously not familiar with—or did not consider—Judge Alexander's qualifications and tenacity.

Alexander's would-be opponent, Justice Susie Sharp, was initially intrigued by her. Both women had overcome obstacles to become pioneering women in the legal field. After Sharp's first encounter with Alexander in 1960, she wrote to a cousin describing "a colored lady lawyer," who was "the best Negro lawyer in the state." And Sharp, known for being conservative and no-nonsense in the courtroom, could not help but notice Alexander's fashion sense, saying, "She wears a different and more striking outfit every day—shoes, hat, bag, complete outfit entirely different."[10]

Fourteen years later, Sharp focused more on Alexander's viability as a candidate than on her wardrobe. Democratic Party workers, however, seemed stumped as to why Judge Alexander decided to run. In a party memo it was speculated that "Elrita [sic] made a very last-minute decision to file without any working arrangement or even any warning to the party leaders; and she said she did it because the other Republican who filed doesn't have a college degree.... Elrita does not expect much support from the party.... Evelyn said she really couldn't tell for certain just what the real motives were."[11] The memo failed to note that Alexander had filed to run before her primary opponent did, which negates the claim that she filed in response to his lack of credentials.[12] Alexander did, however, make her announcement to run seemingly without consultation. Although she was qualified for the position, the move left her colleagues on both sides of the aisle stumped. Perhaps others felt what Judge Alexander did not publicly acknowledge—that the odds of a woman, let alone a Black woman, being elected to a statewide seat in North Carolina in 1974 were extremely low. Elreta Alexander had overcome some high barriers in her career, so perhaps she saw little reason to believe she could not overcome one more. Per usual, Alexander kept her true motives and feelings closely guarded.

As would be the case with many North Carolina voters, Justice Sharp's racism contributed to her perception of Judge Alexander. In 1974 Sharp did not describe Alexander as favorably as she had in 1960. Like many white southerners, Sharp was adamantly against federal intervention in desegregation, calling the *Brown v. Board of Education* decision "the greatest calamity to befall the South since reconstruction." Sharp also said, "You simply cannot judge animals by human standards"—referring to African Americans in her courtroom.[13] She viewed Alexander's nontraditional courtroom style and the Judgment Day program as "disturbing."[14] Regarding Alexander's campaign, Sharp wrote to her nephew, "Half the folks think her candidacy is merely an effort to advertise herself for some other job; the other half are so appalled at the prospect that she might become C[hief] J[ustice]."[15]

Justice Sharp's assessment of the reasons for and the reaction to Judge Alexander's candidacy in some circles was probably spot-on. Increased name recognition for Alexander, as well as touting of her achievements, served as a beneficial side effect of running for office. Alexander surely knew that Sharp would be a difficult, if not impossible, opponent to beat. Using the campaign as a means to advertise herself for a federally appointed judgeship would have been a strategic and logical move. Sharp was also undoubtedly correct that conservative southern Democrats were horrified by the thought that an African American woman, known for her performative style and informal court, could possibly become the state's supreme court chief justice. Many conservatives in the Republican Party apparently felt the same way.

When Judge Alexander decided to run for chief justice as a Republican in 1974, she faced a different political landscape than in her first election in 1968, as the "great white switch" had continued to change North Carolina's electorate. The antiquated views of old southern Democrats, like Sharp, had become less prominent in their party. Not all conservatives, however, were convinced that the Republican Party was the best fit. Social conservatives remained divided in party affiliation, as evidenced by Democratic senator Sam

Ervin, who during his career defended Jim Crow laws and mounted a vigorous opposition to the Equal Rights Amendment.[16] Jesse Helms of North Carolina had joined the Republican Party in 1970 and was elected to the U.S. Senate in 1972, replacing Strom Thurmond as "the most conspicuously unreconstructed Republican senator from the South."[17] Additionally, in 1973, James E. Holshouser Jr. had become North Carolina's first Republican governor since 1896, and North Carolina and the rest of the South had voted Republican in the 1968 and 1972 presidential elections. The emergence of Republicanism made North Carolina a viable two-party state, making Alexander's candidacy on the Republican ticket seem logical, but at the same time it was odd because of her race and the GOP's increasing embrace of traditionalism and racial and gender intolerance.[18] In 1974, Alexander faced an electorate swept up in a backlash to the liberalism of the 1960s and an embrace of the conservativism of the 1970s.

The electoral shift in North Carolina was in line with political trends throughout the South. In 1968, the year of Alexander's first election in Guilford County, Richard Nixon had implemented his southern strategy in an attempt to solidify a voting bloc in the South. He deliberately pandered to white conservative voters with threats of increasing racial equality and a loss of "southern values."[19] Turmoil throughout the country and the embrace of civil rights drove many white southerners out of the Democratic Party. Nixon capitalized on this by using phrases such as "law and order," "states' rights," and "forced busing," and he created an image of a "silent majority" of white voters beleaguered by what they saw as a country spinning into disorder, with an increasing crime rate and drug subculture.[20] Many members of this so-called silent majority saw the advancement of civil rights for Black citizens as the cause of this disarray. By 1974, Nixon's southern strategy was reflected in an emerging Republican South and had firmly landed the Republican Party on the wrong side of civil rights issues.

As much as Nixon capitalized on the fears of conservative whites, he did make some attempt to attract the Black electorate, particularly the votes of college-educated, middle-class African Americans like Alexander. Using the language of the politics of respectability, Nixon made appeals to Black capitalists, particularly well-educated African Americans who owned businesses, embraced the concept of self-help, and voiced concerns regarding the economy.[21] Despite this, in 1968 Nixon only received 10 percent of the Black vote. His meager appeals to middle-class African Americans could not overcome the racist rhetoric of conservatives like Strom Thurmond and Jesse Helms.[22]

Those African Americans who still had allegiance to the Republican Party saw promise in Nixon's "Black Cabinet," a loose coalition of Black Republican appointees who promoted a largely economic agenda focusing on the needs of middle-class African Americans.[23] Black officials in the Nixon White House, however, largely had silent roles and did not feel able to speak out against objectionable policies. Nixon's Black appointees also miscalculated the appeal of a Republican-led "economic civil rights movement" since the "Black silent majority" was much smaller than they thought.[24]

Alexander's remaining with the Republican Party was in line with other African Americans who remained. She felt that integration was key to Black success, and so did others, despite the difficulty that the emergence of Republican conservatives like Barry Goldwater brought. Prominent Black Tennessee Republican George W. Lee expressed a sentiment similar to Alexander's: "During my Goldwater fight in San Francisco [in 1964] . . . I was a lone individual down there. . . . Somebody had to stay there in the Republican Party and fight, and fight with the hope that the Republican Party wouldn't be made a party of ultra-conservatism and further than that, a party for the white man."[25] Alexander maintained that an integrated party was the only way for Black people to have a voice and succeed.[26]

As the Republican Party moved increasingly toward the right, many Black party members, like Judge Alexander, remained focused on civil rights. Black Republicans often formed alliances with the remaining white liberals and moderates in the GOP ranks, and they focused on civil rights struggles such as fair employment, school desegregation, housing, and voting. And like Alexander, many of these Black Republicans were leaders in their local communities and ran competitive political campaigns in state and local elections. While the black-and-tan Republicans had largely dissipated after the 1964 nomination of Barry Goldwater as the Republican presidential candidate, some African Americans remained in the party, and several years later they were optimistic about Nixon's Black capitalism initiatives and his appointment of African Americans to executive-level positions.[27] Like the views of Elreta Alexander, the reasoning of other Black Republicans to remain with the party was complicated.

Along with the members of Nixon's Black Cabinet, Judge Alexander might have miscalculated the strength of Black Republicans to gain Black votes. The national numbers were certainly stacked against them. In 1970, seven African American Republican candidates had run for congressional, senatorial, or gubernatorial seats. In contrast, there were thirty-six African American

Democrats who ran.[28] Alexander was a part of a shrinking minority that held many of the ideological values, such as respectability and uplift, that she grew up with. Many Black Republicans worked for "an alternative economic and civil rights movement" rooted in those politics. Some Black Republicans also maintained that it was their responsibility to stay in the Republican ranks and "reform the party," a sentiment Alexander had echoed when she joined the party in 1968.[29]

The increasingly tepid relationship between African Americans and Republicans was an issue both the state and national parties faced, hurting Alexander's electability. As the Black electorate expanded after the passage of the Voting Rights Act in 1965, Thruston Morton, a U.S. senator from Kentucky and chair of the Republican National Committee, cautioned his fellow Republicans to not alienate potential GOP voters: "The negro in the South is going to vote.... The sound foundation for Republicanism [is] not based on racism.... You don't have to go down there and wave the Confederate flag." Some in North Carolina had a similar attitude. Robert Gavin, who lost the governor's race to Democrat Dan Moore in 1964, commented that he did not want the North Carolina GOP to be a "racist or a lily-white party."[30] Many Republicans in the Deep South, however, felt that courting the Black vote would be a futile endeavor, and Republican policies and ideologies, particularly on civil rights issues such as school desegregation, continued to estrange potential Black voters from the GOP. While the Republican Party was in flux, it was losing its battle to attract Black voters.

Despite the party's recent electoral successes in North Carolina, being an African American woman in the Republican Party had a negative impact on Alexander's statewide campaign. In 1968, the changing political climate and her reputation likely had helped Alexander win her district court seat in Guilford County. But it was improbable that an African American woman on the Republican primary ballot in 1974 could obtain the votes of the same men and women who opposed social and racial equality in the South. Judge Alexander surely understood these dynamics, although at the time of her filing she had no primary opponent. She also understood that the vast majority of African Americans who would vote for her in the general election would be Democrats or independents. In 1974 there was a great deal of African American dissatisfaction with the Democratic Party, as there was in 1968, which helped Alexander's chances of winning the Black vote in the general election since many might cross the political line to vote for a Black Republican.[31] Black voters' dissatisfaction with the Democrats, however, would not help

Alexander overcome the race and gender biases of conservative Republicans in the primary. At the time, North Carolina had a closed primary system, in which a voter had to be a registered member of a party in order to vote in its primary.[32]

At the time of her filing, Judge Alexander probably felt confident in her ability to secure the Republican nomination without the Black vote since she was the only Republican candidate for chief justice. She had the qualifications to be a North Carolina Supreme Court justice, and even if she lost in the general election, the campaign would serve to promote her name for other positions. Alexander did not have an uncontested primary for long though. Her white opponent, James Newcomb, sixty-five, hailed from the small town of Williamston in eastern North Carolina and was undoubtedly unqualified to be a supreme court justice. The father of ten, he described himself as a "Christian family man." After dropping out of school in the seventh grade, he had finished high school at age twenty-two before taking a series of odd jobs, including lighthouse keeper, before settling down as a fire extinguisher salesman. His only political experience was a failed bid for a seat on the Wilson County Board of Commissioners in 1954.[33] Newcomb's lack of qualifications compared to Judge Alexander, however, did not seem to dampen his confidence in his ability to secure the Republican nomination.

James Newcomb saw himself as an "everyman" and felt he represented the majority of North Carolinians. The subtext of his statements reveals that Newcomb was one of the many working-class white voters who felt disillusioned with liberal policies and the advancement of civil rights in the 1960s. During the campaign he stated that there had "been a drift in our state for over 50 years to treat the people that make up the backbone of our society with a growing indifference.... The rich can protect themselves. The poor are generally taken care of. That leaves the vast majority which make up the backbone of our state. I speak with authority when I say that I represent all the people, including that vast majority."[34] The "vast majority" that Newcomb spoke of were the same people who made up Nixon's white silent majority. These voters did not participate in political protests, but were fed up with having to defend their values, such as hard work, traditional family structures, and patriotism.[35] In North Carolina, this group also supported individuals like Newcomb's political role model, Justice I. Beverly Lake. Lake was an ardent segregationist who as late as 1987 stated he was "not personally enthused about women lawyers."[36] Newcomb's embrace of conservative principles was part of the backlash to the rise of civil rights movements for African

Americans and women, movements that threatened white masculinity. He did not see his lack of legal qualifications as a hindrance, but rather viewed his candidacy as an attempt to return to the values important to the "backbone" of society—white men who saw themselves as increasingly marginalized.[37] Additionally, by 1974, the Watergate scandal and government dishonesty regarding U.S. involvement in Vietnam had led many conservatives to believe that government was not the solution to the nation's ills, but rather the problem.[38] A political and legal neophyte such as Newcomb, with no prior connections to government, found a voice among North Carolina's rural white conservative electorate.

Newcomb's lack of educational or legal qualifications was not a barrier to his candidacy. Surprisingly, having a college degree, let alone a law degree, was not necessary in order to become a judge in the state of North Carolina at that time. The only requirements were that the candidate had to be twenty-one years of age and a qualified, registered voter.[39] Newcomb publicly stated that he was allowing God to steer his campaign, leading the Democratic candidate, Justice Susie Sharp, to conclude that he was probably "a religious fanatic and . . . his purpose in filing was to prevent a woman from becoming chief justice." Newcomb certainly relied on divine intervention to be the driving force behind his campaign because he put little effort into the election. His campaign literature consisted only of a one-page "Pledge to the Voters of North Carolina," in which he touted his lack of legal experience as an asset.[40] His pledge was distributed among the people on Newcomb's regular sales route, and the only press he received pointed out the unlikelihood of his election. The idea of a high school graduate beating an experienced attorney and judge with an Ivy League education seemed as unlikely to the press as it did to most educated observers.

While James Newcomb relied on God to steer his campaign in the primary, Judge Alexander relied on hard work. The *Asheville Citizen-Times* detailed her tour of western North Carolina in April and touted her achievements in the legal field.[41] She created an arsenal of campaign literature with the same slogan she had used in her district court races—"The symbol of justice is a woman"—next to a picture of a Lady Justice statue. In one campaign flyer, Judge Alexander presented a side-by-side comparison of her achievements versus those of Newcomb. Alexander listed her degrees, while Newcomb's column said "No college or law education." Under legal experience, judicial experience, electoral experience, and awards, Alexander had long lists while the Newcomb column said simply "none."[42] Additionally, Judge Alexander, who was fifty-five years old, was eligible to serve the entire eight-year term. Newcomb, at age sixty-five, was not. In 1972, North Carolina voters had approved a constitutional amendment requiring that the North Carolina General Assembly recommend age limits for justices and judges, which was set at age seventy-two. If elected, Newcomb would be forced to retire before completing a full term.[43]

Even had Judge Alexander's campaign literature not highlighted Newcomb's startling lack of qualifications, the media certainly did. Two days before the Republican primary, the *Greensboro Daily News* endorsed her for the nomination: "District Judge Elreta Alexander, who is well known and respected by her friends and associates here in Greensboro, is the clear choice for the Republican nomination. Her primary opponent... is without any legal or judicial credentials of any kind."[44] The *Raleigh News and Observer* stated, "District Judge Elreta M. Alexander of Greensboro is obviously a better choice for Republican voters than her opponent, who has no legal training.... The record shows her to be intellectually competent, fair-minded and admirably committed to the rule of law."[45] Newcomb defended his lack of formal education by comparing himself with Abraham Lincoln. "The balance of my education came very similar to the way Abe Lincoln received his; therefore, I can understand and appreciate our people with less than a college degree or other advanced training," he said.[46] Newcomb's Lincoln comparison was less than convincing, and Alexander and Sharp geared up for a historic, all-woman contest for the highest judicial post in the state, discounting his candidacy. The North Carolina Republican electorate, however, thwarted those plans.

In the May 7, 1974, Republican primary, James Newcomb, the fire extinguisher salesman, beat Judge Elreta Alexander, an experienced legal professional, for the Republican nomination with 59.16 percent of the vote.[47] Politicos and media commentators alike immediately began to conjecture why Alexander had lost. Justice Susie Sharp, winner of the Democratic primary, speculated that it all came down to gender: "People hadn't heard of either one but they knew one was a man and the other a woman so they voted for the man."[48] Sharp's other theory was that because Alexander had presented herself as a credible candidate, people had been forced to vote for Newcomb to ensure a Sharp victory. She stated, "Everybody who voted for Mr. Newcomb was really voting for me."[49] It is true that many voters throughout North Carolina did not know who Judge Alexander was, but even fewer knew of Newcomb. Alexander, throughout her career, had received statewide press, especially when she became the first African American woman in the nation to become an elected district court judge. Anna Hayes in a biography of Justice Susie Sharp states that the North Carolina Republican Party did not devote any resources to Alexander's campaign because the party leaders believed she would beat the unqualified Newcomb.[50] But since the party devoted no resources to the race, it could not be sure that voters, especially in western North Carolina, knew that Alexander was the more qualified candidate.

Alexander in her campaign materials had ensured that voters knew her gender by including pictures of herself. Her race, however, was presented more vaguely. One piece of campaign literature showed her behind the bench with her robe on. Another included a head shot of Alexander looking sternly into the camera, her blonde wig and intricate blouse hard to miss. The blonde wig lightened Alexander's overall complexion, making her race potentially ambiguous. Traditionally, Black hair is second only to skin tone as a racial signifier in a country that categorizes human worth on a Black-white binary. While Alexander was already known in Guilford County for her wigs, in this election she had to appeal to a larger electorate—and to Republicans who had fled the Democratic Party precisely because of racial issues. The media coverage of the campaign consistently identified her as a "Negro" woman, leaving even uninformed voters certain of her race. There has, however, historically been "degrees" of Blackness, with lighter skin being less objectionable to white people.[51] The blonde wig might have been a strategic move to soften the initial reaction of some white voters to a Black candidate, although that seems unlikely given Alexander's vow as a Columbia Law student that she would never try to "pass." If there was any strategy behind the blonde wig, however, it was lost on the North Carolina Republican electorate.

Judge Alexander received an outpouring of support after her primary loss. Representative Richardson Preyer, a Democrat from Greensboro, wrote, "I was appalled at the outcome in your race. This is the worst result in an election that I have ever heard of." John E. Hall, an attorney from North Wilkesboro in the northwestern corner of North Carolina, wrote, "I am totally ashamed of the Republicans of the State of North Carolina. The Republican Party has turned its back on the only decent thing that has happened to it in some time." A. W. Houtz, an aluminum manufacturer who conducted business with Newcomb in Elizabeth City in northeastern North Carolina, wrote, "In my fifteen years of active service to the Republican Party of North Carolina (most of them as County Chairman) I have seldom been ashamed of my party affiliation. The results of your failure to become our candidate in last week's primary was one of them."[52] The letters, which came from all areas of North Carolina, suggest that Alexander was more well known across the state than some initially thought.

Other supporters of Judge Alexander specifically acknowledged that her loss was a racial issue. A white housewife in High Point, North Carolina, wrote that she and her husband had voted for Alexander in the primary: "We think you are doing a terrific job and were shocked that Republicans voted so poorly.... I praise God for you and for people like you—no matter what color of skin one is born with—what a ridiculous way to judge a person."[53] The most telling letter came from E. S. Schlosser Jr., an attorney in Greensboro, who wrote, "I am sorry, truly sorry. I don't understand, but I am afraid I do understand. I am sorry."[54] Facing the reality that such an accomplished person, regardless of race or gender, could lose to an unqualified salesman was difficult for many, although they understood that racism and sexism remained powerful factors in politics.

Even if Alexander had won the Republican primary, issues of race probably would have been a factor in the general election versus Justice Sharp. Sharp, a white woman who was comfortable with the power structure in Raleigh, would likely have had the support of white conservatives who did not want a Black woman in charge of the highest court in North Carolina. Rufus Edmisten, the North Carolina attorney general at the time, later said that in 1974, a Black woman on the North Carolina Supreme Court was a "pipe dream": she would not have had the support of the Raleigh political establishment.[55] Alexander might have found more support in the North Carolina Democratic Party, but despite her credentials she likely would not have had enough support to beat a more establishment candidate such as Susie Sharp.

Regardless of the reasons behind Judge Alexander's primary loss, the Republican Party had to deal with the backlash. The media swiftly took aim at the party establishment and Republican voters. In an article that stated Alexander's loss could be attributed to "racism, sexism, or gross ignorance. Take your pick," Republican state senator Bob Somers offered a rationale for GOP voting patterns: "In any race where neither candidate is particularly well known, the voters will almost always choose the one whose name is phonetically most appealing, and James or Jim is obviously more appealing than Elreta."[56] Attributing the loss of an election to phonetics indirectly ascribes the defeat to sexism and/or racism. Elreta was obviously a feminine name, and it was not a name traditionally associated with white women. James or Jim had no racial connotations, but they were masculine names that white voters could be comfortable with. According to Somers and others, in the closed Republican primary, a masculine name won.

The fact that Alexander's qualifications could not secure her the Republican nomination troubled many in the judicial system. As a result of the GOP primary, many people in North Carolina, including Justice Sharp, began to openly question how judges should be elected. The fact that the Republican nominee to be the supreme court chief justice was an uneducated fire extinguisher salesman led to calls that requirements be established in order for one to run for judge. The first and most obvious requirement was that the candidate have a law degree. An editorial in the *Winston-Salem Journal* called for the selection of judges to be removed from the electoral process.[57] Calls for Republican officeholders to publicly repudiate Newcomb increased. Many believed that James Newcomb should not have beaten Judge Elreta Alexander, yet he did. The fear that he could also beat Justice Susie Sharp began to swell, especially if sexism was a major factor behind Alexander's loss.

While the North Carolina Republican Party had not supported either candidate in the primary, it was lambasted for selecting such an unqualified nominee. It became increasingly obvious that if the party supported Newcomb, the GOP would face increased backlash. One by one, the leaders of the North Carolina Republican Party publicly withdrew their support of Newcomb. Thomas Bennett, the state GOP chair, released a statement: "A Supreme Court justice has to write formal opinions that require substantial scholarship as far as legal theory goes. With this in mind, Mr. Newcomb does not have this kind of background. Therefore, in my judgement, personally as an attorney and as a political leader, I cannot in good faith recommend (Mr. Newcomb) for election as chief justice."[58] This statement made it clear to his fellow Republicans that they too should not vote for the Republican candidate.

Other Republican officials offered lukewarm support for the party's nominee. Senator Jesse Helms stated that he would not officially endorse Newcomb for the chief justice position, but he would not attack him either: "I'm sure that the people, when they go to the polls, will evaluate the candidates on the basis of their qualifications and decisions."[59] The primary results obviously had not dampened Helms's faith in North Carolina voters. Republican governor Jim Holshouser made a similar statement: he was endorsing neither Newcomb nor Sharp, and he would not say which candidate he would cast his vote for.[60] While there were no public endorsements of Newcomb from the North Carolina GOP, it did not endorse Sharp either. While this is not surprising considering that political parties rarely endorse the nominees of an opposing party, Newcomb's lack of support highlights the difficult position the primary results created for the North Carolina GOP.

The loss marked the first major professional failure for Judge Elreta Alexander, and she had little to say about the results of the primary election. She did not release a statement at the time nor did she discuss the defeat or even her motivation for running in the first place in interviews she gave later in her life. When asked by the *Raleigh News and Observer* if the Republican Party should have endorsed her in the primary, she stated, "If a person is clearly not qualified, if a person clearly cannot fill the job and if the party position is that they can't take sides, then I don't know what to say." Alexander declined to support Newcomb, and she also refused to state that race or gender were factors in her loss.[61] Perhaps Alexander did not want to ignite a controversy, or perhaps she was hurt and wanted to put the election in her past. For a woman who had achieved such professional success despite society's problems with her race and gender, it could have been hard to admit she had failed to clear these hurdles for the first time. Her law partner in the 1980s and 1990s stated that Alexander never discussed the race, and he believed it had been a difficult time for her.[62] Whatever her reasons for not discussing the 1974 race for supreme court chief justice, Alexander resumed her judicial duties in Greensboro and moved on with her life.

The Democratic candidate, however, quickly turned her focus toward the general election. Susie Sharp, born July 7, 1907, was eleven years older than Judge Alexander. Unlike Alexander, Sharp grew up relatively poor in Rockingham County, North Carolina. Her father, James, had been a teacher and a lawyer in Reidsville, while her mother, Annie, raised Susie and her siblings. In 1929, she was the only woman in her class to receive a law degree from the University of North Carolina at Chapel Hill (UNC). After working for the law school at UNC and with her father in private practice, she was appointed by Governor Kerr Scott to the superior court bench, and in 1962 Governor Terry Sanford appointed her as an associate justice on the North Carolina Supreme Court. She was the first woman to serve in both roles and was elected to the supreme court post in 1966.[63] With a legal career spanning more than forty years, Sharp was a recognizable figure to the voters of North Carolina.

Despite Sharp's name recognition and the bad press Newcomb received, the salesman still felt he could translate his primary win into a general election victory. Newcomb claimed that if elected to the high court, he would "depend on his own common sense, reference books, a knowledge of human nature, help from the other judges and God in making his decisions."[64] Newcomb's lack of qualifications, however, continued to be well publicized throughout the state. With no support from the Republican Party and no major endorsements, it became virtually impossible for Newcomb to beat Justice Sharp.

In addition to Newcomb's handicaps, Sharp had timing on her side. The general election was held three months after President Gerald Ford was sworn into office following the Watergate scandal, and many voters were briefly disillusioned with Ford's pardon of Nixon for the former president's possible crimes while in office. Nationally, Democrats made large gains in the U.S. House of Representatives and nominal gains in the U.S. Senate. In North Carolina, Democrat Robert Morgan defeated Republican William Stevens for a seat in the U.S. Senate, and Rufus Edmisten handily beat Republican William Carson for the North Carolina attorney general seat.[65]

Justice Sharp did not take any chances with her campaign though. North Carolina, as a whole, was conservative when it came to cultural issues. The state had never elected a woman to a major office.[66] She was afraid of straight-ticket voting on the part of Republicans and ran a hard campaign in an attempt to dispel voter ignorance and gender bias, which she saw as her real opponent.[67] Sharp made sure her qualifications were advertised in newspapers and on television and radio across the state, and she used her extensive legal connections to ensure she had a campaign presence in all one hundred North Carolina counties.[68] On November 5, 1974, Susie Sharp won 74 percent of the vote statewide, making her the first woman supreme court chief justice in North Carolina history, and the first popularly elected woman state supreme court chief justice in the country. As Sharp biographer Anna Hayes states, she could not stop every Republican from voting a straight ticket, nor could she avoid the fact that some voters would prefer the name "Jim" over the name "Susie," but she won.[69] The day after the election Judge Alexander sent Sharp a telegram: "Congratulations to you and the voters of our state for their good judgement. Best Wishes, Elreta Melton Alexander."[70] Justice Sharp obviously had the vote of the woman who should have been her opponent.

Sharp spent the next six years pushing for the establishment of judicial standards in North Carolina. The 1974 election for supreme court chief justice needed to lead to changes in the way judges were selected in the state. Many realized that if a salesman with a high school degree could earn a quarter of a million votes in a midterm election, he could have come much closer to winning had there been a presidential election and more straight-ticket voters.[71] In 1975, legislation was introduced for a constitutional amendment requiring judges to be licensed attorneys. The measure failed that year and two other times, in 1977 and in 1979, despite Chief Justice Sharp's strong endorsement.[72] Finally, in 1980 the voters of North Carolina approved a constitutional amendment establishing that all justices and judges of state courts should be licensed attorneys before they could be elected or appointed to the bench.[73] The law now ensured that a judge with Elreta Alexander's credentials would never lose to someone so blatantly unqualified as James Newcomb.

Judge Alexander had tried to move on from the defeat, but the use of a racial slur to describe her in 1975 was like salt on an open wound. During an oral argument before the U.S. Supreme Court on April 21, 1975, North Carolina's assistant attorney general, Jean A. Benoy, referred to Alexander as a "Negress Judge."[74] Benoy was arguing in defense of a North Carolina law making the death penalty mandatory for particular crimes. His racialized language led to a tense exchange with Justice Thurgood Marshall, the first African American to serve on the Supreme Court. Benoy stated that "there's not one aspect of racial overtones in the system of justice in the State of North Carolina." When Justice Marshall asked Benoy how many African Americans were in North Carolina's judicial system, Benoy responded, "I believe there—I don't know if the last Negress, there was a Negro woman who was a judge." Thurgood Marshall was flabbergasted: "A Neg-what?" Benoy repeated the term: "A Negress . . . a Negro woman who was a judge in Guilford County." "You're still using 'Negress' down there?" asked Marshall. "Well, Your Honor, I'm a Caucasian, and I see nothing wrong with using the word 'Negro.' That's the name of a race of people."[75]

The Benoy-Marshall exchange made national news, and Judge Alexander wasted no time issuing a response. In traffic court, Alexander stated that she was "disappointed and upset very much that a distinguished public official of this state would make such a statement, one that can be interpreted only by intelligent persons as a derogatory one."[76] Other attorneys echoed Alexander's disgust. Reginald L. Frazier, a prominent Black attorney in New Bern, North Carolina, wrote to Judge Alexander, "Black lawyers in North Carolina have a long history of being politically impotent and inert. You and a few others who dared to struggle for power and recognition, should be publicly applauded, not castigated for being a 'Nigger in Law.' The pathetic reality, is that, Benoy might have felt it professional[ly] permissible to refer to you as a negress."[77] Letters also came from Raleigh and Washington, D.C., praising

Alexander for her handling of the situation. Even North Carolina attorney general Edmisten said that because of Benoy, he had "never been so embarrassed in my life."[78] Jean Benoy never apologized to Alexander.

While the powers-that-be in Raleigh too often failed to recognize Judge Alexander and her accomplishments, others throughout the country took note of her pioneering status. A made-for-television movie titled *Soul on the Bench* was in development with Hollywood producer Marian Rees.[79] While they were in negotiations with ABC, however, issues over one of the writers permanently halted the project. The interest in Alexander's story highlights the recognition that her home state was slow to give her. The demise of the project was probably yet another blow to Judge Alexander.

Issues with her ex-husband, Tony, continued to dominate her personal life. Tony never completely recovered from the stabbing incident in Hawaii. While he was well enough to resume his duties as a doctor at L. Richardson Hospital, he was plagued by chronic ill health. Elreta attributed a large part of Tony's health problems to the fact that he never gave up his womanizing and heavy drinking. Yet after the divorce, she remained the person he went to for friendship and emotional support.[80]

In late July 1975, after making his morning rounds, he complained that he felt faint. He started to drive home but fell unconscious before even leaving the hospital parking lot. His car drifted into a ditch, and he was "completely deranged" by the time the police arrived. When Elreta arrived at the hospital from a trial in High Point, she found Tony in a hospital bed smoking a cigarette. Doctors thought he might have had a heart attack, and he had received a significant blow to the head from the car accident. He was in and out of delirious states. After further examination, they found two blood clots on Tony's brain. He recovered, but in August 1976 another blood clot was discovered in his leg.[81]

Elreta still felt that Tony needed to address his alcoholism as the basis of his ongoing health issues. In consultation with Greensboro psychiatrist Dr. Raouf Badawi, Elreta got Tony into the Menninger Clinic in Topeka, Kansas, to receive treatment for his physical and psychological needs. At Menninger, however, doctors discovered that the blood clots on Tony's brain had returned, and they needed to perform surgery quickly. By the time Elreta and Girardeau arrived, doctors had discovered two additional blood clots in Tony's lungs and needed to clear those before they could operate on his brain. The doctors suggested that Tony be airlifted back to Greensboro, and Elreta informed him as to what was going on. Tony told her, "You can't do me any good. . . . Don't you think I know what's wrong with me? Go ahead and take care of Girardeau. We've been through so much." Elreta was not going to give up on her first love though.[82]

When the Alexanders arrived back in Greensboro, Tony's condition suddenly improved. He was more lucid and began eating on his own again, but doctors at L. Richardson Hospital were hesitant to operate. Elreta called the Menninger Clinic to inform the doctors there of the situation. They informed her that lucidity often comes before death and that Tony needed to be operated on immediately. She had Tony transferred to Cone Hospital, which was now integrated, where he fell into a coma after his surgery. For six weeks Tony was in and out of consciousness, and Elreta was informed that he would never fully recover. She had him transferred to a long-term care facility, where he died less than a day later, on November 17, 1976, at the age of sixty-one.[83]

Elreta oversaw all the preparations for Tony's funeral, which in true Alexander fashion was an over-the-top affair. For his burial, Elreta dressed Tony in his surgical garb, stethoscope in hand. She knew that "all he really cared about in life was his medicine. And despite all that was wrong with him, he never made a mistake in his medicine." For twenty-four hours before the private funeral, Elreta had Tony lie in state, and she later said that more than ten thousand people came to see him.[84] Even Tony's burial, however, was not free of drama. Elreta Alexander alleged that the Greensboro funeral home in charge of the arrangements had broken Tony's legs to fit him inside a regular coffin but had charged her for an oversized coffin. Tony had stood at about six foot four. Elreta was so convinced that the funeral home had defrauded her that she had her former associate, Jerry Pell, oversee the exhumation of the body—only to find out that, indeed, the funeral home had used an oversized coffin.[85] Perhaps the focus on her political race over the previous two years had made Judge Alexander more openly assertive if there was a chance that racism would negatively impact her. The dispute with the funeral home was a sign of her increasing turmoil.

Even in the midst of Tony's illness and subsequent death, Judge Alexander had announced her plan to seek reelection. Running as a Republican and with no Democratic opposition, she easily retained her judgeship with minimal hassle.[86] But also during this trying time Alexander faced perhaps her most significant career controversy. On August 23, 1976, William Raulston, twenty-one, was arrested and charged with felony possession of marijuana. Raulston was a young white man from Jamestown, North Carolina, just southeast of Greensboro. After his arrest, a preliminary hearing was scheduled for October 1976 with Judge Alexander presiding, but the case was continued. In December of that year, the case landed on one of Alexander's Judgment Days. Alexander handed down sentences on Judgment Days for cases in which a plea had been accepted or a preliminary hearing had been held. Neither had occurred in the Raulston case. Judge Alexander was on vacation on the scheduled Judgment Day, so the case was rescheduled again. Additionally, because it was a felony, a district court judge could not legally pass a sentence in the case. In March 1977, the grand jury returned a bill of indictment against Raulston while the case was still pending on Judge Alexander's docket. In April, copies of the indictment were placed on the district court calendar, as opposed to the superior court docket as was customary when a true bill of indictment was returned.[87]

The complicated case involved many actors, but Judge Alexander became the focus of a potential judicial misconduct accusation, although the situation began as a simple error. On April 25, 1977, assistant district attorney Joseph Williams signed a bill of information, an indictment waiver, in which Raulston acknowledged the felony charges against him. Accompanying the waiver was a transcript of a plea bargain agreement. However, it should not have been valid because the felony indictment had not been remanded to the district court by the superior court. Nevertheless, the plea was signed by Donna Amos, the deputy clerk of court in High Point. In May 1977, after the Raulston case had appeared on Judge Alexander's calendar three previous times, she sentenced Raulston to fifty hours of volunteer work. The following week Elreta Alexander requested the Raulston files for review, met with district attorney Ray Alexander, and ordered that the documents be incorporated with the superior court files on the case, having determined that she had passed judgment on a felony that rightfully belonged in superior court. The case then went to superior court judge Thomas Seay, and Raulston's attorney, Arch Schoch, requested that Elreta Alexander's verdict stand because a retrial would constitute double jeopardy.[88] For the next several months, confusion over the validity of the bill of indictment and Judge Alexander's role in the matter made local headlines.

Perhaps Alexander's biggest mistake was failing to check on whether the bill of indictment had been dismissed. In September 1977, Judge Seay subpoenaed Judge Alexander and Joseph Williams, at that time also a district court judge, to testify about their handling of the Raulston case. Alexander and Williams filed motions to dismiss the subpoenas. In her motion, Alexander carefully detailed her handling of the case, acknowledging that after she became aware of the situation she agreed the case should be in superior court. She asked, "When did it become improper for a judge to correct an error?" Alexander also stated that "this unprecedented procedure [the subpoena] was probably inspired by the clerk of this court, J. P. Shore, and his administrative assistant, Mrs. Betty Withers."[89]

Joseph "J. P." Shore, clerk of the Superior Court of Guilford County, and Elreta Alexander had long had a contentious relationship. In an interview, Alexander recalled that early in her career superior court judges were hard on her, and judges and attorneys would snicker when she walked in the courtroom. According to Alexander, Shore did not like her but tolerated a male Black attorney "because he Uncle Tommed."[90] Shore, born in 1911, grew up in a time when Jim Crow notions of racial etiquette required Black deference to whites. He was a member of the Democratic Party when the party still promoted racial segregation. Shore was first sworn in as a deputy clerk in the superior court in 1932, more than a decade before Alexander made history as the first African American woman to practice law in North Carolina.[91] Alexander also had run-ins with Shore's assistant, Betty Withers. During the Yoes trial, when Alexander filed the appeal, Withers questioned if Alexander had served it to the district attorney. Alexander was astounded that "Betty has an 8th grade education, but she's giving me lessons in the law."[92] Animosity between Shore and Alexander ran deep.

After Alexander and Williams filed their motions to quash the subpoenas, Judge Seay denied them. In October 1977, Judge Alexander was placed under investigation by the North Carolina Judicial Standards Commission after someone lodged a confidential complaint against her. Not taking any chances with her career, Alexander drove to Massachusetts to the home of noted trial lawyer F. Lee Bailey. Bailey's most recent high-profile client was newspaper heir Patricia Hearst. Bailey agreed to represent Alexander, sensing that Shore wanted to get rid of her. He said that he found Alexander to be courageous, articulate, and someone who "didn't buckle under" to threats. Alexander's retention of Bailey as counsel made news in Greensboro and sent a message "not to fool" with the judge, as "it'll be expensive."[93]

At the end of November, the North Carolina Judicial Standards Commission cleared Judge Alexander of any wrongdoing. The whole experience, however, left her bitter. She refused to talk to the local newspaper, the *Greensboro Record*, saying only, "You people have done nothing but lied, lied, lied. . . . You haven't wanted to do anything but look at records and make up lies. So don't call me anymore."[94] She spoke more at length with the *High Point Enterprise*, which reported that Alexander was concerned with the way her involvement in the case was handled. She claimed her phone had been tapped and that mail was stolen from her mailbox. She also had heard from a reliable source that North Carolina Bureau of Investigation agents wanted to "get Judge Alexander at any cost" and that "she wouldn't be around much longer." Her appeal to North Carolina attorney general Rufus Edmisten for an investigation went nowhere, and the attorney general's office stated her claims were unfounded.[95]

The previous five years had been difficult for Alexander. She had not received the nomination for Middle District Court judge in 1972, had lost the North Carolina Supreme Court Republican primary in 1974, had been subjected to the "Negress" comment in 1975, experienced Tony's death in 1976, and had to deal with the Raulston affair. Later, Alexander rarely discussed the truly painful events in her life. While she was open about her tumultuous relationship with Tony, she never discussed the death of her parents, the 1974 loss, or the Raulston case in any depth. Although she claimed in interviews that she never had set out to change the legal system in North Carolina, she took tremendous pride in her accomplishments and obviously felt deeply about the career disappointments and controversies.

There are strong links between racism and heightened trauma. Many of Judge Alexander's professional setbacks during the 1970s were laden with racial overtones. Psychology professor Robert T. Carter argues that experiencing racism is an assault on one's sense of self. As a form of defense, it is common to become vigilant, even paranoid, to prepare oneself for future racist incidents.[96] From Alexander's first day at Columbia Law School, race was central to how society viewed her, even if it was not central to how she viewed herself. The disappointments of the 1970s possibly altered Alexander's self-perception, as she deeply felt the racial injustices that contributed to her setbacks during these years.

Controversy resurfaced in May 1978, when her old feud with the Guilford County clerk of the superior court, Joseph Shore, made headlines again. In open court, Alexander criticized several lawyers, calling them "weak-kneed" for signing Shore's campaign advertisement, and said she no longer considered those attorneys to be friends. The incident was another dark moment in what had been an admired career. The *Greensboro Record* opined that "Judge Alexander is entitled to her political views, even political grudges. As one of the nation's first black female lawyers, to say nothing of her pioneering as a black female judge, she has struggled much, and her feud with Mr. Shore has been one of long standing, carrying bitter racial overtones. But she should never let partisan political prejudices... intrude into her conduct on the bench."[97]

Despite Judge Alexander's atypical behavior, she was recommended to the administration of President Jimmy Carter for a slot on the Fourth Circuit Court of Appeals after she submitted an application to the selection committee. Her resume listed her numerous awards, community boards she served on, and the many firsts in her distinguished career. There is no evidence, however, that Alexander was seriously considered for the position.[98] Alexander stated that she was never contacted by the selection committee and that out of the fourteen candidates, she was the only one not to receive an interview.[99] There were no women and only one other African American considered. The head of the North Carolina Association of Black Lawyers, Michael Lee, requested a more balanced list of nominees, which was supported by the Judicial Selection Project. Again not wanting to address her race and gender, Alexander stated that she "doesn't have the slightest idea why she wasn't interviewed" and added she was not going to worry about it.[100]

Even if she no longer made headlines for her career successes, her personality and legendary status in the Greensboro community was still recognized. In 1979, local newspapers still recounted her story from minister's daughter to groundbreaking legal scholar. She kept her trademarks that made her a well-recognized and beloved figure in the community. Her attire and personality remained a source of public interest. As she walked down the hallways of the Guilford County Courthouse, she spoke with county employees she had known for years. She would often stop to chat: "Hello darlin', when did you get new glasses?" Or "Your hair sure looks nice today, sweetheart. How'd you learn to fix it that way?" She personified the role of southern Black lady, and Greensboro did not forget the obstacles she had overcome to achieve her position. "I belong to the people," she would say. "The people love me." Continued interest in Alexander also gave her a chance to reflect on her life and career, including her adoration of her father, J. C. Melton; the death of her best friend, Katharine Tynes, when she was sixteen; and her marriage to Dr. Tony Alexander, which she described as a "traumatic 30 years." She also now began to gush over her new love, whom she described as a man of "dignity and a wonderful sense of humor."[101]

On August 22, 1979, Elreta Melton Alexander became Elreta Alexander-Ralston, marrying John D. Ralston, a white, retired Internal Revenue Service officer. Alexander was sixty, while the groom was seventy. The wedding was at Guilford Park Presbyterian Church, where Ralston was an elder. At the time, interracial marriage in North Carolina, while legal, was not typical. Judge Alexander addressed the issue directly: "I have to love everybody because I'm visibly kin to them all.... My name is Melton and I am the melting pot that America represents. I was the American Indian, and I represent the European who came and took my lands and ran me into the hills, I was the African who tilled the soil, and probably I am a little Asiatic, if my father told the truth in the cool of the evening." The race issue was "never a big deal to us," she stated. She said Ralston made her happier than she ever thought she could be, and their marriage was simply "two old people who get along and chose to spend their last years together."[102] While Alexander claimed that race was not important, her marriage to a white man made news and made a statement.

After her marriage, she continued to work. On October 15, 1979, Judge Alexander-Ralston announced she would seek reelection to her seat on the state district court, and she would "rely on her record over the past 11 years as a judge."[103] Shortly after her campaign announcement, Greensboro found itself in the national spotlight again. On the morning of November 3, 1979, the Communist Workers Party (CWP) held a Death to the Klan march, for which it had obtained the proper permits. Although four Greensboro police officers were assigned to protect the marchers, they were suspiciously several blocks away when members of the Ku Klux Klan and the American Nazi Party arrived. The CWP marchers banged on the cars of Klan members, and a confrontation ensued, resulting in the shooting deaths of five CWP members.[104] Judge Alexander-Ralston was a part of the subsequent legal proceedings.

The event that became known as the Greensboro Massacre elicited strong feelings regarding race and class in the community. Compared to many others in the court system, Alexander-Ralston displayed fairness and perhaps a bit of sympathy to the CWP marchers who appeared before her. On July 31, 1980, the widows of two of the victims, Signe Waller and Dale Sampson, were arrested for disrupting a Greensboro City Council meeting, accusing the city of not doing enough to prevent the deaths of their husbands and expressing frustration over city leaders' praise of the Greensboro Police Department. On August 6, CWP leader Nelson Johnson was arrested and charged with contempt of court for disturbing a hearing regarding his bail on riot charges stemming from the November 3, 1979, shooting. Johnson was sentenced to twenty days in jail for contempt, but he was released into his attorney's custody pending appeal and a promise to not disrupt any more public meetings. District attorney Michael Schlosser argued that Johnson's bail should be raised from $15,000 to $100,000, and it was. After his bond was raised, Johnson was arrested again for assaulting an officer with his elbow when he was taken from the courtroom. Judge Alexander-Ralston obviously disagreed with the exorbitant bail, and the next morning, August 7, she reduced Johnson's bond to $200, citing the fact that he had never hurt anyone or disrupted her courtroom. Alexander-Ralston had known Johnson since his days as a student at the North Carolina Agricultural and Technical University in the late 1960s and said she was confident Johnson would appear in court. On September 26, Alexander-Ralston found Johnson not guilty of assaulting a police officer. Then, on October 6, 1980, she found Waller and Sampson guilty of disrupting the city council meeting on July 31 but postponed their sentencing for sixty days and ordered the women not to disrupt any more public meetings during that time. In December another judge fined the women twenty-five dollars each plus court costs.[105] These sentences were more than any member of the Ku Klux Klan received; all of the Klan members charged with murder were acquitted. The hearings around the Greensboro Massacre were some of the last she would preside over as a district court judge.

On January 16, 1981, Judge Elreta Alexander-Ralston announced that she planned to retire from the bench. Not yet sixty-two, she sent her notice to North Carolina governor Jim Hunt that her last day as a judge would be April 1, 1981, ten years before state law would require her retirement. The news came as a shock to many colleagues and court officials. As she was known to do during Judgment Day sentencing, Alexander-Ralston quoted the Bible in her statement: "To everything there is a season, and a time to every purpose under the heaven: a time to be born and a time to die; a time to plant, and a time to pluck up that which is planted."[106] Alexander-Ralston said that she wanted to travel, write a book, spend time with her husband, and return to private practice. Governor Hunt accepted her resignation and noted, "Judge Alexander-Ralston has served with great distinction on the District Court bench. She has been an unfailing advocate of fairness, firmness and compassion. On behalf of the people, I congratulate her on a great career and wish her well in retirement." Alexander-Ralston stated that she would miss the bench, but true to form she also noted that "she wouldn't look back."[107]

CONCLUSION

Remembering "Judge A"

THE REVEREND J. C. MELTON was always proud of his youngest child, going so far as to offer her services to his parishioners: "Daddy would ask me a legal point concerning some of these Negros whose white lawyers weren't defending them very well. Out of respect for my father, once or twice I answered his question." Many of the white attorneys, according to Alexander, did not take up civil rights causes. But Alexander's legal expertise did not come for free. She eventually told her father: "You are subconsciously telling that fellow and every other Negro they can pay a white lawyer and get my services free. You're still telling them that white is right, better than Negro. If I don't protect my own integrity, nobody's going to.... The point is: I won't play second fiddle, even if I lose money."[1] For many in the Greensboro community, Elreta Alexander-Ralston is remembered for this integrity and never playing second. In addition to her integrity, personality, and series of firsts, she is also remembered for opening doors for other African American women in the legal field.

Her departure from the bench did not signal her departure from the legal profession. In 1981, Judge Alexander-Ralston, Donald Speckhard, Donald's brother Stanley, and Alexander-Ralston's former law partners Jim and Jerry Pell formed their own law firm.[2] Back in private practice, Alexander-Ralston prioritized domestic cases, rarely turning anyone down. According to Donald Speckhard, "She didn't get paid a lot of times ... [and] she sort of was a crusader. [She believed] the millionaire and pauper should have the same type of representation and she provided that."[3]

Although she was no longer a judge, the local newspapers continued to opine on Alexander-Ralston's remarkable career and her comings and goings. She was praised for her performative style and her innovation, including the Judgment Day program, even though it had been discontinued. When asked what she was up to with her free time, Alexander-Ralston said, "I ain't up to *nothin'.*" She enjoyed watching *Jeopardy!* "because it reminds her how dumb she is" and frequently turned down interview requests because there were "plenty of other idiots to write about." She mulled writing an autobiography, and Margaret Avery, the Academy Award–winning actress from *The Color Purple*, expressed interest in making a movie based on Alexander-Ralston's life. Ultimately, neither the autobiography nor the movie materialized. Stories about Alexander also touched on some of the difficulties of the 1970s, including missing out on the 1972 appointment during the Nixon years and the 1974 election loss.[4]

Through her hard work and determination, Elreta Alexander-Ralston had achieved a level of success that could hardly have been dreamed of at the time of her birth in 1919. Although she was blessed with the privileges of a middle-class upbringing and extraordinary intelligence, overcoming the hurdles of race and gender in the mid-twentieth-century South was no small feat. The professional and societal structures she encountered inside and outside the courtroom, however, would not allow her to ascend to the professional level she sought. In the 1970s and then in private practice in the 1980s, Alexander-Ralston called out injustices when she saw them, whether in the chambers of the U.S. Supreme Court or in domestic cases. Nothing could stop the admiration that many in the Greensboro community had for "Judge A."

Even those who did not initially love Alexander-Ralston as a jurist grew to love her as a person. Her law partner Donald Speckhard was one of those people. "She wasn't my favorite judge," he said later in an interview. As a young attorney appearing before Judge Alexander in 1970, Speckhard had represented a man in a divorce case who, it was revealed, had given champagne to some of his high school students. Stemming from her personal experience, there were two things Judge Alexander did not like: husbands and minors drinking alcohol. "I felt she was picking on me and maybe she was," Speckhard said, "but if you represent the husband, for heaven's sake, don't get Judge A!"[5] As the years went on, however, Donald Speckhard and Elreta Alexander-Ralston became friends and colleagues.

Aside from her career, her son, Girardeau, was the central focus in Alexander's life. Her attention increased after his schizophrenia became apparent in the mid-1960s. Judge Alexander spent much of her free time researching schools and treatment plans for Girardeau and pampered him endlessly. The coddling Girardeau received from his mother, however, went beyond what was healthy, as her son grew increasingly violent and physically abusive. "You could tell where he had hit her. But she would never, in a million years, do anything about [it].... She just grinned and bore it," said Speckhard.[6] Girardeau seemed to be reenacting Dr. Tony Alexander's abuse. And as with Tony, Elreta Alexander allowed the abuse to continue. With a mentally ill son, as opposed to an alcoholic husband, the situation was not one where she could leave the house or the country.

By the 1980s Girardeau's violent outbursts were well known outside the Alexander-Ralston household. One minute, he would smile at strangers, and the next he would explode. Despite her best efforts to keep him happy, she could not control his increasingly violent behavior. Alexander-Ralston tried to appease her son, buying him a small house where a series of caretakers watched him. Over time one of those caretakers, Eula Mae Rankin, became increasingly concerned and weary of Girardeau.[7] In October 1990, Girardeau stabbed Rankin to death while his mother was out of town. There was no trial at the time because Girardeau was declared mentally unfit and was placed in a state mental hospital. In 1994, superior court judge Catherine Eagles deemed Girardeau mentally competent to stand trial. He pled guilty to second degree murder and was sentenced to fifteen years in prison. Worried he would not receive the proper treatment in prison, Judge Alexander-Ralston sat alone in the snack room of the Guilford County Courthouse. As her eyes filled with tears, she said, "I wasn't pleased ... but it'll work itself out, I guess." Girardeau did not end up in prison, however, but in a group home in Burlington, North Carolina, where he resided until he died on August 28, 2003.[8] His mother had been unable to stop her son's mental illness from taking over his life.

John Ralston, Elreta's second husband, had died in October 1983. In 1993 Alexander-Ralston had suffered a heart attack while defending a client in court. The heart attack left her dependent on a cane to walk. She called old age an "inconvenience" and continued to work another two years.[9] The stress of Girardeau's ordeal also took its toll on Alexander-Ralston. "Her health was not very good for the last five years," said Donald Speckhard. "I think she was worn out.... We would go see her and you could tell that she was declining as time went on. She still maintained her dignity and demeanor and everything else, but the lifetime episodes with Girardeau I'm sure couldn't have helped."[10]

Upon her retirement in 1995 from private practice at age seventy-six, Alexander-Ralston's portrait was hung in room 2A of the Guilford County Courthouse. "I am overwhelmed and nervous by all the accolades," she said. "But I think I deserve most of them!" Colleagues recalled her creation of the Judgment Day program, along with her being a partner in the South's first integrated law firm and the first African American woman to argue a case before the North Carolina Supreme Court.[11] But it was her outgoing personality, courtroom performances, and commitment to serving the people that her colleagues most remembered.

Judge Elreta Melton Alexander-Ralston died on March 14, 1998, just short of her seventy-ninth birthday. She had requested that there be no funeral, and her ashes were buried in a small grove behind a nursing home in Greensboro.[12] As he later reflected on his personal and professional relationship with Alexander-Ralston, Donald Speckhard stated, "She pioneered doing what she wanted to do and she wasn't doing it because she wanted to be the first Black person to do this or do that or be remembered in that vein only. She believed in what she did and she certainly caused a lot of changes in Guilford County just by being who she was."[13] Fellow attorneys remembered her as a brilliant legal scholar and as a tough but fair judge. Her long obituary in the *Greensboro News and Record* declared, "Her influence will be felt for years," and it predicted that even without her accomplishments she would have been remembered for her forceful and outgoing personality.[14]

The draining final years of her life did not define the legacy of Elreta Alexander-Ralston. With Girardeau's legal troubles weighing heavily on her, her story did not have a happy ending that reflected her accomplished and extraordinary life. Yet in Greensboro, North Carolina, the people who remember her today do not immediately recall her last few years. Those who lived through the height of her career remember a headstrong and outspoken member of the community. Some recall her wardrobe and her chauffeur-driven car. Others remember her ministerial style of dispensing justice. Everyone recalls her outgoing personality. And whether or not they immediately identify her as a civil rights pioneer, the mention of Judge Elreta Alexander-Ralston often brings a smile to the face of those whom she impacted.[15]

In the twenty-first century, there are few visible reminders of Alexander-Ralston. Her face is included in a mural at the downtown Greensboro Public Library, and there is a small plaque and picture at the Greensboro History Museum. The spaces she integrated bear no reminder of her. The Southeastern Building in downtown Greensboro, where Alexander-Ralston was part of the first integrated law firm in the South, is now luxury apartments. Her home in Starmount Forest is now a residential health care facility for individuals with developmental disabilities. Young adults or newcomers to Greensboro are unaware of Elreta Alexander-Ralston. She lives on, however, in the memories of her contemporaries.

Those in the legal community remember Alexander as an exceptional jurist. Justice Henry Frye noted that he did not know anybody who could cross-examine a witness like Alexander, and nobody challenged her unless they absolutely knew she was wrong.[16] Jerry Pell said she had the "courage of her conviction" and that her legal philosophy could be found in her Judgment Day program. She actively encouraged young Black defendants to get an education, knowing that prison and fines do not help reform young offenders. Instead, "she had kids in the emergency room mopping up blood."[17] She changed lives with the Judgement Day program. Many juveniles who went through the program became ministers, attorneys, and business professionals because one daring judge gave them a second chance. Deferred prosecution, as pioneered in Alexander's Judgment Day program, is now part of state statutes around the country.

Because of Elreta Alexander-Ralston, a new generation of Black women attorneys could reach the same professional heights and higher. In 1980, Karen Galloway Bethea-Shields was elected the first African American woman judge from Durham County, North Carolina. Although she never personally met Judge Alexander, Bethea-Shields counts her among her inspirations, stating that Alexander made the path easier for her.[18] And thirty-two years after Alexander lost her primary race for North Carolina Supreme Court chief justice, a Black woman was finally elected to that court. In February 2006, Governor Mike Easley appointed Patricia Timmons-Goodson to the North Carolina Supreme Court, and she was then elected by the voters in November 2006; she served until 2012. Timmons-Goodson is another jurist who credits Alexander with blazing a trail others could follow. She once stated, "We owe [Alexander] a debt of gratitude for opening doors that had been closed to a significant segment of our community."[19]

Governor Roy Cooper appointed Cheri Beasley as the twenty-ninth chief justice of the North Carolina Supreme Court—the first African American woman to hold the position—and she was sworn in on March 7, 2019, forty-five years after Elreta Alexander lost to an uneducated fire extinguisher salesman in the GOP primary. As with Judges Bethea-Shields and Timmons-Goodson, Alexander was a role model and inspiration for Beasley: "I often think about what that journey was like for her personally. . . . I'm certain that it was onerous, insulting and demoralizing to some extent. . . . What we cannot forget was how she was in her quiet moments. It takes a lot of stamina, courage and ingenuity to be the one to come forth. [She was] determined to do what was right. [I have] no doubt her service has had an impact on my ability to serve and my service."[20] Unfortunately, in the 2020 elections Justice Beasley lost by 401 votes as she ran to keep her position as chief justice. The voters of North Carolina have yet to elect a Black woman to that position.

On the state and national levels, Black women have reached career statuses unimaginable during the height of Alexander-Ralston's career. In 1992 Eva Clayton became the first African American woman to represent a North Carolina district in the U.S. House of Representatives and the first African American elected to Congress from North Carolina since 1901.[21] In 2007 Yvonne Johnson became the first African American mayor of the city of Greensboro. On November 8, 2014, President Barack Obama nominated Loretta Lynch to be the U.S. attorney general. Lynch, a Greensboro, North Carolina, native, was the first African American woman to serve in that role. All of these women undoubtedly journeyed down a long path to reach their groundbreaking positions. But having Elreta Alexander-Ralston come before them meant one less barrier to surmount.

Slowly, as African American women continue to break new barriers, unsung pioneers like Alexander-Ralston are being remembered. In November 2020, in her first speech as vice president–elect, Kamala Harris honored the Black women who "are too often overlooked but so often prove they are the backbone of democracy."[22] A month later, Judge Alexander-Ralston was honored for her status as the first Black woman to graduate from Columbia Law School. In her remarks, Assistant Dean Andrea Saavedra stated that women of color who enter Columbia Law School are not alone because Alexander-Ralston walked before them:

> Formidable talent, character, and fortitude [were] required of her to break down the many barriers she faced as a woman, an African American woman, a law student, an attorney and, finally, a jurist, particularly in the Jim Crow South. . . . She lived by example and proved her talents in the courtroom, over and over again, both as a trial lawyer and as a judge. She was admired by men

and women alike, of all races. And, importantly, she chose to run for judicial office to improve the administration of justice.[23]

Alexander-Ralston broke down those barriers at a time when a woman, let alone a Black woman, was not expected to reach such professional heights. Because of her series of firsts, Alexander-Ralston deserves credit as a pioneering woman and African American. But it is how she approached her career and what she accomplished after that series of firsts that make her a civil rights pioneer. In some ways, Elreta Alexander-Ralston did not work toward any specific agenda, except being the best attorney and judge she possibly could, but she treated every case as though it were a civil rights case. Her dedication to civil rights for all people, especially African Americans and women, led her to fundamentally change the North Carolina legal system. Alexander prevented civil rights violations by ensuring that African Americans were represented on Guilford County juries. She changed the lives of many juveniles by giving them a chance at rehabilitation. Even one of her most painful professional moments, the 1974 campaign loss, ensured that North Carolina would in the future elect qualified judges. Regardless of what else individuals remember her for, it can be agreed that without Alexander, the history of Guilford County and of North Carolina would be a little less interesting and less fair. In a career full of firsts, Elreta Melton Alexander-Ralston's most significant accomplishment was her commitment to civil rights and challenging the status quo.

Alexander saw changing the law and the legal system as her way of helping African Americans during the civil rights movement. Because of this view, she drew attention to herself, both positive and negative. She saw that the justice system needed more creativity, and she knew that such change would make those who maintain the status quo uncomfortable. Ultimately, Alexander had to decide if she was going to get caught up in procedure or if she was going to help people. She chose to help. She was always the woman who stood out from the crowd, and she became a model for other African American women who wanted a legal career.[24] But by the end of the 1970s, Alexander had become weary of carrying the weight: "After a while you get tired of being a pioneer, and you want to have peace."[25] Unfortunately, the circumstances of her personal life did not allow for much peace.

Elreta Alexander-Ralston represents many individuals who have been left out of the traditional civil rights narrative. Many of them did not conform to our traditional notions of activism. Or maybe their impact was more on a local or state level. Judge Alexander-Ralston refused to be stymied by the professional options available to an African American woman in the segregated South. She was not a "reluctant pioneer," and she consistently took professional and personal risks and accepted new challenges with respectability and her trademark style.[26] She knew who she was, and she forged her own path. Many times she won, but when she lost she quietly and stoically moved on with her life and career. Jerry Pell stated that "she stood out as someone of superior character, in my opinion."[27] She was always the daughter of the Reverend J. C. and Alain Melton, the precocious girl who was not afraid to chastise her teacher for making fun of those less fortunate. She lived her life with autonomy and agency, led by a strong moral compass and a desire to change the status quo.

In 2012 Justice Patricia Timmons-Goodson delivered a public tribute to Judge Alexander-Ralston. In preparation for her remarks, Timmons-Goodson spoke with Jim Holshouser, North Carolina's Republican governor from 1973 to 1977. He said of Alexander-Ralston, "As the drama is unfolding, you don't get the big picture. But when you look back, at the end of the day, [hers] was a remarkable journey."[28] With the benefit of hindsight, we can all appreciate Elreta Melton Alexander-Ralston's remarkable journey and her place in history.

ACKNOWLEDGMENTS

In this book about a strong, extraordinary woman, it is only fitting that I first give credit to the strong, extraordinary women who made this book happen. First, Anya Jabour took me on as a graduate student in 2010 when I desperately needed someone to invest in me as an academic. She mentored me and shaped me into a historian. I owe all of this to her. Additionally, my contract with the University of Georgia Press would have never happened without Keri Leigh Merritt. Not only is her work inspiring, but on a personal level, her support has helped sustain me; she provides a guiding light for scholars outside the traditional tenure track. This book would have never happened without her.

This project has been a decade-long labor of love, and I owe many people thanks for their guidance and expertise. I first encountered Elreta Alexander while a graduate student in the History Department at the University of Montana. In addition to Dr. Jabour, I owe a debt of gratitude to Tobin Miller Shearer, whose work in the pursuit of racial justice continues to inspire me. My educational foundation was cemented at Catawba College in Salisbury, North Carolina, where Michael Bitzer and Gary Freeze served as my advisors. Twenty years later, they both continue to serve as mentors and friends, and I am deeply grateful.

At the University of North Carolina at Greensboro I had the privilege of working with scholars who believed in this project and provided academic and moral support. In particular, Charles Bolton, my dissertation advisor, and Omar Ali guided my dissertation on Judge Alexander to completion. Other professors who took the time to provide editorial support include Mark Elliott, Greg O'Brien, and Anne Parsons. Dawn Avolio, Laurie O'Neil, and Kristina Wright all helped keep me on track as I completed my Ph.D. And my cohort—Hannah Dudley-Shotwell, Justina Licata, Jamie Mize, and Joseph Ross—provided invaluable support and friendship.

As with any biography, a considerable amount of research went into examining and contextualizing Elreta Alexander's life. The staff of the Martha Blakeney Hodges Special Collections at the University of North Carolina at Greensboro, particularly Erin Lawrimore and Stacey Krim, maintain the papers of Judge Alexander, which provided the foundation of this book. Thank you also to the kind staff at the Wilson Library at the University of North Carolina at Chapel Hill, which houses the Southern Historical and North Carolina Collections. Thank you to Jocelyn Wilk at the Columbia University Archives and to Sabrina Sondhi, who was at the Arthur W. Diamond Law Library at Columbia. Sabrina generously researched, scanned, and emailed documents to me when I could not travel to New York. Todd Johnson at the Johnston County Historical Society and the entire staff at the Greensboro History Museum have also been generous with their time and resources. I thoroughly enjoyed talking with Afrique Kilimanjaro, who provided access to decades of editions of the *Carolina Peacemaker*. My high school friend Laura Fiaschetti Crooks helped me dig through papers in the back room of the Alexander County Library in Taylorsville, North Carolina. And the staff at the North Carolina State Archives graciously kept North Carolina Supreme Court records on hold for an entire summer so they would be available when I traveled to Raleigh.

Several people have been gracious enough to sit down with me to discuss their memories of Elreta Alexander. Her profound impact on civil rights and the legal community lives on in the memories of F. Lee Bailey, Cheri Beasley, Karen Bethea-Shields, Rufus Edmisten, Henry Frye, Gerald Pell, Donald Speckhard, and Patricia Timmons-Goodson. Thank you all for your time and sharing your thoughts.

Karen L. Cox, Hannah Dudley-Shotwell, Shannon Frystak, Justina Licata, Austin McCoy, and Keri Leigh Merritt served as insightful readers and editors. I'm so fortunate to have you all as fellow historians and, most important, close friends.

The phenomenal staff at the University of Georgia Press took my dissertation and helped me turn it into a book. Specifically, Mick Gusinde-Duffy has been an editor, sounding board, and cheerleader for this project. I am truly blessed to have had him on board. Beth Snead and Jon Davies at the press and copyeditor Merryl A. Sloane helped see it through to publication. I am so grateful for the time and attention they dedicated to this manuscript.

As this book has drawn closer to completion, several people have taken a renewed interest in Elreta Alexander's life. The wonderful folks at Columbia

Law School, in particular Kimberlé Crenshaw, Dean Gillian Lester, Dean Andrea Saavedra, and especially Nancy Goldfarb, have helped introduce Judge Alexander to wider audiences. Nancy McLaughlin at the *Greensboro News and Record* and Rodney Dawson at the Greensboro History Museum have brought Alexander to fresh audiences in her hometown.

Portions of this material were previously published in Summey, "Redefining Activism: Judge Elreta Alexander Ralston and Civil Rights Advocacy in the New South," *North Carolina Historical Review* 90, no. 3 (July 2013): 237–58. Much of the editing and revisions for this book were done from my home in Greensboro, North Carolina, in 2020 in the midst of great uncertainty and anxiety. The COVID-19 pandemic and the deaths of George Floyd, Breonna Taylor, and other people of color at the hands of police forced me to examine my position as an educated white woman living on the west side of Elm Street in Greensboro. My Greensboro experience will never be that of a young Elreta Alexander, who grew up only a couple of miles from where I wrote this but under the restrictions of Jim Crow. As Black Americans have died at a disproportionate rate from the pandemic, it is clear that the dreams of Judge Alexander have yet to be realized. I hope that this book is only the first of many that will be written about her. The addition of multiple perspectives will enrich our understanding of Alexander and other pioneering Black women professionals and activists.

Finally, this book would have never happened without the love and support of my family. My father, Billy Summey, my intellectual touchstone, passed away before the publication of this work. His love of the humanities ultimately set me on this path. Yet it was my mom, Sally Stoffel Summey, who read every word multiple times before it was published. My brother and sister, Gene and Sarah Summey, always remind me of my most embarrassing and humbling moments when I need them to. My mother-in-law, Trisha Clayton Abee, and Lisa Herrick provided much-needed childcare. And my beloved dog, Grits, has been by my side—usually snoring—as I've written.

But of course those who supported me the most through the home stretch are my husband, Graham Abee, and our children, Hannah and Marshall. This book, along with everything else I do, is for them.

NOTES

Introduction

1. Rick Stewart and Greta Tilley, "Judge Alexander-Ralston Planning to Retire April 1," *Greensboro Record*, January 16, 1981, A1.
2. Throughout most of her career, Elreta Alexander-Ralston was known as Elreta Melton Alexander, or as "Judge A" while she was on the bench. Mostly, I refer to her as Alexander.
3. Alexander interview, July 13, 1977, box 5, folder 11, Alexander Collection.
4. Johnson, *Appropriating Blackness*, 9.
5. D. D. Jackson, *Judges*, 134.
6. Ransby, *Ella Baker and the Black Freedom Movement*, 1–2.
7. Ritterhouse, *Growing Up Jim Crow*; Shaw, *What a Woman Ought to Be and to Do*; Berrey, *Jim Crow Routine*.
8. Collins, "Social Construction," 191.
9. Crenshaw, "Demarginalizing the Intersection," 209.
10. Morello, *Invisible Bar*, 148–50.
11. McLeod, *Daughter of the Empire State*; Motley, *Equal Justice under Law*.
12. Ruth Whitehead Whaley, for example, a North Carolina native, was the first Black woman to graduate from Fordham Law School in 1924 and was also the first to pass the North Carolina bar exam. She never practiced law in North Carolina, however, as her professional career was based in New York.
13. Burke, *All for Civil Rights*, 171, 181.
14. Ransby, *Ella Baker and the Black Freedom Movement*.
15. Farrington, *Black Republicans*; Rigueur, *Loneliness of the Black Republican*.
16. See Brown, *Belles of Liberty*; Chafe, *Civilities and Civil Rights*.
17. Thomas and Boisseau, *Feminist Legal History*, 1.
18. Hayes, *Without Precedent*, 348; Alexander-Ralston interview.

Chapter 1. A Respectable Childhood

1. Alexander interview, May 19, 1977, box 5, folder 8, Alexander Collection.
2. Alexander-Ralston interview; May 1921 registration of deed, 1927 contract giving up Fuller Street property, 1933 *Johnston County v. J. C. Melton et al.*, suit over the

property, all in Johnston County Register of Deeds, N.C. According to records from the Johnston County Register of Deeds, the Meltons were involved in several real estate transactions between May 1920 and May 1921. The 1920 Census lists the family as living on Caswell Street next to the First Missionary Baptist Church. There is a quit claim deed dated June 1920 in the name of J. C. Melton on Fuller Street in Smithfield. There is also a March 1921 deed made out to J. C. Melton for property on Belmont Avenue and a May 1921 indenture regarding the Fuller Street property.

3. Alexander interview, May 19, 1977. This account does not coincide with U.S. Census records, and there is not conclusive evidence for the existence of a marriage certificate for John and Narcissus Melton. The 1870 Census records list Narcissus and her mother, Kittie Flood, as "mulatto." My labeling of her family members as "white" is based on Alexander's descriptions later in life. In 1875, a ban on interracial marriage was inscribed in the North Carolina Constitution. The specific date of the inception of North Carolina's antimiscegenation law, however, is disputed among scholars. Laws enacted in 1715 prevented free Black people from voting and from marrying whites. Franklin, *Free Negro in North Carolina*, 10.

4. Alexander interview, May 19, 1977. According to Franklin, "At the time of the taking of the first census in 1790, there were 5,041 free Negroes in North Carolina.... By 1800, the number of free Negroes had grown to 7,043, at which time the slave population was 133,296 and the total population 478,103. The majority of these free Negroes were concentrated in twenty-five coastal and piedmont counties." Franklin, *Free Negro in North Carolina*, 14. Also see Milteer, *North Carolina's Free People of Color*, 140–41; Smallwood, "History of Native American and African Relations"; Heinegg, *Free African Americans*.

5. The number of children in the Melton family matches U.S. Census records. The Census of 1900 lists John T. Melton as having married Martha A. Melton in 1889. Joseph C. Melton, eighteen, is listed as a member of the household. The whole family is listed as Black. Also see Alexander interview, May 19, 1977.

6. Jenkins, "Historical Study of Shaw University," 22, 49.

7. Alexander interview, May 19, 1977; U.S. Department of the Interior, National Park Service, National Register of Historic Places Inventory—Nomination Form, http://www.hpo.ncdcr.gov/nr/HF0386.pdf.

8. Alexander interview, May 19, 1977. Census records for Alain Reynolds's mother, Emma Turner, list her as either Black or "mulatto." The 1910 U.S. Census record for her father, Robert E. Reynolds, lists him as "mulatto" and being a farmer. No records list him as white. Paul Heinegg also includes an analysis of the Reynolds family in *Free African Americans*, 558.

9. Higginbotham, *Righteous Discontent*, 41. The Proceedings of the Baptist State Convention of North Carolina in 1922, 1923, and 1924 list J. C. Melton as pastor of Shiloh Baptist Church in Scotland Neck, North Carolina. Church history provided by Loyal Baptist Church, Danville, Virginia, via email to author, October 22, 2015.

10. Key, *Southern Politics in State and Nation*, 206; Chafe, *Civilities and Civil Rights*, 5–6.

11. Jones, *Labor of Love, Labor of Sorrow*, 220. There are several articles in the *Chicago Defender* that mention J. C. Melton participating in community spiritual events in Greensboro, including "'Vision' Subject at A&T Vespers," December 28, 1935, 10; "3rd Convocation at A&T Called Best in History," September 5, 1936, 3; "Dr. Patterson Addresses Dudley Day Celebration," November 9, 1940, 3. See also Alexander-Ralston interview, 9.

12. Du Bois, "Talented Tenth"; Gaines, *Uplifting the Race*, 2.

13. Gaines, *Uplifting the Race*, xiv. There are many secondary sources that examine the Black middle class in the early twentieth century. See Gilmore, *Gender and Jim Crow*; Shaw, *What a Woman Ought to Be and to Do*; Higginbotham, *Righteous Discontent*.

14. Ritterhouse, *Growing Up Jim Crow*, 5; Hale, *Making Whiteness*, 124; Alexander interview, November 6, 1977, box 5, folder 13, Alexander Collection.

15. Ritterhouse, *Growing Up Jim Crow*, 17; A. Walker, "New Takes on Jim Crow."

16. Clegg, *Troubled Ground*, 8, 184; Ritterhouse, *Growing Up Jim Crow*, 6, 17; Alexander-Ralston interview, 13.

17. Carolina Theatre, "History," http://www.carolinatheatre.com/carolina-theatre-history.aspx; conversation with Pell; Alexander interview, May 19, 1977.

18. Shaw, *What a Woman Ought to Be and to Do*; Faircloth, *Teaching Equality*; Alexander-Ralston interview, 8.

19. Alexander interview, May 19, 1977.

20. Jones, *Labor of Love, Labor of Sorrow*, 110–16, 129, 172–73; Shaw, *What a Woman Ought to Be and to Do*, 23, 24; White, *Ar'n't I a Woman?*

21. Alexander interview, May 19, 1977.

22. Ibid.; Alexander-Ralston interview, 10.

23. Summers, "Diagnosing the Ailments of Black Citizenship"; R. T. Carter, "Racism and Psychological and Emotional Injury."

24. Sernett, *African American Religious History*, 134; Alexander-Ralston interview, 3.

25. Frazier, *Negro Church in America*; Lincoln and Mamiya, *Black Church*; Higginbotham, *Righteous Discontent*, 176.

26. Alexander interview, May 19, 1977; Millicent Rothrock, "Neighborhood Communities Evolved with Distinct Identities," *Greensboro News and Record*, September 15, 1990.

27. Clegg, *Troubled Ground*, 8, 184.

28. Chafe, *Civilities and Civil Rights*, 18–19.

29. Batchelor, *Guilford County Schools*; Anderson, *Education of Blacks in the South*, 156.

30. Alexander interview, May 19, 1977

31. Alexander casually mentions a number of people in her interviews. In many instances, I was unable to determine their full names.

32. Collier-Thomas and Turner, "Race, Class, and Color"; Alexander interview, May 19, 1977.

33. Gaines, *Uplifting the Race*; Gilmore, *Gender and Jim Crow*; Roberts, *Pageants, Parlors, and Pretty Women*.

34. Norwood and Monroe, "Thoughts on Bullying and Colorism"; Alexander interview, May 19, 1977.

35. Alexander-Ralston interview, 12.

36. Chafe, *Civilities and Civil Rights*, 16.

37. Higginbotham, *Righteous Discontent*, 44; United Institutional Baptist Church, "Pastoral History of United Institutional Baptist Church," Greensboro, N.C. (church records).

38. Wilmore, *Black Religion and Black Radicalism*, 3; "Pastoral History of United Institutional Baptist Church."

39. Alexander interview, May 19, 1977.

40. Ritterhouse, *Growing Up Jim Crow*, 4; Alexander-Ralston interview, 9.

41. Shaw, *What a Woman Ought to Be and to Do*, 2–3.

42. Gibbs, *History of the North Carolina Agricultural and Technical College*, 2–5; University Archives, Bluford Library, North Carolina Agricultural and Technical State University, "A&T History," http://www.library.ncat.edu/resources/archives/history.html (accessed June 29, 2021).

43. Chafe, *Civilities and Civil Rights*, 17–18, 20.

44. "A&T History"; Fortieth Annual Catalogue (1934–1935) of the Agricultural and Technical College of North Carolina; Alexander interview, May 19, 1977; Perkins, "Bound to Them by a Common Sorrow." Majoring in music was fairly common for women of the Black middle class, as detailed in Shaw's *What a Woman Ought to Be and to Do*. Many intended to pursue careers as professional performers or private music instructors.

45. "Eighty Students on Honor Roll for First Quarter," *Register* 29, no. 3 (February 1935), 1; "Winter Honor Roll Announced," *Register* 30, no. 6 (May 1936), 1; "Four Tie for High Honors as List Is Announced," *Register* 31, no. 5 (February 1937), 6; "So Help Me," and "The Voice Speaks," *Register* 30, no. 2 (November 1935), 3. All issues of the *Register* can be found in University Archives, F. D. Bluford Library, North Carolina Agricultural and Technical State University, Greensboro.

46. Alexander interview, May 19, 1977; Alrige, "Guiding Philosophical Principles"; Frazier, *Black Bourgeoisie*, 94.

47. "The Ivy Leaf Club," *Register* 18, no. 5 (May 1934), 4; "Young Women Hold Appreciation Hour," *Register* 29, no. 3 (February 1935), 1; "Choral Club Gives 'The Christ Child,'" *Register* 29, no. 2 (December 1935), 1; "Senior Education Students in Program," *Register* 31, no. 2 (November 1936), 1.

48. Alexander interview, May 19, 1977; Shaw, *What a Woman Ought to Be and to*

NOTES TO CHAPTER ONE 159

Do, 47. The Waugh family was also of multiracial ancestry. According to Alexander, Lee Waugh was of Cherokee and white descent, while Lavinia's mother, Caroline, was of white and African American descent.

49. Alexander interview, May 12 and 19, 1977, box 5, folders 7, 8, Alexander Collection; "The Voice of the Skull," *Register* 30, no. 4 (January 1936), 3; "Campus Chatter," *Register* 21, no. 3 (December 1936), 2.

50. Alexander interview, May 19, 1977.

51. Katharine Tynes's official death certificate states that she mistook a bottle of Yager's Liniment for medicine and drank a portion, which killed her. Her death was ruled accidental, but Alexander stated a number of times that it was suicide. Alexander interview, May 19, 1977.

52. Alexander interview, May 12 and 19, 1977; Meharry Medical College, "About Meharry," 2016, https://www.mmc.edu/about/.

53. Shaw, *What a Woman Ought to Be and to Do*, 144, 175–76; Alexander interview, May 12, 1977.

54. Alexander interview, May 12, 1977.

55. Ibid.

56. Ibid. Patricia Carter's *Everybody's Paid but the Teacher* states that by 1931, "77% of all U.S. school districts had instituted bans on married women teachers" (97). This was most notable in smaller towns, like Chester, South Carolina. Carter also states that the justification behind the ban was the belief that "the married woman's true place was in the home" (100).

57. Alexander interview, May 12, 1977; High School Principals' Annual Reports, 1938–1939, North Carolina Department of Public Instruction, Division of Negro Education, State Archives of North Carolina, http://digital.ncdcr.gov/cdm/ref/collection/p16062coll13/id/49911 (accessed January 25, 2020); Cal Bryant, "Sunbury Salute," *Roanoke-Chowan News Herald*, August 23, 2015, https://www.roanoke-chowan newsherald.com/2015/08/23/sunbury-salute/.

58. Alexander interview, May 12, 1977; Teague and Teague, "Happy Plains School." The information compiled by the Teagues lists Elereta [*sic*] N. Melton as having been on the faculty during the 1939–1940 school year.

59. Meharry Medical College, "1940 Meharry Medical College Commencement," http://diglib.mmc.edu/omeka/items/show/191 (accessed July 11, 2016).

60. Curwood, *Stormy Weather*, 56–58.

61. Alexander interview, May 12, 1977; Bailey, *From Front Porch to Back Seat*, 4; Curwood, *Stormy Weather*, 31–32.

62. Letter from F. D. Bluford, box 1, folder 1, Alexander Collection.

63. Alexander interview, May 12, 1977; Chafe, *Civilities and Civil Rights*, 24–25.

64. Alexander-Ralston interview, 21; Chafe, *Civilities and Civil Rights*, 25.

65. Alexander interview, May 12, 1977.

66. Ibid. For information on Black women's work during World War II, see White, *Too Heavy a Load*; Jones, *Labor of Love, Labor of Sorrow*.

Chapter 2. Between Two Worlds

1. Alexander interview, May 12, 1977, box 5, folder 7, Alexander Collection.
2. Alexander-Ralston interview; Alexander interview, May 12, 1977; Alexander interview, May 20, 1977, box 5, folder 9, Alexander Collection.
3. Goebel, *History of the School of Law*.
4. Levy, *Political Life of Bella Abzug*, 27; Annual Report of the President and Treasurer to the Trustees with Accompanying Documents for the Academic Year Ending June 30, 1943; Report of the Dean of the School of Law; and Columbia University, One Hundred and Ninety First Annual Commencement, June 5, 1945, Series: Contents List, box 13, Commencement Collection, 1758, folder 1, 1945, all in Rare Books and Manuscripts, Butler Library, Columbia University Archives, New York; Motley interview.
5. Jones, *Labor of Love, Labor of Sorrow*, 196–200.
6. Alexander interview, May 12, 1977. Many applications to Columbia Law School during this time were accompanied by photographs of the applicants. While her application and photograph have not been found in archives, it is likely that Alexander's application included a picture.
7. Alexander interview, May 12, 1977.
8. Goebel, *History of the School of Law*, 351; Alexander interview, May 20, 1977,..
9. See Berebitsky, *Sex and the Office*; Crenshaw, "Whose Story Is It Anyway."
10. Historical Biographical Files, ser. 1, box 217, folder 4, Rare Books and Manuscripts, Butler Library, Columbia University, New York.
11. Motley interview.
12. Alexander, "Student's Plan for Peace." The United Nations was formally established on October 24, 1945, one year and six months after Alexander's paper was written. The International Labour Organization is now a U.N. agency.
13. Alexander, "Student's Plan for Peace," 6, 12.
14. Alexander interview, May 20, 1977. In her oral history, Alexander refers to Paul B. Hays. Columbia Law, however, only has a record of Professor Paul R. Hays during the time Alexander was a law student.
15. Alexander interview, May 20, 1977; Motley, *Equal Justice under Law*, 58.
16. Alexander interview, May 20, 1977.
17. Alexander interview, July 13, 1977, box 5, folder 11, Alexander Collection.
18. Alexander interview, June 16, 1977, box 5, folder 10, Alexander Collection; Hobbs, *Chosen Exile*, 136.
19. Hobbs, *Chosen Exile*, prologue; Alexander interview, July 13, 1977.
20. Jones, *Labor of Love, Labor of Sorrow*, 214.
21. Alexander interview, June 16, 1977.
22. Alexander interview, May 20, 1977.
23. An Act to Provide Graduate and Professional Courses for the Negroes of North Carolina, H.B. 18, chapter 65, *Public Laws and Resolutions Passed by the General As-*

sembly at Its Extra Session of 1938 and at Its Regular Session of 1939 (Raleigh: State of North Carolina, 1939), 88.

24. Alexander interview, June 16, 1977. I have not been able to confirm that North Carolina would pay for African Americans to attend law school out of state nor have I found the specific statute stating African Americans must be exceptional and meritorious. However, according to historian Sarah Thuesen, the Murphy Bill (1939) established "a system of out-of-state aid ... whereby black students who wished to obtain graduate degrees offered at UNC but not at NCC or A&T could apply for state scholarship[s] to pursue those programs elsewhere." Thuesen, *Greater than Equal*, 115. Also see Alexander-Ralston interview, 25.

25. Alexander interview, May 20, 2017; Timmons-Goodson, "Darlin', the Truth Will Set You Free."

26. Alexander interview, May 20, 1977.

27. Ibid.

28. Ronald Smothers, "Hope Stevens, 77, Harlem Leader, Lawyer, and Businessman, Is Dead," *New York Times*, June 25, 1982, http://www.nytimes.com/1982/06/25/obituaries/hope-stevens-77-harlem-leader-lawyer-and-businessman-is-dead.html; Holland, *From Harlem with Love*.

29. Alexander interview, June 16, 1977.

30. Alexander-Ralston interview, 31; Timmons-Goodson, "Darlin', the Truth Will Set You Free."

31. Alexander-Ralston interview, 31.

32. Ibid., 29.

33. Timmons-Goodson, "Darlin', the Truth Will Set You Free."

34. This story is recalled by Pierce Rucker's daughter Mary Lewis Rucker Edmunds in her book, *Recollections of Greensboro*. Alexander recalls the same story almost identically in her oral interviews..

35. Pye, "Legal Subversives."

36. Davis, "Role of Black Colleges and Black Law Schools."

37. Alexander interview, July 13, 1977.

38. Ibid.; Alexander-Ralston interview, 26.

39. Alexander interview, July 13, 1977. Boyd in *Jim Crow Nostalgia* discusses political patronage, and she states that many Black elites were beholden to their white patrons.

40. "The Struggle for Civil Rights," http://www.learnnc.org/lp/editions/nchist-postwar/6031 (accessed May 18, 2017).

41. Chafe, *Civilities and Civil Rights*, 17.

42. Ibid., 26.

43. Ibid., 28.

44. Speckhard interview.

45. Conversation with Pell; Alexander interview, July 13, 1977, box 5, folder 11, Al-

exander Collection. Henry Frye in 1963 became the first Black attorney to join the Greensboro Bar Association.

46. "News of Interested to Colored People," *High Point Enterprise*, May 11, 1952, 9A; Negro Citizen's Council flyer, 1948, box 5, folder 18, Alexander Collection.

47. Alexander interview, July 13, 1977.

48. Newspaper clippings, box 3, folder 2, Alexander Collection; Frye interview.

49. Chafe, *Civilities and Civil Rights*, 44–45. Also see Batchelor, *Race and Education in North Carolina*.

50. Alexander interview, October 23, 1977, box 5, folder 12, Alexander Collection. Gaston Street is now Friendly Avenue.

51. Friedman and Holzman, "Performing the World"; Alexander-Ralston interview, 88.

52. Alexander interview, July 13, 1977.

53. Summey, "Redefining Activism."

54. Berrey, *Jim Crow Routine*, 2, 8–9.

55. Lamson, *Few Are Chosen*, 127; Summey, "Redefining Activism."

56. Alexander interview, July 13, 1977. Dr. Simkins and others were arrested in 1955 for trying to play golf again at Gillespie Park, instead of Nocho Park. Gillespie temporarily shut down shortly after the decision in *Simkins v. City of Greensboro* ordered the city's recreational facilities to desegregate. When the course reopened in 1962, Simkins was the first to tee off. Usher, "Golfers"; Simkins interview; Scott Michaux, "Civil Rights: George Simkins," *Greensboro News and Record*, April 15, 2000.

57. Alexander interview, July 13, 1977; Alexander interview, November 6, 1977, box 5, folder 13, Alexander Collection. During this time, southern states rebuked federal standards of payment to prevent the equal treatment of white and Black children. See Abramovitz's *Regulating the Lives of Women*.

58. "High Court Heeds 1st Negro Woman to Argue Case," *Greensboro Daily News*, July 1, 1955, 12; "Supreme Court Hears Negro Woman Lawyer," *Greensboro Record*, May 10, 1955, B3. The ruling in *State v. Davis* was handed down on June 30, 1955. Alexander was the sole attorney for the appellants.

59. Covington, *Henry Frye*, 47.

60. Correspondence, box 1, folder 2, Alexander Collection.

61. "Attorney Speaks Here Today," *High Point Enterprise*, May 11, 1952, 9A.

62. Newspaper clippings, box 3, folder 2, Alexander Collection.

63. Correspondence, box 1, folder 4, Alexander Collection.

64. S. Walker, *Style and Status*, 3.

65. Kelley, *Race Rebels*, 64, see also 50; correspondence from Lord & Taylor, box 1, folder 4, Alexander Collection; Roberts, *Pageants, Parlors, and Pretty Women*, 8, 11; S. Walker, *Style and Status*, 6–7.

66. Alexander-Ralston interview, 19; conversation with Pell.

67. Sanders-McMurtry and Haydel, "Linking Friendship and Service Education"; Alexander interview, November 6, 1977; Parker, *History of the Links*; S. A. Jackson,

"I've Got All My Sisters with Me"; newspaper clippings, box 1, folders 4–6, Alexander Collection.

68. "High School Activities," *Chicago Defender*, March 19, 1960, 17.

69. *Daily Defender*, March 12, 1958, 5; "Twelve Local Names Added to Who's Who in Women," *Greensboro Daily News*, July 30, 1961, B9.

70. Chafe, *Civilities and Civil Rights*, 102.

71. Alexander interview, November 6, 1977.

72. Correspondence, box 1, folder 4, Alexander Collection.

73. "Negro Doctor Withdraws Bid for Medical Society," *Greensboro Record*, October 24, 1960, B1.

74. "Greensboro, North Carolina, Group Files Historic Suit against Hospital Exclusion," *Journal of the National Medical Association* 54, no. 2 (March 1962): 259, http://www.ncbi.nlm.nih.gov/pmc/articles/PMC2642370/pdf/jnma00684-0131a.pdf. Also see Smith, *Health Care Divided*, 83.

75. Chafe, *Civilities and Civil Rights*, 36.

76. Smith, *Health Care Divided*, 106–7; *Simkins v. Moses H. Cone Memorial Hospital*, 211 F. Supp. 628 (M.D.N.C. December 5, 1962); Karen Kruse Thomas, "Simkins v. Cone," http://ncpedia.org/simkins-v-cone (accessed July 26, 2016).

77. Alexander interview, July 13, 1977. Alexander in her oral history did not provide a date for this incident. The Irving Park Delicatessen was purchased from its original owners in 1962.

Chapter 3. Changing the System

1. Alexander-Ralston interview; *State of North Carolina v. Charles Yoes and Willie Hale, Jr. (Alias Willie Haile, Jr.) and Leroy Davis*, Supreme Court of North Carolina, 271 N.C. 616; 157 S.E.2d 386; 1967 N.C. Lexis 1259, November 1, 1967, filed (hereafter *North Carolina v. Yoes, Hale, and Davis*).

2. Alexander interview, November 6, 1977, box 5, folder 13, Alexander Collection.

3. Ibid.

4. Superior Court Transcript, Supreme Court Original Cases, Fall 1967, cases 613–59, box 15, State Archives of North Carolina, Raleigh; Alexander interview, November 6, 1977.

5. Loevy, *Civil Rights Act of 1964*.

6. Alexander interview, November 6, 1977.

7. Ibid.

8. DuRocher, *Raising Racists*, 133–34; Dorr, *White Women, Rape, and the Power of Race*, 7.

9. Hall, "The Mind That Burns."

10. H. Rosen, *Terror in the Heart of Freedom*, 72.

11. Ibid., 173.

12. Ibid., 195.

13. For instances of rape-related lynchings, see Hodes, *White Women, Black Men*.

14. Dorr, *White Women, Rape, and the Power of Race*, 213; H. Rosen, *Terror in the Heart of Freedom*, 172.

15. Hall, "The Mind That Burns."

16. Barnett, *Dangerous Desire*, xxix.

17. Alexander interview, November 6, 1977.

18. "Four Ordered for Trial on Charges of Rape," *High Point Enterprise*, July 14, 1964, B1.

19. Don Follmer, "Rape Defendants Given Life Terms," *High Point Enterprise*, December 19, 1964, 12.

20. Superior Court Transcript, Supreme Court Original Cases, Fall 1967, cases 613-59; "Rare Rape Charged Filed against Guilford Woman," *Greensboro Record*, January 12, 1965, B1.

21. Alexander interview, November 6, 1977.

22. Greenberg, *Race Relations and American Law*, 336.

23. Franklin and McNeil, *African Americans and the Living Constitution*, 237-38.

24. Brownmiller, *Against Our Will*, 215.

25. Alexander interview, November 6, 1977.

26. Charles Price, "Constitutionality to Be Challenged of State's Criminal Assault Statute," *Greensboro Record*, October 27, 1964, B1.

27. "Subpoenas Ordered Recalled," *Greensboro Daily News*, October 29, 1964, B1.

28. Superior Court Transcript, Supreme Court Original Cases, Fall 1967, cases 613-59; "Arguments, Motions Slow Trial," *Greensboro Daily News*, December 18, 1964, B1.

29. Article I, section 17, of the North Carolina Constitution in 1964 stated that "no person ought to be taken, imprisoned or disseized of his freehold, liberties, or privileges, or outlawed or exiled, or in any manner deprived of his life, liberty or property, but by the law of the land."

30. North Carolina General Statutes, 1951, §§ 14-21: regarding punishment for rape "every person who is convicted of ravishing and carnally knowing any female of the age of twelve years or more by force and against her will, or who is convicted [of] unlawfully and carnally knowing and abusing any female child under the age of twelve years, shall suffer death: Provided, if the jury shall so recommend at the time of rendering its verdict in open court, the punishment shall be imprisonment for life in the State's prison, and the court shall so instruct the jury." The statutes were not amended until 1973.

31. Superior Court Transcript, Supreme Court Original Cases, Fall 1967, box 15.

32. *North Carolina v. Yoes, Hale, and Davis*.

33. Ibid.

34. "Fair Jury Selection Procedures."

35. Don Folmer, "Trial of Four for Rape Called in Greensboro Court," *High Point Enterprise*, November 30, 1964, B1.

36. Alexander interview, November 6, 1977.

37. *North Carolina v. Yoes, Hale, and Davis*.

38. "Tax List Distinctions Injected in Grand Jury Selection Test," *Greensboro Record*, December 2, 1964, box 3, folder 3, Alexander Collection.

39. Alexander interview, November 6, 1977.

40. Fukurai and Krooth, *Race in the Jury Box*, 3, 153; Benokraitis and Griffin-Keene, "Prejudice and Jury Selection."

41. "Arguments, Motions Slow Trial," *Greensboro Daily News*, December 18, 1964, B1.

42. Superior Court Transcript, Supreme Court Original Cases, Fall 1967, cases 613–59.

43. Ibid.; "2 Alternate Jurors Still to Be Chosen," *Greensboro Daily News*, December 14, 1964, B1; "Rape Trial Jurors Take Seats Today," *Greensboro Record*, December 14, 1964, B1.

44. Alexander interview, November 6, 1977.

45. Alexander-Ralston interview, 84.

46. Alexander interview, November 6, 1977.

47. Ibid. In 1970, Charles Yoes petitioned for a writ of habeas corpus and cited Judge Gambill's use of the word "nigger" during the trial. "Convicted Rapist Petitions for Writ," *Greensboro Record*, March 18, 1970, C11.

48. Alexander interview, November 6, 1977.

49. D. D. Jackson, *Judges*, 122, 367; "W. Harold Cox, Federal Judge in Mississippi, Dies," *Washington Post*, February 28, 1988, https://www.washingtonpost.com/archive/local/1988/02/28/w-harold-cox-federal-judge-in-mississippi-dies/5e9bbbc1-b66d-49f4-9734-b05ddff6143e/?utm_term=.6ac197c683b3.

50. Superior Court Transcript, Supreme Court Original Cases, Fall 1967, cases 613–59.

51. Alexander interview, November 6, 1977.

52. Konradi, *Taking the Stand*, 8; Brownmiller, *Against Our Will*, 372.

53. Superior Court Transcript, Supreme Court Original Cases, Fall 1967, cases 613–59.

54. Ibid.

55. Ibid.; Konradi, *Taking the Stand*, 103; Alexander interview, November, 6, 1977.

56. For examinations of changing sexual norms in the twentieth century, see Bailey, *From Front Porch to Back Seat*; Cahn, *Sexual Reckonings*; Odem, *Delinquent Daughters*.

57. Alexander interview, November 6, 1977.

58. Brownmiller, *Against Our Will*, 220.

59. Superior Court Transcript, Supreme Court Original Cases, Fall 1967, cases 613–59.

60. Alexander interview, November 6, 1977.

61. MacKinnon, *Women's Lives, Men's Laws*, 131.

62. Superior Court Transcript, Supreme Court Original Cases, Fall 1967, cases 613–59.

63. Alexander interview, November 6, 1977. Charles Yoes later accused Sheriff Jones

of discussing the case with jurors during the trial. "Convicted Rapist Petitions for Writ," *Greensboro Record*, March 18, 1970, C11.

64. Superior Court Transcript, Supreme Court Original Cases, Fall 1967, cases 613–59.

65. DuRocher, *Raising Racists*, 141.

66. Alexander interview, November 6, 1977.

67. Superior Court Transcript, Supreme Court Original Cases, Fall 1967, cases 613–59.

68. Alexander-Ralston interview, 84; Don Folmer, "Rape Defendants Given Life Terms," *High Point Enterprise*, December 19, 1964, 12.

69. Superior Court Transcript, Supreme Court Original Cases, Fall 1967, cases 613–59.

70. Folmer, "Rape Defendants Given Life Terms," 12.

71. Holt McPherson, "Good Morning," *High Point Enterprise*, December 20, 1964, clipping in box 3, folder 3, Alexander Collection.

72. "Four Negroes Appeal Pauper Conviction," *Greensboro Daily News*, January 13, 1965, A8.

73. "Judge Turns Down Move by Rapists," *Greensboro Daily News*, January 15, 1965, A16.

74. Alexander interview, November 6, 1977.

75. Ibid.

76. Ibid.

77. "High Court Upholds Sentences," *Greensboro Record*, November 2, 1967, B2. Defendant Julian Hairston did not appeal to the North Carolina Supreme Court.

78. Superior Court Transcript, Supreme Court Original Cases, Fall 1967, cases 613–59.

79. *North Carolina v. Yoes, Hale, and Davis*.

80. Christensen, *Paradox of Tar Heel Politics*, 198.

81. Alexander interview, November 6, 1977; "Rumors of Assault Case Denied by Sheriff Jones," *Greensboro Record*, August 24, 1964, A4.

82. Alexander-Ralston interview, 89.

83. Benjamin Taylor, "Jail 'Bug' Device Evokes Surprise," *Greensboro Daily News*, February 28, 1967, A1.

84. North Carolina General Statutes § 9-1 states, "There shall be appointed in each county a jury commission of three members. One member of the commission shall be appointed by the senior regular resident superior court judge, one member by the clerk of superior court, and one member by the board of county commissioners."

85. Alexander interview, November 6, 1977.

86. Ibid.; Jim Schlosser, "'Judge A' Paved Way—With Style," *Greensboro News and Record*, March 15, 1998, A1; conversation with Pell. Julius Chambers, James Ferguson, and Adam Stein later claimed that their law firm in Charlotte, North Carolina, was the first integrated law firm in the South. Theirs was established in 1968, according to the

North Carolina Heritage Calendar (https://ncheritagecalendar.com/honorees/julius-chambers-james-ferguson-adam-stein/), while Alston, Alexander, Pell, and Pell was established in 1966.

87. Alexander interview, December 4, 1977, box 5, folder 14, Alexander Collection.
88. Alexander interview, November 6, 1977.
89. "Judge Alexander Logs Firsts in School, State," undated clipping, box 4, folder 2, Alexander Collection.

Chapter 4. Turbulence at Home

1. Copy of letter sent to Girardeau "Tony" Alexander, box 1, folder 1, Alexander Collection.
2. Ibid.
3. Hine, "Rape and the Inner Lives of Black Women."
4. Curwood, *Stormy Weather*, 7.
5. Jones, *Labor of Love, Labor of Sorrow*, 100.
6. Alexander interview, May 19, 1977, box 5, folder 8, Alexander Collection.
7. Ibid.
8. Higginbotham, *Righteous Discontent*, 176.
9. Ibid., 134.
10. Floyd, *Floyd's Flowers*, 253.
11. Copy of letter sent to Tony Alexander.
12. Alexander interview, May 19, 1977.
13. Alexander interview, May 12, 1977, box 5, folder 7, Alexander Collection.
14. Estate of Dr. Girardeau Alexander, Inter Vivos Transfers of Properties to Former Wife, Elreta Melton Alexander, Alexander Collection, MSS 223, box 4, folder 8.
15. Alexander interview, May 20, 1977, box 5, folder 9, Alexander Collection.
16. Charron, *Freedom's Teacher*, chap. 3.
17. Curwood, *Stormy Weather*, 6.
18. White, *Ar'n't I a Woman?*, 44.
19. Charron, *Freedom's Teacher*, 83.
20. Curwood, *Stormy Weather*, 18.
21. Gilmore, *Gender and Jim Crow*, 18.
22. Curwood, *Stormy Weather*, 15.
23. Ibid., 18.
24. Gilmore, *Gender and Jim Crow*, 62.
25. Ibid., 76.
26. H. Rosen, *Terror in the Heart of Freedom*, 122.
27. Copy of letter sent to Tony Alexander.
28. Curwood, *Stormy Weather*, 3.
29. R. Rosen, *World Split Open*, 9.
30. Ibid., 186.
31. Gordon, *Heroes of Their Own Lives*, 23.

32. R. Rosen, *World Split Open*, 13.
33. Alexander interview, December 4, 1977, box 5, folder 14, Alexander Collection.
34. Alexander interview, October 23, 1977, box 5, folder 12, Alexander Collection.
35. Ibid.
36. Estate of Dr. Girardeau Alexander.
37. Ibid. In the estate documents, the date of the beating is listed as "December 1959 or 1960."
38. Moynihan and U.S. Department of Labor, *Negro Family*, 5.
39. Alexander interview, May 20, 1977.
40. Alexander interview, July 13, 1977, box 5, folder 11, Alexander Collection.
41. Conversation with Pell.
42. Curwood, *Stormy Weather*, 29.
43. For example, in 1874 North Carolina courts decided that in order to bring a criminal indictment against a husband, the battery had to be bad enough to cause permanent injury, endanger the life of the wife, or be excessively malicious. U.S. Commission on Civil Rights, *Under the Rule of Thumb: Battered Women and the Administration of Justice*, January 1982, https://www.nlm.nih.gov/exhibition/confronting violence/assets/transcripts/OB12012_200_dpi.pdf; Eleanor Alexander, *Lyrics of Sunshine and Shadow*, 9.
44. Gelles, "Violence in the Family"; Schechter, *Women and Male Violence*, 22–23.
45. Estin, "Golden Anniversary Reflections."
46. Schechter, "Roots of the Battered Women's Movement."
47. Curwood, *Stormy Weather*, 54.
48. H. Rosen, *Terror in the Heart of Freedom*, 6.
49. Ibid., 191–92.
50. Curwood, *Stormy Weather*, 4.
51. Copy of letter sent to Tony Alexander.
52. Alexander interview, July 13, 1977.
53. Ehrenreich, *Hearts of Men*, 120.
54. Curwood, *Stormy Weather*, 149.
55. Alexander interview, January 22, 1978, folder 15, box 5, Alexander Collection.
56. Alexander interview, December 4, 1977.
57. Alexander interview, October 23, 1977.
58. Alexander interview, November 6, 1977, box 5, folder 13, Alexander Collection.
59. Ibid.
60. Correspondence, box 1, folder 4, Alexander Collection.
61. Alexander interview, December 4, 1977.
62. Letter to McNeil Smith of Greensboro from Erwin Griswold, dean of Harvard Law School, box 1, folder 5, Alexander Collection.
63. Alexander interview, December 4, 1977.
64. Ibid.

65. Letter to Tony Alexander, box 1, folder 6, Alexander Collection. Colonel Walter Burch was a friend of the family who served as an intermediary between Tony and Elreta. He is mentioned in "History of the Greensboro Police Department," https://www.greensboro-nc.gov/home/showpublisheddocument/43813/637038917960430000 (accessed July 27, 2021).
66. Alexander interview, December 4, 1977.
67. Hine, "Rape and the Inner Lives of Black Women."
68. Curwood, *Stormy Weather*, 7.
69. Ibid., 91.
70. Ibid., 97.
71. "Final Rites Held for Greensboro Minister," *Future Outlook*, January 19, 1968, A1.
72. Cooper, "Problems and Possibilities."
73. R. Rosen, *World Split Open*, 315, 337.
74. Curwood, *Stormy Weather*, 31.
75. Nakonezny, Schull, and Rodgers, "Effect of No-Fault Law."
76. Alexander interview, May 19, 1977.

Chapter 5. A Reluctant Pioneer?

1. Eleanor Kennedy, "New Judge Reluctant Pioneer," *Greensboro Daily News*, December 1, 1968, E1, E6.
2. Jonathan Yardley, "About Books," *Greensboro Daily News*, August 20, 1967, D3.
3. Alexander, *When Is a Man Free?*, 13.
4. Ibid., 8.
5. Ibid., 26.
6. Alexander interview, December 4, 1977, box 5, folder 14, Alexander Collection.
7. Amanda Lehmert, "1940 Deeds May Block Rezoning," *Greensboro News and Record*, March 1, 2012, https://greensboro.com/news/1940-deeds-may-block-rezoning/article_5f492f13-0326-58e2-933d-79aebb1c4b50.html; Alexander interview, December 4, 1977; Rothstein, *Color of Law*, 147.
8. Conversation with Pell; Alexander interview, December 4, 1977, Alexander, *When Is a Man Free?*, 9.
9. Conversation with Pell; Alexander interview, December 4, 1977.
10. Chafe, *Civilities and Civil Rights*, 7; Cunningham, *Klansville, U.S.A.*, 160–72.
11. Alexander interview, December 4, 1977.
12. James Ross, "Mrs. Alexander, Local Lawyer, Plans to Reveal Political Intentions Monday," *Greensboro Daily News*, February 17, 1968, A10.
13. Black and Black, *Rise of Southern Republicans*, 1–4; Crespino, *Strom Thurmond's America*, 165–84.
14. Black and Black, *Rise of Southern Republicans*, 3.
15. Correspondence between Alexander and Washington, box 1, folder 3, Alexander Collection.

16. Alexander interview, November 6, 1977, box 5, folder 13, Alexander Collection.

17. Jim Schlosser, "'Judge A' Paved Way—With Style," *Greensboro News and Record*, March 15, 1998, A1.

18. Farrington, *Black Republicans*, 140; Rigueur, *Loneliness of the Black Republican*, 5–9.

19. Campaign statement, box 5, folder 16, Alexander Collection.

20. Campaign advertisement and brochure, ibid.

21. "Elreta Alexander Will Run for Dist. Judge in Guilford," *Register*, no. 6, n.d., box 3, folder 4, Alexander Collection.

22. "The County Ballot Deserves Study Removed from Clamor," *Greensboro Record*, October 30, 1968, A14.

23. Alexander interview, November 6, 1977.

24. Jo Spivey, "Guilford Goes for Nixon, Votes Preyer over Osteen," *Greensboro Record*, November 6, 1968, 1.

25. Joe Brown, "5 Democrats, 1 Republican Winners in Judgeship Race," *High Point Enterprise*, November 6, 1968, C1.

26. "Over 110,000 Registered to Vote in County Today," *Greensboro Daily News*, November 5, 1968, A3.

27. Edmonds, *Negro and Fusion Politics*.

28. John Marshall Stevenson, "A New Day Has Dawned: Frye to Legislature; Alexander to District Court," *Carolina Peacemaker*, November 9, 1968, box 3, folder 4, Alexander Collection.

29. Frye interview.

30. D. D. Jackson, *Judges*, 111.

31. Ibid., 253.

32. Alexander interview, December 4, 1977; "Democrats, Woman Leading in Guilford Judgeship Race," *Greensboro Daily News*, November 8, 1968, B1; "Court Strikes Down 2 N.C. Vote Laws," *Greensboro Daily News*, January 14, 1972, A1.

33. "State Voting Laws Attacked by Blacks," *Greensboro Record*, December 1, 1970, A9. Debates over numbered seats continued in North Carolina. See *Gingles v. Edmisten*, 590 F. Supp. 345, 359–64 (E.D.N.C. 1984); *Thornburg v. Gingles*, 478 U.S. 30 (1986).

34. Kennedy, "New Judge Reluctant Pioneer," E1, E6.

35. Ibid.

36. Chambers, *Having It All?*, 47–49.

37. Conversation with Pell; Goldstein, *Price of Whiteness*, 194–99; Sacks, "How Did Jews Become White Folks?"; "Obituaries," *Greensboro News and Record*, posted August 28, 1995, http://www.greensboro.com/obituaries/article_f222d13a-a8a5-5ea8-83bc-f56057fd7c2e.html.

38. Speckhard interview.

39. Alexander-Ralston interview, 90.

40. Ibid.
41. John Lowe, "Judgement Day in High Point Gives Young Another Chance," *High Point Enterprise*, December 29, 1977, 1–2B.
42. Blomberg and Lucken, *American Penology*, 63, 99.
43. Schlossman, *Love and the American Delinquent*, 137; Feld, *Bad Kids*, 55.
44. Knupfer, *Reform and Resistance*, 2.
45. Ibid., 14.
46. Blomberg and Lucken, *American Penology*, 80.
47. Ibid., 93.
48. Ross, "Rethinking the Road to Gault."
49. Feld, *Bad Kids*, 89.
50. Ibid., 66.
51. Speckhard interview.
52. Alexander-Ralston interview, 91.
53. Lyman, *Great African-American Women*, 186; "Judgement Day Unique for Guilford County," *Greensboro Daily News*, September 24, 1978, E8; Alexander-Ralston interview, 91–92.
54. Marable, *Race, Reform, and Rebellion*, 3; Thompson, "Why Mass Incarceration Matters."
55. Bill Rhodes Weaver, "Judge Feels Program against Drugs Success," *Greensboro Daily News*, March 26, 1973, B1.
56. "'Judgement Day' Today for Continued Cases," *Greensboro Daily News*, July 12, 1974, B6.
57. Lowe, "Judgement Day in High Point," 1–2B.
58. D. D. Jackson, *Judges*, 110, 111.
59. Ross, "Rethinking the Road to Gault."
60. "Court Overrules 'Judgement Day,'" *Salisbury Sunday Post*, September 10, 1978, box 4, folder 1, Alexander Collection.
61. Corriero, *Judging Children as Children*, 180.
62. National Institute of Law Enforcement and Criminal Justice, *Determinate Sentencing: Reform or Regression? Summary Report* (Washington, D.C.: Law Enforcement Assistance Administration, U.S. Department of Justice, 2008), 64.
63. Alexander-Ralston interview, 3.
64. Steve Berry, "Chief Judge Supports First Offenders Statute," *Greensboro Daily News*, October 2, 1979, B2.
65. "Judgement Day—Over?," *Greensboro Record*, April 15, 1980, A6.
66. Morris, "Contemporary Prison."
67. Don Folmer, "Her Honor's Philosophy: 'Every Judge Must Push Own Shovel,'" *High Point Enterprise*, May 10, 1969, 2A.
68. Newspaper clippings, box 3, folder 5, Alexander Collection.
69. Kelso Gillenwater, "Judge Says War Training Causes Problems as GIs Ad-

just to Peace," *Greensboro Daily News*, September 25, 1969, box 3, folder 5, Alexander Collection.

70. D. D. Jackson, *Judges*, 125–26.

71. Ross, "Mrs. Alexander, Local Lawyer," A10.

72. C. A. Paul, "People, Places & Things," *Greensboro Daily News*, March 11, 1973, D6.

73. Ford, "Harlem's 'Natural Soul'"; Weitz, "Women and Their Hair"; Banks, *Hair Matters*.

74. Folmer, "Her Honor's Philosophy," 2A.

75. Richard Moore, "Self Respect Urged at A&T," *Greensboro Daily News*, May 31, 1969, B1.

76. Phyllis McLeod, "Town Rich in Feminine Resources," *Greensboro Record*, January 3, 1970, 3.

77. "UNC-G Faculty Wives Arranging 'Encounter,'" *Greensboro Daily News*, March 1, 1970, D6; "What's Happening," *Greensboro Record*, March 4, 1970, B1.

78. "CBS Commentator Will Speak to Girls State," *Greensboro Daily News*, June 13, 1970, 4; Wilson Davis, "Girls State Elects First Black Leader in History," *Greensboro Daily News*, June 24, 1972, 4; "Sen. Ervin to Address Girls State," *Greensboro Record*, June 5, 1973, 6; "Girls State to Convene 36th Session," *Greensboro Record*, June 2, 1975, 7; "300 to Attend Girls State Here," *Greensboro Daily News*, June 9, 1976, A10; "300 Seniors Coming to Girls State Here," *Greensboro Daily News*, June 6, 1978, B3; "Hunt, Edmisten among Speakers for Girls State," *Greensboro Daily News*, June 3, 1979, B6; "Tar Heel Girls State Opens Here Sunday," June 12, 1981, B1.

79. Crenshaw, "Demarginalizing the Intersection."

80. Bryan Haislip, "North Carolina's First Negro Jurist Has Originality," *Gastonia Gazette* and *Robesonian*, October 27, 1971.

81. Farrington, *Black Republicans*, 189; Goldman, *Picking Federal Judges*, 223–24.

82. Goldman, *Picking Federal Judges*, 223–24; "Alexander Out of Judge Picture?," *Greensboro Record*, January 27, 1972, and "Appointment Politics and Judge Alexander," *Greensboro Record*, January 12, 1972, both in box 3, folder 8, Alexander Collection.

83. Goldman, *Picking Federal Judges*, 223–24; "Why Should Longevity Enter into It?," *Greensboro Record*, February 2, 1972, A14; Ned Cline, "Mrs. Alexander a Top Prospect for Judge Seat," *Greensboro Daily News*, January 7, 1972, B1; Steve Berry, "GOP Rates Osteen, Ward, Gavin Top Judge Choices," *Greensboro Daily News*, February 6, 1972, A1.

84. Molly Sinclair, "An Idea Whose Time Had Come: The Judge That Won without a Campaign," *Miami Herald*, April 22, 1972, 5B.

85. Alexander interview, December 4, 1977.

86. Ibid.

87. Alexander interview, January 22, 1978, box 5, folder 15, Alexander Collection.

88. Alexander-Ralston interview, 85.

Chapter 6. Attempting the Impossible

1. Alexander interview, July 13, 1977, box 5, folder 11, Alexander Collection.
2. Brent Hackney, "Best Candidate Doesn't Always Win," *Salisbury Post*, May 12, 1974, box 3, folder 10, Alexander Collection.
3. Campaign materials, box 5, folder 16, Alexander Collection. This document appears in a newsletter, presumably released by the Alexander campaign, under the heading "Judge Alexander Runs for Chief Justice Post," and was reprinted with the permission of the *Carolina Times*.
4. *Greensboro Record*, February 25, 1974, box 2, folder 1, Alexander Collection.
5. Hayes, *Without Precedent*, 2.
6. Campaign materials, box 5, folder 16, Alexander Collection.
7. Hayes, *Without Precedent*, 351.
8. Alexander correspondence with Thomas Bennett, January 1974, box 2, folder 1, Alexander Collection.
9. Hayes, *Without Precedent*, 504n65; Rip Woodin, "Newcomb Victory Revives Judicial Standards Issue," *Greensboro Daily News*, May 19, 1974, A1.
10. Hayes, *Without Precedent*, 348.
11. Memo between North Carolina Democratic Party workers, folder 326, Susie Sharp Papers. The Evelyn mentioned in the memo is likely Evelyn Crutchfield, who in 1974 ran for Guilford County commissioner as a Republican. "6 in Republican Primary," *High Point Enterprise*, May 5, 1974, C1.
12. "Newcomb Seeks Office Higher Court," box 3, folder 10, Alexander Collection; Jack Scism, "Judge Alexander Joins Race," *Greensboro Daily News*, February 26, 1974, A1. Newcomb's filing was reported on February 27, 1974, a couple of days after Alexander made her announcement.
13. Hayes, *Without Precedent*, 198.
14. Ibid., 349.
15. Ibid., 351.
16. Spruill, *Divided We Stand*, 112–13.
17. Black and Black, *Rise of Southern Republicans*, 103.
18. Bullock and Rozell, *New Politics of the Old South*, 142–45; Eamon, *Making of a Southern Democracy*.
19. Black and Black, *Rise of Southern Republicans*, 210.
20. Schoen, *Nixon Effect*, 91, 100.
21. Rigueur, *Loneliness of the Black Republican*, 137.
22. Ibid., 138.
23. Ibid., 139.
24. Ibid., 174.
25. Farrington, *Black Republicans*, 140.
26. Jim Schlosser, "'Judge A' Paved Way—With Style," *Greensboro News and Record*, March 15, 1998, A1.
27. Farrington, *Black Republicans*, introduction, 189.

28. Rigueur, *Loneliness of the Black Republican*, 175.
29. Ibid., 5, 178.
30. Thurber, *Republicans and Race*, 252.
31. Alexander interview, December 4, 1977, box 5, folder 14, Alexander Collection; Walton, *Black Republicans*, 165–66.
32. Kimberly J. McLarin, "High Court Strikes Down 'Closed' Party Primaries," *Greensboro News and Record*, December 11, 1986, A1.
33. Hayes, *Without Precedent*, 350.
34. Harry Stapleton, "Newcomb Sees Victory in N.C. Justice Race," *Greensboro Daily News*, May 13, 1974, B1.
35. Schoen, *Nixon Effect*, 101.
36. Robert B. Cullen, "State Judicial Reform Dead This Year?," *Greensboro Record*, May 14, 1975, A19; Lake interview.
37. Fine et al., "(In)Secure Times."
38. Esty, "North Carolina Republicans."
39. Hayes, *Without Precedent*, 505n81.
40. Ibid., 350–51.
41. *Asheville Citizen-Times*, April 11, 1974, and other newspaper clippings, box 2, folder 1, Alexander Collection.
42. Campaign materials, box 5, folder 16, Alexander Collection.
43. Hayes, *Without Precedent*, 334; North Carolina Constitution, Article IV, section 8.
44. "Judges Recommended," *Greensboro Daily News*, May 5, 1974, D4; newspaper clippings, box 3, folder 10, Alexander Collection.
45. Quoted in Hayes, *Without Precedent*, 353–54n102.
46. Rip Woodin, "Only GOP Court Primary Is for Chief Justice," Rockingham edition of *Greensboro Daily News*, April 30, 1974, B1.
47. "Legal Novice Beats Judge," unidentified newspaper, May 8, 1974, and other newspaper clippings, box 3, folder 10, Alexander Collection.
48. Hayes, *Without Precedent*, 354.
49. Ibid., 355.
50. Ibid., 354.
51. Mercer, "Black Hair/Style Politics"; Roberts, *Pageants, Parlors, and Pretty Women*, 4.
52. Box 2, folder 1, Alexander Collection.
53. Correspondence from Beth Riddle, June 4, 1974, box 2, folder 1, Alexander Collection. In her letter, Riddle described herself as a "white housewife in her 30s."
54. Box 2, folder 1, Alexander Collection.
55. Conversation with Edmisten.
56. Hackney, "Best Candidate Doesn't Always Win."
57. "Disavowing Newcomb," *Winston-Salem Journal*, May 16, 1974, 4.
58. Ibid.

59. Wayne Woodlief, "Helms Won't Endorse Newcomb Bid," *Raleigh News and Observer*, May 13, 1974, box 3, folder 10, Alexander Collection.
60. "GOP Leaders Shun Court Nominee," *Raleigh News and Observer*, May 14, 1974, box 3, folder 10, Alexander Collection.
61. Ibid.
62. Speckhard interview.
63. Hayes, *Without Precedent*, 302.
64. Harry Stapleton, "Newcomb Sees Victory in N.C. Justice Race," *Greensboro Daily News*, May 13, 1974, B1.
65. Eamon, *Making of a Southern Democracy*, 163.
66. Christensen, *Paradox of Tar Heel Politics*, 289.
67. Hayes, *Without Precedent*, 356–57.
68. Ibid., 353.
69. Ibid., 365–66.
70. Ibid., 508n163.
71. Ibid., 380.
72. Ibid., 381.
73. Ibid., 385.
74. *Fowler v. North Carolina*, 428 U.S. 904 (1976).
75. The full text of the Benoy-Marshall exchange can be found in Mandery, *Wild Justice*, 327–28.
76. Bill Rhodes Weaver, "District Judge Finds 'Negress' Offensive," *Greensboro Daily News*, April 24, 1975, B1.
77. Correspondence from Reginald L. Frazier, April 30, 1975, box 2, folder 2, Alexander Collection.
78. Conversation with Edmisten.
79. Correspondence with Marian Rees, September 8, 1975, box 2, folder 2, Alexander Collection.
80. Alexander interview, January 22, 1978, box 5, folder 15, Alexander Collection.
81. Ibid.
82. Ibid.
83. Alexander interview, January 22, 1978.
84. Ibid.
85. Conversation with Pell.
86. Joe McNulty, "Ten Democrats Competing for Seats on Bench," *Greensboro Daily News*, August 1, 1976, D2.
87. Rick Stewart, "Judges Want Subpoenas Dismissed against Them," *Greensboro Record*, September 26, 1977, B1; Stan Swofford, "Hopscotch Pot Case Probe Set," *Greensboro Daily News*, September 3, 1977, B1.
88. Stewart, "Judges Want Subpoenas Dismissed"; Swofford, "Hopscotch Pot Case."
89. Stewart, "Judges Want Subpoenas Dismissed"; Stan Swofford, "Judges Say Subpoenas Mock Justice," *Greensboro Daily News*, September 27, 1977, A1.

90. Alexander interview, July 13, 1977, box 5, folder 11, Alexander Collection.
91. "Joseph P. Shore Is Sworn In as Clerk Here," *Greensboro Daily News*, December 2, 1932, 18.
92. Alexander interview, November 6, 1977.
93. Conversation with Bailey; Rick Stewart and Rosemary Yardley, "Judge Facing State Scrutiny?," *Greensboro Record*, October 21, 1977, A1.
94. Rick Stewart, "Alexander Says Judicial Panel Has Cleared Her," *Greensboro Record*, December 1, 1977, box 3, folder 13, Alexander Collection.
95. John Lowe, "Judge Claims Exoneration in Raulston Trial Incident," *High Point Enterprise*, November 30, 1977, box 3, folder 13, Alexander Collection.
96. R. T. Carter, "Racism and Psychological and Emotional Injury."
97. "Courtroom Politics," *Greensboro Record*, May 4, 1978, A12.
98. A Guide to the Microfilm Edition of Civil Rights during the Carter Administration, 1977–1981, part 1: Papers of the Special Assistant for Black Affairs, section B, reel 14, 0637, box 49, Judgeships [2], 1978–1979, Papers of Louis Martin, Jimmy Carter Presidential Library and Museum, Atlanta, Ga.
99. Rick Stewart, "Appeals Court List Could Change," *Greensboro Record*, March 7, 1979, B2.
100. Ibid.
101. Greta Tilley, "Judge Alexander at 60: Certain of Who She Is, Why She's Here," *Greensboro Record*, August 20, 1979, A1.
102. Ibid.
103. "Judge Alexander-Ralston Announces Re-Election Bid," *Greensboro Daily News*, October 16, 1979, B1.
104. Jack Scism, "Four Die in Klan-Leftist Shootout," *Greensboro Daily News*, November 4, 1979, A1. Four CWP members died at the scene, and a fifth died two days later of his injuries.
105. Lindsey Gruson, "CWP Chief Wins Two, Loses One," *Greensboro Daily News*, August 8, 1980, D1; "CWP Leader Is Acquitted," *Greensboro Daily News*, September 27, 1980, A14; Winston Cavin, "Judge Delays Sentencing," *Greensboro Daily News*, October 7, 1980; "Two Fined for Council Disruption," *Greensboro Daily News*, December 5, 1980, B4; Waller, *Love and Revolution*, 319.
106. Ecclesiastes 3:1–2, King James Version.
107. Rick Stewart and Greta Tilley, "Judge Alexander-Ralston Planning to Retire April 1," *Greensboro Record*, January 16, 1981, A1. This article erroneously stated that Judge Alexander retired eight years before she was required to, but the mandatory retirement age was seventy-two.

Conclusion

1. Alexander interview, July 13, 1977, box 5, folder 11, Alexander Collection.
2. Speckhard interview. The law firm they created is still named Alexander-Ralston, Speckhard and Speckhard.

3. Speckhard interview.

4. Andy Duncan, "Judge A," *Greensboro News and Record*, May 22, 1988, G1.

5. Speckhard interview.

6. Ibid.

7. Jim Schlosser and Virginia Demaree, "Patients' Violence Hard to Predict," *Greensboro News and Record*, October 13, 1990, https://greensboro.com/patients-violence-hard-to-predict/article_11966a2d-a466-5e98-8320-73c6466b3d0e.html.

8. Jim Schlosser, "Ex-Judge's Son Charged in Death," *Greensboro News and Record*, October 8, 1990, https://greensboro.com/ex-judges-son-charged-in-death/article_ddfa10c3-b3d9-5d69-9c72-e6da671052b8.html; Anubha Anand, "For Killing His Caretaker, Mentally Ill Man Guilty of Murder," *Greensboro News and Record*, June 15, 1994, BH2; Anubha Anand, "Mentally Ill Man Sent to Prison," *Greensboro News and Record*, June 13, 1994, https://greensboro.com/mentally-ill-man-sent-to-prison/article_8d24c707-51a9-5e52-a159-ab8d7a4d0e35.html; Speckhard interview; Ancestry.com, North Carolina, Death Indexes, 1908–2004.

9. Anita McDivitt, "Pioneer 'Judge A' Retires from Law," *Greensboro News and Record*, July 8, 1995, B1.

10. Speckhard interview.

11. Ibid.

12. Ibid.

13. Ibid.

14. Jim Schlosser, "'Judge A' Paved Way—With Style," *Greensboro News and Record*, March 15, 1998, A1.

15. Anecdotal evidence based on informal conversations with various community members.

16. *African-American Female Pioneers in Search of Justice and Equality*, video, 1990, produced by the North Carolina Association of Black Lawyers, in North Carolina Collection, Wilson Library, University of North Carolina, Chapel Hill.

17. Conversation with Pell.

18. Conversation with Bethea-Shields.

19. Timmons-Goodson's remarks to the Greensboro Bar Association, February 17, 2011 http://nealrobbins.com/greensboro/wp-content/uploads/2011/03/Justice-T-G-GBA-Address.pdf (accessed May 3, 2011).

20. Conversation with Beasley.

21. "Clayton, Eva M.," History, Art, and Archives: U.S. House of Representatives, http://history.house.gov/People/Detail/11065 (accessed August 14, 2017).

22. Kathleen Ronayne, "Harris Pays Tribute to Black Women in 1st Speech as VP-Elect," *Associated Press*, November 7, 2020.

23. Remarks by Andrea C. Saavedra, "The Extraordinary Life and Legacy of the Honorable Elreta Alexander '45," Alumni of Color Virtual Event, Columbia Law School, December 9, 2020.

24. Conversation with Bethea-Shields.

25. Alexander interview, November 6, 1977.
26. Timmons-Goodson, "Darlin', the Truth Will Set You Free."
27. Conversation with Pell.
28. Timmons-Goodson, "Darlin', the Truth Will Set You Free," 174.

BIBLIOGRAPHY

Manuscript Collections

Elreta Alexander Collection. MSS 223, Martha Blakeney Hodges Special Collections and University Archives, University Libraries, University of North Carolina, Greensboro.
Rare Books and Manuscripts, Butler Library, Columbia University, New York.
Register. University Archives, F. D. Bluford Library, North Carolina Agricultural and Technical State University, Greensboro.
Supreme Court Original Cases, Fall 1967. State Archives of North Carolina, North Carolina Department of Natural and Cultural Resources, Raleigh.
Susie Sharp Papers. Collection no. 04898, Southern Historical Collection at the Louis Round Wilson Special Collections Library, University of North Carolina, Chapel Hill.

Interviews and Conversations

Alexander-Ralston, Judge Elreta. Interview by Anna Barbara Perez, February 18 and March 4, 1993. Interview no. J-0018, Southern Oral History Program Collection no. 4007, Southern Historical Collection, Wilson Library, University of North Carolina, Chapel Hill.
Bailey, F. Lee. Conversation with Virginia L. Summey, March 14, 2017. Notes in possession of the author.
Beasley, Cheri. Conversation with Virginia L. Summey, March 17, 2020. Notes in possession of the author.
Bethea-Shields, Karen. Conversation with Virginia L. Summey, May 26, 2017. Notes in possession of the author.
Edmisten, Rufus. Conversation with Virginia L. Summey, April 26, 2017. Notes in possession of the author.
Frye, Henry. Interview by Virginia L. Summey, July 22, 2011. Notes in possession of the author.
Lake, I. Beverly, Sr. Interview by Charles Dunn, September 8, 1987. Interview no. C-0043, Southern Oral History Program Collection no. 4007, Southern Historical Collection, Wilson Library, University of North Carolina, Chapel Hill.

Motley, Constance Baker. Interview by Kitty Gellhorn, 1978. Interview no. NXCP88-A910, Rare Book and Manuscript Library, Butler Library, Columbia University, New York.
Pell, Gerald. Conversation with Virginia L. Summey, May 29, 2014. Notes in possession of the author.
Simkins, George. Interview by Karen Kruse Thomas, April 6, 1997. Interview no. R-0018, Southern Oral History Program Collection no. 4007, Southern Historical Collection, Wilson Library, University of North Carolina, Chapel Hill.
Speckhard, Donald. Interview by Virginia L. Summey, July 29, 2011. Notes in possession of the author.
Timmons-Goodson, Patricia. Interview by Virginia L. Summey, July 28, 2011. Notes in possession of the author.

Books, Articles, and Dissertations

Abramovitz, Mimi. *Regulating the Lives of Women: Social Welfare Policy from Colonial Times to the Present.* Abingdon, England: Routledge, 2018, 238–65.
Alexander, Eleanor. *Lyrics of Sunshine and Shadow: The Tragic Courtship and Marriage of Paul Laurence Dunbar and Alice Ruth Moore.* New York: New York University Press, 2001.
Alexander, Elreta Melton. "A Student's Plan for Peace," April 1944. Arthur W. Diamond Law Library, Columbia University, New York.
———. *When Is a Man Free?* Philadelphia, Pa.: Dorrance, 1967.
Alrige, Derrick P. "Guiding Philosophical Principles for a Du Boisian-Based African American Educational Model." *Journal of Negro Education* 68, no. 2 (Spring 1999): 182–99.
Anderson, James D. *The Education of Blacks in the South.* Chapel Hill: University of North Carolina Press, 1988.
Bailey, Beth L. *From Front Porch to Back Seat: Courtship in Twentieth-Century America.* Baltimore, Md.: Johns Hopkins University Press, 1988.
Banks, Ingrid. *Hair Matters: Beauty, Power, and Black Women's Consciousness.* New York: New York University Press, 2000.
Barnett, Pamela E. *Dangerous Desire: Literature of Sexual Freedom and Sexual Violence since the Sixties.* London: Routledge, 2004.
Batchelor, John E. *The Guilford County Schools: A History.* Winston-Salem, N.C.: John F. Blair, 1991.
———. *Race and Education in North Carolina: From Segregation to Desegregation.* Baton Rouge: Louisiana State University Press, 2015.
Benokraitis, Nijole, and Joyce A. Griffin-Keene. "Prejudice and Jury Selection." *Journal of Black Studies* 12, no. 4 (June 1982): 427–49.
Berebitsky, Julie. *Sex and the Office: A History of Gender, Power, and Desire.* New Haven, Conn.: Yale University Press, 2012.
Berrey, Stephen A. *The Jim Crow Routine: Everyday Performances of Race, Civil*

Rights, and Segregation in Mississippi. Chapel Hill: University of North Carolina Press, 2015.

Black, Earl, and Merle Black. *The Rise of Southern Republicans*. Cambridge, Mass.: Belknap, 2002.

Blomberg, Thomas G., and Karol Lucken. *American Penology: A History of Control*. New York: Aldine de Gruyter, 2000.

Boyd, Michelle. *Jim Crow Nostalgia: Reconstructing Race in Bronzeville*. Minneapolis: University of Minnesota Press, 2008.

Brown, Linda Beatrice. *Belles of Liberty: Gender, Bennett College, and the Civil Rights Movement in Greensboro, North Carolina*. Greensboro, N.C.: Women and Wisdom Press, 2013.

Brownmiller, Susan. *Against Our Will: Men, Women, and Rape*. New York: Simon and Schuster, 1975.

Bullock, Charles S., III, and Mark J. Rozell. *The New Politics of the Old South: An Introduction to Southern Politics*. Lanham, Md.: Rowman and Littlefield, 1998.

Burke, William Lewis. *All for Civil Rights: African American Lawyers in South Carolina, 1868–1968*. Athens: University of Georgia Press, 2017.

Cahn, Susan K. *Sexual Reckonings: Southern Girls in a Troubled Age*. Cambridge, Mass.: Harvard University Press, 2007.

Carter, Patricia Ann. *Everybody's Paid but the Teacher: The Teaching Profession and the Women's Movement*. New York: Teachers College Press, 2002.

Carter, Robert T. "Racism and Psychological and Emotional Injury: Recognizing and Assessing Race-Based Traumatic Stress." *Counseling Psychologist* 35, no. 1 (January 2007): 13–105.

Chafe, William H. *Civilities and Civil Rights: Greensboro, North Carolina, and the Black Struggle for Freedom*. New York: Oxford University Press, 1980.

Chambers, Veronica. *Having It All? Black Women and Success*. New York: Doubleday, 2003.

Charron, Katherine Mellen. *Freedom's Teacher: The Life of Septima Clark*. Chapel Hill: University of North Carolina Press, 2009.

Christensen, Rob. *The Paradox of Tar Heel Politics: The Personalities, Elections, and Events That Shaped Modern North Carolina*. Chapel Hill: University of North Carolina Press, 2008.

Clegg, Claude A. *Troubled Ground: A Tale of Murder, Lynching, and Reckoning in the New South*. Urbana: University of Illinois Press, 2010.

Collier-Thomas, Bettye, and James Turner. "Race, Class, and Color: The African American Disclosure on Identity." *Journal of American Ethnic History* 14, no. 1 (Fall 1994): 5–31.

Collins, Patricia Hill. "The Social Construction of Black Feminist Thought." In *The Black Feminist Reader*, edited by Joy James and T. Denean Sharpley-Whiting. Malden, Mass.: Blackwell, 2000, 183–207.

Cooper, Brittney C. "The Problems and Possibilities of the Negro Woman Intellectual."

In Cooper, *Beyond Respectability: The Intellectual Thought of Race Women*. Champaign: University of Illinois Press, 2017, 115–40.

Corriero, Michael A. *Judging Children as Children: A Proposal for a Juvenile Justice System*. Philadelphia, Pa.: Temple University Press, 2006.

Covington, Howard E., Jr. *Henry Frye: North Carolina's First African American Chief Justice*. Jefferson, N.C.: McFarland, 2013.

Crenshaw, Kimberlé. "Demarginalizing the Intersection of Race and Sex: A Black Feminist Critique of Antidiscrimination Doctrine, Feminist Theory and Antiracist Politics." In *The Black Feminist Reader*, edited by Joy James and T. Denean Sharpley-Whiting. Malden, Mass.: Blackwell, 2000, 208–38.

———. "Whose Story Is It Anyway: Feminist and Antiracist Appropriations of Anita Hill." In *Applications of Feminist Legal Theory*, edited by D. Kelly Weisberg. Philadelphia: Temple University Press, 1996, 826–44.

Crespino, Joseph. *Strom Thurmond's America*. New York: Hill and Wang, 2012.

Cunningham, David. *Klansville, U.S.A.: The Rise and Fall of the Civil Rights–Era Ku Klux Klan*. New York: Oxford University Press, 2013.

Curwood, Anastasia C. *Stormy Weather: Middle-Class African American Marriages between the Two World Wars*. Chapel Hill: University of North Carolina Press, 2010.

Davis, Abraham L. "The Role of Black Colleges and Black Law Schools in the Training of Black Lawyers and Judges." *Journal of Negro History* 70, nos. 1–2 (Winter-Spring 1985): 24–34.

Dorr, Lisa Lindquist. *White Women, Rape, and the Power of Race in Virginia, 1900–1960*. Chapel Hill: University of North Carolina Press, 2004.

Du Bois, W. E. B. "The Talented Tenth." In *The Negro Problem: A Series of Articles by Representative American Negroes of Today*. New York: James Pott, 1903.

DuRocher, Kristina. *Raising Racists: The Socialization of White Children in the Jim Crow South*. Lexington: University of Kentucky Press, 2011.

Eamon, Tom. *The Making of a Southern Democracy: North Carolina Politics from Kerr Scott to Pat McCrory*. Chapel Hill: University of North Carolina Press, 2014.

Edmonds, Helen G. *The Negro and Fusion Politics in North Carolina, 1894–1901*. Chapel Hill: University of North Carolina Press, 1951.

Edmunds, Mary Lewis Rucker. *Recollections of Greensboro*. Greensboro, N.C.: Mary Lewis Rucker Edmunds, 1993.

Ehrenreich, Barbara. *The Hearts of Men: American Dreams and the Flight from Commitment*. New York: Anchor Press/Doubleday, 1983.

Ennis, Carolyn Grantham. *The Historical Heritage of First Missionary Baptist Church, 1866–2008*. Smithfield, N.C.: Carolyn Grantham Ennis.

Estin, Ann Luquer. "Golden Anniversary Reflections: Changes in Marriage after Fifty Years." *Family Law Quarterly* 42, no. 3 (Fall 2008): 333–52.

Esty, Amos. "North Carolina Republicans and the Conservative Revolution, 1964–1968." *North Carolina Historical Review* 82, no. 1 (January 2005): 1–32.

Faircloth, Adam. *Teaching Equality: Black Schools in the Age of Jim Crow*. Athens: University of Georgia Press, 2001.
"Fair Jury Selection Procedures." *Yale Law Journal* 75, no. 2 (December 1965): 322–34.
Farrington, Joshua D. *Black Republicans and the Transformation of the GOP*. Philadelphia: University of Pennsylvania Press, 2016.
Feld, Barry C. *Bad Kids: Race and the Transformation of the Juvenile Court*. New York: Oxford University Press, 1999.
Fine, Michelle, Lois Weis, Judi Addleston, and Julia Marusza. "(In)Secure Times: Constructing White Working-Class Masculinities in the Late 20th Century." *Gender and Society* 11, no. 1 (February 1997): 52–68.
Floyd, Silas Xavier. *Floyd's Flowers; or, Duty and Beauty for Colored Children*. Atlanta, Ga.: Hertel, Jenkins, 1905.
Ford, Tanisha C. "Harlem's 'Natural Soul': Selling Black Beauty to the Diaspora in the Early 1960s." In Ford, *Liberated Threads: Black Women, Style, and the Global Politics of Soul*. Chapel Hill: University of North Carolina Press, 2015, 41–66.
Franklin, John Hope. *The Free Negro in North Carolina, 1790–1860*. Chapel Hill: University of North Carolina Press, 1995.
Franklin, John Hope, and Genna Rae McNeil. *African Americans and the Living Constitution*. Washington, D.C.: Smithsonian Institution Press, 1995.
Frazier, E. Franklin. *Black Bourgeoisie*. Glencoe, Ill.: Falcon's Wing, 1957.
———. *The Negro Church in America*. New York: Schocken, 1964.
Friedman, Dan, and Lois Holzman. "Performing the World: The Emergence of Performance Activism." In *Performance Studies in Motion: International Perspectives and Practices in the Twenty-First Century*, edited by Atay Citory et al. London: Bloomsbury, 2014, 276–87.
Fukurai, Hiroshi, and Richard Krooth. *Race in the Jury Box: Affirmative Action in Jury Selection*. Albany: State University of New York Press, 2003.
Gaines, Kevin. *Uplifting the Race: Black Leadership, Politics, and Culture in the Twentieth Century*. Chapel Hill: University of North Carolina Press, 1996.
Geary, Daniel. *Beyond Civil Rights: The Moynihan Report and Its Legacy*. Philadelphia: University of Pennsylvania Press, 2015.
Gelles, Richard J. "Violence in the Family: A Review of Research in the Seventies." *Journal of Marriage and Family* 42, no. 4 (November 1980): 873–85.
Gibbs, Warmoth T. *History of the North Carolina Agricultural and Technical College*. Dubuque, Iowa: William C. Brown, 1966.
Gilmore, Glenda. *Gender and Jim Crow: Women and the Politics of White Supremacy in North Carolina, 1896–1920*. Chapel Hill: University of North Carolina Press, 1996.
Goebel, Julius, Jr. *A History of the School of Law: Columbia University*. New York: Columbia University Press, 1955.

Goldman, Sheldon. *Picking Federal Judges: Lower Court Selection from Roosevelt through Reagan*. New Haven, Conn.: Yale University Press, 1997.

Goldstein, Eric L. *The Price of Whiteness: Jews, Race, and American Identity*. Princeton, N.J.: Princeton University Press, 2006.

Gordon, Linda. *Heroes of Their Own Lives: The Politics and History of Family Violence, Boston, 1880–1960*. New York: Viking, 1988.

Greenberg, Jack. *Race Relations and American Law*. New York: Columbia University Press, 1959.

Hale, Grace Elizabeth. *Making Whiteness: The Culture of Segregation in the South, 1890–1940*. New York: Vintage, 1998.

Hall, Jacquelyn Dowd. "The Mind That Burns in Each Body: Women, Rape, and Racial Violence." *Southern Exposure* 12, no. 6 (November–December 1984): 61–71.

Hayes, Anna R. *Without Precedent: The Life of Susie Marshall Sharp*. Chapel Hill: University of North Carolina Press, 2008.

Heinegg, Paul. *Free African Americans of North Carolina, Virginia, and South Carolina from the Colonial Period to about 1820*, vol. 2. Baltimore, Md.: Clearfield Company by Genealogical Publishing, 2005.

Higginbotham, Evelyn. *Righteous Discontent: The Women's Movement in the Black Baptist Church, 1880–1920*. Cambridge, Mass.: Harvard University Press, 1993.

Hine, Darlene Clark. "Rape and the Inner Lives of Black Women in the Middle West." *Signs* 14, no. 4 (Summer 1989): 912–20.

Hobbs, Allyson Vanessa. *A Chosen Exile: A History of Racial Passing in American Life*. Cambridge, Mass.: Harvard University Press, 2014.

Hodes, Martha. *White Women, Black Men: Illicit Sex in the Nineteenth-Century South*. New Haven, Conn.: Yale University Press, 1997.

Holland, Joseph H. *From Harlem with Love: An Ivy Leaguer's Inner City Odyssey: A Memoir*. New York: Lantern, 2012.

Houck, Davis W., and David E. Dixon, eds. *Women and the Civil Rights Movement, 1954–1965*. Jackson: University Press of Mississippi, 2009.

Jackson, Donald Dale. *Judges: An Inside View of the Agonies and Excesses of an American Elite*. New York: Atheneum, 1974.

Jackson, Shirley A. "I've Got All My Sisters with Me: Black Women's Organizations in the Twenty-First Century." In *Black Greek-Letter Organizations in the Twenty-First Century: Our Fight Has Just Begun*, edited by Gregory S. Parks. Lexington: University of Kentucky Press, 2008, 233–50.

Jenkins, Clara. "A Historical Study of Shaw University, 1865–1963." Ed.D. diss., University of Pittsburgh, 1965.

Johnson, E. Patrick. *Appropriating Blackness: Performance and the Politics of Authenticity*. Durham, N.C.: Duke University Press, 2003.

Jones, Jacqueline. *Labor of Love, Labor of Sorrow: Black Women, Work, and the Family from Slavery to the Present*. New York: Basic, 2010.

Kelley, Robin D. G. *Race Rebels: Culture, Politics, and the Black Working Class.* New York: Free Press, 1994.
Key, V. O. *Southern Politics in State and Nation.* 1949; repr., Knoxville: University of Tennessee Press, 1984.
Knupfer, Anne Meis. *Reform and Resistance: Gender, Delinquency, and America's First Juvenile Court.* London: Routledge, 2001.
Konradi, Amanda. *Taking the Stand: Rape Survivors and the Prosecution of Rapists.* Westport, Conn.: Praeger, 2007.
Lamson, Peggy. *Few Are Chosen: American Women in Political Life Today.* Boston: Houghton Mifflin, 1968.
Levy, Alan H. *The Political Life of Bella Abzug, 1920-1976: Political Passions, Women's Rights, and Congressional Battles.* Lanham, Md.: Lexington, 2013.
Lincoln, C. Eric, and Lawrence H. Mamiya. *The Black Church in the African-American Experience.* Durham, N.C.: Duke University Press, 1990.
Loevy, Robert D., ed. *The Civil Rights Act of 1964: The Passage of the Law That Ended Racial Segregation.* Albany: State University of New York Press, 1997.
Lyman, Darryl. *Great African-American Women.* New York: Gramercy, 1999.
MacKinnon, Catharine A. *Women's Lives, Men's Laws.* Cambridge, Mass.: Belknap, 2005.
Mandery, Evan J. *A Wild Justice: The Death and Resurrection of Capital Punishment in America.* New York: Norton, 2013.
Marable, Manning. *Race, Reform, and Rebellion: The Second Reconstruction in Black America, 1945-1990.* Jackson: University Press of Mississippi, 1991.
McLeod, Jacqueline A. *Daughter of the Empire State: The Life of Judge Jane Bolin.* Urbana: University of Illinois Press, 2011.
Mercer, Kobena. "Black Hair/Style Politics." *New Formations* 1, no. 3 (Winter 1987): 33-54.
Milteer, Warren Eugene, Jr. *North Carolina's Free People of Color, 1715-1885.* Baton Rouge: Louisiana State University Press, 2020.
Morello, Karen Berger. *The Invisible Bar: The Woman Lawyer in America, 1638 to the Present.* Boston: Beacon, 1986.
Morris, Norval. "The Contemporary Prison, 1965-Present." In *The Oxford History of the Prison: The Practice of Punishment in Western Society,* edited by Norval Morris and David J. Rothman. New York: Oxford University Press, 1995, 227-59.
Motley, Constance Baker. *Equal Justice under Law: An Autobiography.* New York: Farrar, Straus and Giroux, 1998.
Moynihan, Daniel P., and U.S. Department of Labor. *The Negro Family: The Case for National Action.* Washington, D.C.: Office of Policy Planning and Research, U.S. Department of Labor, 1965.
Nakonezny, Paul A., Robert D. Schull, and Joseph Lee Rodgers. "The Effect of No-Fault Law on the Divorce Rate across the 50 States and Its Relation to Income, Ed-

ucation, and Religiosity." *Journal of Family and Marriage* 57, no. 2 (May 1995): 477–88.

Norwood, Kimberly Jade, and Carla R. Monroe. "Thoughts on Bullying and Colorism in Black Women's Remembered Experiences." In *Race and Colorism in Education*, edited by Carla Monroe. New York: Routledge, 2016, 24–38.

Odem, Mary E. *Delinquent Daughters: Protecting and Policing Adolescent Female Sexuality in the United States, 1885–1920*. Chapel Hill: University of North Carolina Press, 1995.

Parker, Marjorie H. *The History of the Links, Incorporated*. Washington, D.C.: National Headquarters of the Links, 1982.

Perkins, Linda M. "'Bound to Them by a Common Sorrow': African American Women, Higher Education, and Collective Advancement." *Journal of African American History* 100, no. 4 (Fall 2015): 721–47.

Pye, David Kenneth. "Legal Subversives: African American Lawyers in the Jim Crow South." Ph.D. diss., University of California, San Diego, 2010.

Ransby, Barbara. *Ella Baker and the Black Freedom Movement: A Radical Democratic Vision*. Chapel Hill: University of North Carolina Press, 2003.

Rigueur, Leah Wright. *The Loneliness of the Black Republican: Pragmatic Politics and the Pursuit of Power*. Princeton, N.J.: Princeton University Press, 2015.

Ritterhouse, Jennifer. *Growing Up Jim Crow: How Black and White Southern Children Learned Race*. Chapel Hill: University of North Carolina Press, 2006.

Roberts, Blain. *Pageants, Parlors, and Pretty Women: Race and Beauty in the Twentieth-Century South*. Chapel Hill: University of North Carolina Press, 2014.

Rosen, Hannah. *Terror in the Heart of Freedom: Citizenship, Sexual Violence, and the Meaning of Race in the Post-Emancipation South*. Chapel Hill: University of North Carolina Press, 2009.

Rosen, Ruth. *The World Split Open: How the Modern Women's Movement Changed America*. New York: Penguin, 2000.

Ross, Daniel A. "Rethinking the Road to Gault: Limiting Social Control in the Juvenile Court." *Virginia Law Review* 98, no. 2 (April 2012): 425–77.

Rothstein, Richard. *The Color of Law: A Forgotten History of How Our Government Segregated America*. New York: Liveright, 2017.

Sacks, Karen Brodkin. "How Did Jews Become White Folks?" In *Race*, edited by Steven Gregory and Roger Sanjek. New Brunswick, N.J.: Rutgers University Press, 1994, 78–102.

Sanders-McMurtry, Kijua, and Nia Woods Haydel. "Linking Friendship and Service Education and Philanthropy among the Black Elite, 1946–60." In *The Educational Work of Women's Organizations, 1890–1960*, edited by Anne Meis Knupfer and Christine A. Woyshner. New York: Palgrave Macmillan, 2008, 179–92.

Schechter, Susan. "The Roots of the Battered Women's Movement: Personal and Political." In *Applications of Feminist Legal Theory*, edited by D. Kelly Weisberg. Philadelphia: Temple University Press, 1996, 296–305.

———. *Women and Male Violence: The Visions and Struggles of the Battered Women's Movement*. Boston: South End, 1982.

Schlossman, Steven L. *Love and the American Delinquent: The Theory and Practice of "Progressive" Juvenile Justice, 1825–1920*. Chicago, Ill.: University of Chicago Press, 1977.

Schoen, Douglas E. *The Nixon Effect: How Richard Nixon's Presidency Fundamentally Changed American Politics*. New York: Encounter, 2016.

Sernett, Milton C., ed. *African American Religious History: A Documentary Witness*. Durham, N.C.: Duke University Press, 1999.

Shaw, Stephanie J. *What a Woman Ought to Be and to Do: Black Professional Women Workers during the Jim Crow Era*. Chicago, Ill.: University of Chicago Press, 1996.

Smallwood, Arwin D. "A History of Native American and African Relations from 1502 to 1900." *Negro History Bulletin* 62, nos. 2–3 (April–September 1999): 18–31.

———. "A Walk into Greensboro's Past: Warnersville, 1865 to the Present." Presentation at the Greensboro Historical Museum, Greensboro, N.C., October 18, 2015.

Smith, David Barton. *Health Care Divided: Race and Healing a Nation*. Ann Arbor: University of Michigan Press, 1999.

Spruill, Marjorie J. *Divided We Stand: The Battle over Women's Rights and Family Values That Polarized American Politics*. New York: Bloomsbury, 2017.

Summers, Martin. "Diagnosing the Ailments of Black Citizenship: African American Physicians and the Politics of Mental Illness, 1895–1940." In *Precarious Prescriptions: Contested Histories of Race and Health in North America*, edited by Laurie B. Green, John McKiernan-Gonzales, and Martin Summers. Minneapolis: University of Minnesota Press, 2014, 91–114.

Summey, Virginia. "Redefining Activism: Judge Elreta Alexander Ralston and Civil Rights Advocacy in the New South." *North Carolina Historical Review* 90, no. 3 (July 2013): 237–58.

Teague, Sanford, and Celia Teague. "Happy Plains School." 2006. Unpublished paper in Alexander County Library, Taylorsville, N.C.

Thomas, Tracy A., and Tracey Jean Boisseau, eds. *Feminist Legal History: Essays on Women and Law*. New York: New York University Press, 2011.

Thompson, Heather Ann. "Why Mass Incarceration Matters: Rethinking Crisis, Decline, and Transformation in Postwar American History." *Journal of American History* 97, no. 3 (December 2010): 703–34.

Thuesen, Sarah Caroline. Greater than Equal: African American Struggles for Schools and Citizenship in North Carolina, 1919–1965. Chapel Hill: University of North Carolina Press, 2013.

Thurber, Timothy N. *Republicans and Race: The GOP's Frayed Relationship with African Americans, 1945–1974*. Lawrence: University Press of Kansas, 2013.

Timmons-Goodson, Patricia. "Darlin', the Truth Will Set You Free: A Tribute to Judge Elreta Melton Alexander." *Elon Law Review* 4, no. 1 (2012): 151–74.

Usher, Jess. "The Golfers: African American Golfers of the North Carolina Piedmont and the Struggle for Access." *North Carolina Historical Review* 87, no. 2 (April 2010): 158–93.

Walker, Anders. "New Takes on Jim Crow: A Review of Recent Scholarship." *Law and History Review* 36, no. 1 (February 2018): 173–79.

Walker, Susannah. *Style and Status: Selling Beauty to African American Women, 1920–1975*. Lexington: University of Kentucky Press, 2007.

Waller, Signe. *Love and Revolution: A Political Memoir: People's History of the Greensboro Massacre, Its Setting and Aftermath*. Lanham, Md.: Rowman and Littlefield, 2002.

Walton, Hanes, Jr. *Black Republicans: The Politics of the Black and Tans*. Metuchen, N.J.: Scarecrow, 1975.

Weitz, Rose. "Women and Their Hair: Seeking Power through Resistance and Accommodation." *Gender and Society* 15, no. 5 (October 2001): 667–86.

White, Deborah Gray. *Ar'n't I a Woman? Female Slaves in the Plantation South*. New York: Norton, 1999.

———. *Too Heavy a Load: Black Women in Defense of Themselves, 1894–1994*. New York: Norton, 1999.

Wilmore, Gayraud S. *Black Religion and Black Radicalism: An Interpretation of the Religious History of African Americans*. Maryknoll, N.Y.: Orbis, 1998.

INDEX

Abzug, Bella, 37
agitprop drama, 48
Alexander, Elreta Melton, 78–93, 143–50; burn injuries of, 43, 81, 86; at Columbia Law School, 34, 35–42, 81, 148; as commencement speaker, 113; death of, 146; as district court judge, 77, 102–11, 115–18, 136–37; divorce of, 78–81, 92–93; early life of, 12–34; father of (see Melton, Joseph Cleveland); grandparents of, 13; at Greensboro law firm, 77, 112, 143; on Greensboro Massacre trials, 142; at Harlem law firm, 43–45; international travel by, 90–91; on interracial marriage, 141; later years of, 145–46; as librarian, 33; marriage of, 2, 9–10, 31, 78–93; middle name of, 13; mother of, 1, 8, 13–20, 80, 88, 90; musical talent of, 18–19, 28; as N.C. Supreme Court candidate, 119–32; racial epithet used against, 134–35; Raulston scandal and, 136–39; as registered Republican, 100–102, 115–16; remarriage of, 140–41; retirement of, 142, 146; "A Student's Plan for Peace," 39; teaching career of, 2, 30; *When Is a Man Free?*, 7–8, 95–97, 113; wigs of, 112–13, 129
Alexander, Girardeau, III (son), 54, 85, 106; death of, 145; father's stabbing by, 116–17; mental illness of, 89–90, 97–98, 144–45
Alexander, Girardeau "Tony" (husband), 2, 9–10, 68; courtship of, 28–30; discrimination lawsuits of, 55–56; divorce of, 78–81, 92–93; hospital lawsuit of, 55–56, 88; later years of, 135–36; marriage of, 2, 9–10, 31, 78–93; medical education of, 30, 32; military service of, 37; parents of, 28–29, 36, 83; son's stabbing of, 116–17
Allen, Sylvia, 114

Alpha Kappa Alpha sorority, 27
Alpha Phi Alpha fraternity, 28
Alston, Ed, 77
American Baptist Home Mission Society, 14
American Nazi Party, 141
Amos, Donna, 137
Anderson, James, 22
anti-Semitism, 106
Avery, Margaret, 144

Badawi, Raouf, 135
Bailey, F. Lee, 138
Baker, Ella, 6, 37
Bearden, Romare, 42
Beasley, Cheri, 147–48
Bennett, Thomas, 121, 131
Bennett College, 7, 26, 46
Benoy, Jean A., 134–35
Berrey, Stephen A., 4, 49
Bethea-Shields, Karen Galloway, 147
Birth of a Nation (film), 60
Black, Earl, 100
Black, Merle, 100
Black Power movement, 113
Bluford, F. D., 15, 33
Bolin, Jane, 5
Brown, Charlotte Hawkins, 28
Brown, Linda Beatrice, 7
Brown v. Board of Education (1954), 16, 47, 48

Cannon, Ed, 46
Carolina Theatre (Greensboro), 18
Carson, William, 133
Carter, Jimmy, 140
Carter, Robert T., 139
Carver Federal Savings and Loan Association, 43–44

Chafe, William, 7, 8, 99–100
Chambers, Julius, 59
Charron, Katherine, 6
Cherry, Gregg, 45
Civil Rights Act (1964), 59, 100
Clark, Nerie, 82
Clark, Septima Poinsette, 6, 82
class, 13, 25; race and, 16–17, 60. *See also* respectability politics
Clayton, Eva, 148
Collins, Patricia Hill, 4
colorism, 8, 13, 129; at Columbia Law School, 40–41; at Dudley High School, 23–24
Columbia Law School, 2, 40–41, 148; sexual harassment at, 38; during World War II, 8–9, 36–37
Communist Workers Party (CWP), 141
Cook, Mary, 80
Cooper, Roy, 147
Cox, William Harold, 68
Crawford, Harold, 31
Crenshaw, Kimberlé, 4
Cross, Almon R., 72
Curwood, Anastasia C., 10, 89, 92

Darrow, Clarence, 52
Davis, Leroy, 58, 71
Delany, Hubert, 41–42
Delaware-Lackawanna Railroad case, 44
Democratic Party, 100–101, 125
Dent, Harry, 115
Dockerty, Janice, 58, 62
Dolley Madison Award, 114
domestic abuse, 83–87, 91–93
drug laws, 109, 111, 136–37
Du Bois, W. E. B., 16, 53
Dudley, James B., 21
Dudley High School (Greensboro), 21–24, 53
Dyer, Joe, 44

Eagles, Catherine, 145
Easley, Mike, 147
Edmisten, Rufus, 133, 135, 139
Ehrenreich, Barbara, 89

Farmer, James, 6
Farrington, Joshua D., 6
Federal Housing Administration (FHA), 95, 98

feminism, 4, 87, 92–93, 114. *See also* gender
Flood, Narcissus A., 13
Floyd, Silas Xavier, 80
Ford, Gerald, 133
Fourteenth Amendment to U.S. Constitution, 55, 64
Frazier, E. Franklin, 28
Frazier, Reginald L., 134
Frye, Henry, 103, 147

Gambill, Robert M., 63–64, 67; charges of bias against, 68; charges of jury tampering by, 72, 80
Garvey, Amy Jacques, 92
Gates Training School (Sunbury, N.C.), 31–32
Gault, Gerald, 110
Gavin, Robert, 125
gender: domestic abuse and, 83–88, 91–93; feminism and, 4, 87, 92–93; race and, 4–5, 66, 105, 114, 129–32; sexual mores and, 70–71
Georgia bar exam, 46
Gilmore, Glenda, 83
Girl Scouts, 16
Goldwater, Barry, 7, 101, 124
Grady-Truely, Walteen, 105
Great Dismal Swamp, N.C., 13–14
Greensboro Citizens Association, 47
Greensboro Massacre (1979), 141–42

Hairston, Julian, 71
Hale, Willie, 58, 71
Hall, John E., 129
Hamer, Fannie Lou, 6
Hampton, William, 46–47
Harris, Kamala, 148
Hatfield, John B., 110
Hayes, Anna, 129, 133
Hayes-Tilden Compromise (1877), 96
Hays, Paul R., 38–39
Hearst, Patricia, 138
Helms, Jesse, 123–24, 131
Herbin, Lonnie, 62–64, 69–70, 74–75, 76
High, Major S., 51
Hill-Burton Hospital Survey and Construction Act (1946), 55
Hine, Darlene Clark, 10, 79, 91
Holshouser, Jim, 131, 150

Houtz, A. W., 129–30
Hughes, John, 50
Hunt, Jim, 142
Hunter, Juanita, 22
Hurston, Zora Neale, 92

incarceration of African Americans, 109, 111
Ingram, Mack, 61
International Labour Organization, 39
intersectionality, 4–5, 94, 114

Jim Crow laws, 1, 4, 16–17, 96
Johnson, E. Patrick, 2
Johnson, Lyndon B., 59, 100
Johnson, Nelson, 141–42
Johnson, Walter E., Jr., 59, 80–81
Johnson, Yvonne, 148
Jones, Clayton, 59–60, 68, 72, 76
Jones, David Dallas, 18–19
Jordan, Welch, 47
Judgment Day program, 10, 94, 106–11, 137, 144, 147
jury selection process, 57, 59, 63, 65–67, 75
jury tampering, 72
justice, rehabilitative, 107–8
juvenile justice system. *See* Judgment Day program

Kelley, Robin D. G., 52
Kennedy, Robert F., 55
Key, V. O., 15
King, Coretta Scott, 53
King, Martin Luther, Jr., 115
Ku Klux Klan, 3, 99–100, 141–42
Kuykendall, Edward, 117

La Guardia, Fiorello, 5, 41–42
Lake, I. Beverly, 75, 126
Lathrop, Julia, 107
Lee, D. S., 61–62
Lee, George W., 101, 124
Lee, J. Kenneth, 51
Lee, Michael, 140
Lichty, Joseph, 55
Links (women's organization), 52–53, 58, 95, 114
Lott, Arnold S., 54
Lovin, Nellie, 74–75

Lowe, W. Edmund, 74–75
Lyles, Alberta, 58, 62
Lynch, Loretta, 148
lynching, 16, 59, 60, 96
Lytle, Lutie, 5

Malek, Fred, 115–16
Marable, Manning, 109
Marion, Mary Lue, 58, 62, 69–72, 76
marriage, 79, 80, 86–88; couples therapy for, 84; interracial, 14, 53, 141; no-fault divorce and, 93
Marshall, Thurgood, 40, 115, 134
Maxwell, Cassandra E., 5
McCoy, Cleo M., 54
Meharry Medical College (Nashville), 30, 32
Melton, Alain Reynolds, 1, 8, 13–20, 80, 88, 90
Melton, Etta, 19, 27
Melton, John, 13
Melton, Joseph Cleveland "J.C.," 1, 8, 13–20, 79–81, 85, 143; death of, 92, 97; preaching style of, 24–25; stroke of, 75
Melton, Judson, 14, 15, 28, 30
Meredith, James, 6, 50
Michael, Jerome, 38
Montgomery, Dale, 66
Moore, Dan, 125
Morgan, Robert, 133
Morton, Thruston, 125
Motley, Constance Baker, 5, 37; James Meredith and, 50; at NAACP, 40
Moynihan, Daniel Patrick, 86
Murray, Pauli, 37

National Association for the Advancement of Colored People (NAACP), 39–40, 53
National Negro Congress, 43
neo-Nazis, 141
Newcomb, James, 119, 126–32, 134
Nixon, Richard, 103, 126, 127; Ford's pardon of, 133; southern strategy of, 104, 115, 123–24
no-fault divorce law, 93
North Carolina Agricultural and Technical State University, 2, 16, 46; Alexander as commencement speaker at, 113; Alexander as student at, 26; founding of, 26–27; Woolworth's sit-in and, 7, 53–55
North Carolina bar exam, 45

North Carolina Central University, 42
North Carolina Nurses Association, 56

Obama, Barack, 148
Office of Juvenile and Delinquency Prevention, 110–11
Orr, Poindexter, 54

Page, Miles, 41
Palmer Memorial Institute (Sedalia, N.C.), 28
Parham, Asa, 72
Parker, R. Hunt, 75
Parks, Herbert, 51, 80–81
Parks, Rosa, 6
Pell, Gerald "Jerry," 77, 112, 136, 143, 147, 150
Pell, Jim, 77, 143
Pell, Sally, 105–6
performative activism, 2–3, 9, 13, 49–50, 58; agitprop as, 48; Berrey on, 4; Ritterhouse on, 17
Plessy v. Ferguson (1896), 16
Poinsette Clark, Septima, 6, 82
Porgy and Bess, 18
Powell, Richard, 42
Preen, Mildred, 41
Preyer, Richardson, 129
Progressivism, 107–8

race, 49–50; class and, 16–17, 60; gender and, 4–5, 66, 105, 114, 129–32; jury selection process and, 57, 59, 63, 65–67, 75; sentencing disparities and, 59, 62–65; stereotypes of, 59–61, 69, 82–83
racial etiquette, 17, 25, 138
racism, 105, 123; Ku Klux Klan and, 3, 99–100, 141–42; lynching and, 16, 59, 60; "passing" as white and, 40–41, 129; pseudo-scientific theories of, 26; psychological effects of, 139; slavery and, 96–97
Ralston, John D., 141–42, 145
Rankin, Eula Mae, 145
Ransby, Barbara, 3, 6
rape, 69; attempted, 61; as capital crime, 60, 62–65, 73–74; Yoes trial on, 57–77
Raulston, William, 136–37
Rees, Marian, 135
Republican Party, 6–7, 100–101, 115–16, 119–26
respectability politics, 1–3, 6, 52; class and, 13, 16–17, 25, 60; family values and, 79–85, 92–93; Republican Party and, 101, 123
Reynolds, Robert, 15
Rigueur, Leah Wright, 6
Ritterhouse, Jennifer, 4, 17
Rosenwald, Julius, 22
Rucker, Pierce, 45, 46

Saavedra, Andrea, 148–49
Sampson, Dale, 141, 142
Sanford, Terry, 132
Schlosser, Mike, 111
Schoch, Arch, 137
Scott, Kerr, 132
Seay, Thomas, 137, 138
segregation, 13, 16–17; of courtrooms, 2, 49; in Greensboro, 48; housing discrimination and, 98; of schools, 16, 47–48; of water fountains, 2, 49
sentencing disparities, 59, 62–65
sexual harassment, 38
sexual violence. *See* rape
Shands, Dugas, 50
Sharp, James, 132
Sharp, Robert, 33, 34
Sharp, Susie, 120–21, 127, 131–34
Shaw, Stephanie, 4, 26
Shaw University, 8, 14, 26
Shore, Joseph "J.P.," 138, 139–40
Siddle, John, 73
Simkins, George, Jr., 7, 50, 55
Simkins v. Cone (1962), 7, 55–56, 88
Sixth Amendment to U.S. Constitution, 99
slavery, 96–97
Smith, Benjamin, 48
Smith, Young B., 36, 37–38
Somers, Bob, 130
Southern Christian Leadership Conference, 6
Speckhard, Donald, 143, 144, 145–46
Speckhard, Stanley, 143
Stevens, Hope, 43–44
Stevens, William, 133
Student Nonviolent Coordinating Committee, 6
"Student's Plan for Peace, A" (E. M. Alexander), 39
Syphax, Theophilus John Minton, 41

Tarpley, John, 22, 53, 102–3
Taylor, Herman, 38, 39–40
Thurmond, Strom, 100, 123
Timmons-Goodson, Patricia, 147, 150
Tynes, Katharine, 29–30

United Institutional Baptist Church, 15, 25, 79
United Mutual Life Insurance Company, 43
United Negro College Fund, 53
University of North Carolina Law School, 42

Vietnam War, 103, 112, 127
voter registration, 103
voting rights, 46, 68
Voting Rights Act (1965), 100, 103, 125

Waller, Signe, 141, 142
Waller, Yvonne "Vonny," 90–91

Ward, Hiram, 116
Washington, Booker T., 16
Watergate scandal, 127, 133
Waters Institute, 14
Waugh, Lavinia, 28–29, 36
Wettach, Robert, 42
When Is a Man Free? (E. M. Alexander), 7–8, 95–97, 113
White, Fannie, 45, 46
Williams, Joe (judge), 111
Williams, Joseph (district attorney), 137
Wilson, Mick, 58, 59, 62, 68–69
Withers, Betty, 138
Wood, H. A., 66
Woolworth's sit-in (1960), 7, 53–55
World War II, 8–9, 34, 35–37

Yoes, Charles Donald, 57–77, 109, 138